17 HOURS TO GLORY

Extraordinary Stories from the Heart of Triathlon

By Mathias Müller
with Timothy Carlson

Boulder, Colorado

Published in 2008 by Moby Dick Verlag und Media-Services GmbH, Kaistr. 33 / Eckmann-Speicher, D-24103 Kiel under the title *17 Stunden zum Ruhm, Mythos Ironman Hawaii*. Copyright © Moby Dick Verlag, Kiel.
Translation by Mark Deterline

Chapters 4, 5, 6, 9, 13, 14, and 17 written by Timothy Carlson; additional reporting for Chapters 1, 2, 3, 7, 8, 12, and 16 by Timothy Carlson

Ironman® is a registered trademark of World Triathlon Corporation.

Copyright © 2010 VeloPress

3002 Sterling Circle, Suite 100
Boulder, Colorado 80301 USA
(303) 440-0601 · Fax (303) 444-6788 · E-mail velopress@competitorgroup.com

Distributed in the United States and Canada by Ingram Publisher Services

Library of Congress Cataloging-in-Publication Data
Müller, Mathias.
17 hours to glory: extraordinary stories from the heart of triathlon / Mathias Müller with Timothy Carlson.
      p. cm.
      Translation of 17 Stunden Zum Ruhm, Mythos Ironman Hawaii
      ISBN 978-1-934030-43-1 (pbk.: alk. paper)
      1. Ironman triathlons. 2. Triathlon. I. Carlson, Timothy. II. Title.
III. Title: Seventeen hours to glory.
GV1060.73.M85 2010
796.42'57—dc22
                                             2010005357

For information on purchasing VeloPress books, please call (800) 811-4210 ext.2138 or visit www.velopress.com.

This book is printed on 100 percent FSC-certified mixed-sources paper (30 percent post-consumer waste), elemental chlorine free, using soy-based inks.

Cover design by Samira Selod
Cover photo by Getty Images
Interior design by *the*BookDesigners
Fonts used: Diavlo, Folio, and Perpetua

11 12 / 10 9 8 7 6 5 4 3 2

**It is unbelievable how much strength
the soul can give the body.**

—Wilhelm von Humboldt

CONTENTS

PREFACE: BEFORE THE START

Vital statistics: 2.4 miles of swimming, 112 miles of cycling, and 26.2 miles of running. Add open-water swells, relentless sun, hot lava fields, and the *mumuku* winds that can howl at 40 miles per hour, and you have the basic components of Ironman® Hawaii.

If you want to make it here, you must not only prepare your body for the rigors of the race; you must also possess a strong will and the heart of a warrior to help you endure moments of physical and mental weakness. Success does not depend solely on a good training plan.

Anything can happen over the course of Ironman Hawaii and in the lava fields of the Big Island: blisters that form on the soles of your feet, which have been softened by water and sweat; gastrointestinal distress that stems from excessive consumption of electrolyte fluids; dehydration—the other extreme—which begins when your body can't absorb all the liquid you pour into it; cramps; and fatigue, pure and simple. These are just a few of the variables with which every competitor must contend. Not to mention technical issues with the bike, the swim goggles, the running shoes. . . .

Whoever crosses the finish line on Ali'i Drive in Kailua-Kona has won the battle with the course, with all the circumstances outside their control, and often with themselves. Because it's not only the winners of Ironman Hawaii who make history. It's often the underdogs, despite weaknesses and challenges in the struggle to the finish line, who write the most meaningful pages in Hawaii's history books.

It wasn't the story of a winner that popularized Ironman Hawaii beyond U.S. borders and throughout the rest of the world. In 1982, television coverage of a true drama sent unforgettable images around the globe. Julie Moss had victory in sight when her legs gave out just a few feet from the finish line. But giving up never occurred to the young American. Completely dehydrated, she literally crawled toward the finish. And she actually made it. Her unbending will carried her to the line. Not in first place, however: at the last moment, Kathleen McCartney ran past her.

ABC's coverage of the event turned Julie Moss into a hero, an icon, and even a cult figure. The coverage of her struggle was the most widely watched sportscast in the United States that year. "Before that, triathlon in the United States was about as popular as llama racing," wrote the *New York Times*. What made the coverage so unforgettable was her message: "Never give up!"

Through Julie Moss, the sport became something special. Every year there are more and more enthusiasts around the world, inspired by her indomitable spirit, who want to test their physical limits in triathlon. Every year thousands of races of different lengths are organized. Sprint-distance (500-meter swim, 20-kilometer bike, 5-kilometer run) and Olympic-distance (1.5-km swim, 40-km bike, 10-km run) events have done the most to make triathlon accessible to a broader base of active individuals.

For most of these people, however, the dream continues to be Ironman Hawaii. At least once in their lives, they want to hear announcer Mike Reilly's voice as they cross the finish line on Ali'i Drive: "You are an Ironman!" That is the reward for all the effort. That is knighthood. It is the dream that thousands of triathletes would one day like to realize.

Today more than 40,000 athletes try every year to secure a starting spot—a "slot"—for the big event in Kailua-Kona at one of more than 25 qualifying races around the world. In the end only 1,800 starters have the privilege of participating at the Ironman World Championship. Approximately 1,600 will qualify over the same distance in other demanding events, and about 200 applicants are lucky enough to win a spot through an annual lottery drawing.

Participants return home with tales of oppressive heat, hard-fought battles, extreme exertion, and unforgettable experiences from the world's most important triathlon. Even for professional athletes, a victory in Hawaii is more important than an Olympic gold medal. For all these reasons, the race's legendary stature has not only been established but continues to grow.

Today, with our lives often very programmed and predictable, Kona is a place where you can still distinguish yourself as one of a select few. Athletes who finish take strength and self-confidence back with them into everyday life. "Whoever can do this can do anything," explains Peter Reid, three-time Ironman Hawaii champion.

Many agree with him, for athletes must travel a long road before they can succeed in Hawaii: preparation, training, and sacrifice, sometimes over many years. They must qualify and may even need to save money in order to start in Hawaii. And many travel this road in virtual obscurity. Calendars become more ordered, lifestyles grow more disciplined, and obstacles are removed. That which seemed impossible is made possible. The race itself is often just the tip of the iceberg.

It is precisely those athletes whose chances seem poor at the outset who draw most deeply on their internal motivation and determination in order to exceed themselves. They can accomplish things no one thought they could. Having the heart of a warrior is not only the stuff of professional athletes but also applies to ambitious recreational athletes—men and women, young and old, with or without physical handicaps.

It is a tradition for the race to be started by a cannon blast at 7 a.m. At midnight the race is over. The athletes have only 17 hours to cover the 140.6-mile course and realize their dreams. Each chapter of this book shares the story of an athlete who has accomplished something special in the more than three-decade history of Ironman Hawaii. Each has had to chart her or his own journey to Hawaii. And, ultimately, each must race a unique and personal race.

Some readers may believe that the individuals whose stories are contained within these pages are crazy. After all, why would people subject themselves to such punishment? Why not go for a run in the nearby woods when there are people who contest an event like Ironman Hawaii under the most extreme circumstances? But other readers will see these athletes as examples and sources of inspiration.

Even if the following stories do nothing more than serve as entertaining reading, the recurring theme will be difficult to forget. These pages share a powerful message: "Believe in yourself, and you will achieve your goals!"

—*Mathias Müller*

INTRODUCTION

Ironman: a fundamental unit of measure

THE HAWAIIAN IRONMAN Triathlon was, just 32 years ago, the frontier of human endurance. When John Collins, Gordon Haller, and John Dunbar took off into the waters near Honolulu for the first one in 1978, they might have been Columbus, sailing over the horizon, making a bet with the elements that they would not sail off the edge of the known in a foolish quest for the New World.

The distances of this event, like many others that became fundamental units of measurement, were a product of human coincidence. Navy Commander John Collins wanted to settle an argument that raged among swimmers, cyclists, and runners: Who was the fittest at the height of the 1970s fitness revolution? So Collins took the three toughest Hawaiian endurance events, which fortuitously started and finished within close proximity in Waikiki—the annual 2.4-mile Waikiki Rough Water Swim, the 115-mile Around-Oahu Perimeter Bike Race, and the 26.2-mile Honolulu Marathon—and threw them into one package. To make the transitions work out, he chopped 3 miles off the bike ride. This summary act was similar to the settling of the modern marathon distance. In 490 b.c. Pheideppides ran about 40 kilometers, or about 25 miles, from the battlefield of Marathon to Athens to announce the Greek army's victory over the Persians, declaring, "Be joyful! We win!" with his last breath before dying. In the 1900 Olympics in London, organizers thought things would be swell if the queen could start the race from Buckingham Palace, so they added a mile and 385 yards to the event, and that's been the official distance ever since.

For a mile, a league, a yard, a foot, an inch, there are similar stories. The origins of our measurements have always been based on human need. But a unit of measure sticks when it becomes a useful reference for significant human enterprise. Humans consistently reach for new frontiers in science—from flying across the Atlantic to traveling to the moon—and the same happens in sports. The 4-minute mile was thought to be the limit of human capacity, and the marathon was thought to be possible for only a select few. Then came the running revolution, and marathons were choked with runners. It took the Ironman distance to ratchet up the sights of the romantics and capture the imagination once again. Now that frontier has moved on, some say to a land of senseless excess. Hawaii had an Ultraman event 2.5 times the Ironman distance. France has established a Triple Ironman in the Alps, and Mexico has scheduled a sort of Tour de France for the insatiable Ironman, with 16 days to cover 10 times the original Ironman distance: 24 miles of swimming, 1,120 miles of cycling, and 262 miles of running.

But they keep coming back to the Ironman.

The race is first measured with the calendar: a year's worth of effort to train your body to do it. Then it comes down to the clock on race day, which reflects in perfect inverse proportion the number of calendar days you put into it. So, in a world where effort is often ignored or irrelevant, if not downright punished, the Ironman creates a kind of justice and meaning. In one day it burns 3,000 to 9,000 calories, and it drains one to seven gallons of sweat and immeasurable depths of your soul. Just to get ready takes four to eight months of training, covering perhaps 5,000 to 8,000 miles on the bike, hundreds of miles of swimming, and 1,000 to 2,000 miles of running.

As a name it's been popular in other arenas, too. Iron Man Ivan Stewart was fabled for racing around the clock alone in the dusty, rocky wilderness of Baja California off-road races. There are lifeguard Iron Man lifesaving competitions at beaches around the world.

Lou Gehrig was known as the Iron Horse for playing in 2,130 baseball games until disease took him out, and Cal Ripken Jr. took over that mantle as the Iron Man of baseball for breaking Gehrig's record. On the flip side, iron-fisted Soviet dictator Joseph Stalin was also known as the Iron Man, as was Germany's Otto von Bismarck. Iron is essential to our blood and our health. Iron is metal, metaphor, and also myth. Ultimately it is that interior struggle against the objectively monumental task of the Ironman distance that is important.

Mark Allen, six-time Ironman champion, said, "The Ironman is a test of people within themselves. It's so difficult, it works slowly inside you. It forces you to open up your eyes a little bit, and your soul. The way the island is, particularly the Kona side, strips you of everything you put around yourself. You're out there really raw. If you go out there thinking that you're going to crush your competitors and dominate the course, it will slap you down. You have to respect this island and look inside to find your strength."

No matter the difficulty, if the Ironman did not touch the soul, it would not have its enduring popularity, nor would it have created a worldwide phenomenon—there are currently millions of triathletes in over 80 countries. And unless it struck a universal human chord, it would not attract 10 million television viewers in America every year, many of whom rarely get off the couch.

The Ironman event has no intrinsic meaning in itself. Why it still captures the imagination has everything to do with what the people who have done it have brought to it, and its meaning grows every year with the telling of more stories.

And so lies the difficulty and the pleasure in choosing 17 extraordinary persons out of the 50,000 or so who have done Ironman Hawaii. This book—which owes a great debt to the stories of the Ironman that came before, especially Barry McDermott's *Sports Illustrated* epic about Tom Warren's 1979 Ironman victory and Mike Plant's beautiful book *Iron Will*—seeks to explain it all by telling the stories of athletes of extraordinary talent, character, and spirit.

Some—such as Mark Allen, Greg Welch, Thomas Hellriegel, Peter Reid, and Normann Stadler as well as Paula Newby-Fraser, Karen Smyers, Natasha Badmann, and Chrissie Wellington—are among the greatest endurance athletes to ever walk the earth. Others, such as Julie Moss, virtually gave birth to the sport by virtue of their inspiring struggles simply to finish. Some, such as Robert McKeague and Sister Madonna Buder, pushed back the perceived limitations of age with a quantum leap. Others, such as Andreas Niedrig, threw off the shackles of crime and addiction to embrace freedom in the self-discipline of sport. And physically challenged athletes—what a politically correct understatement!—such as Marc Herremans, David Bailey, Carlos Moleda, and Sarah Reinertsen, show us that loss of limb, paralysis, and life-threatening injury cannot defeat the indomitable human heart. All of these stories tell us something important about the human spirit, which does not simply endure but prevails.

In a world where the speed of communication has served to isolate us, where 500 channels of cable have fractured a sense of a shared community, where a high-speed, franchised world has eliminated meaning along with meaningful differences, there remain a few acts that by their very difficulty re-create a more rugged past and renew the fervor of a quest.

The people who tried it were eager for the moral equivalent of a personal war, for acts of individual heroism. They wanted to share the road with others who had caught their admiration, people like the extraordinary athletes in this book. Mark Montgomery, who has started 13 Ironmans, said that the Ironman field reminds him of the kinds of people who settled Australia and America. "The Ironman doesn't interest the average person," he said. "He thinks this is crazy and doesn't give it a second thought. It sorts out those people who have something different going on upstairs. It draws people who have something exceptional."

Sally Edwards, a pioneer in women's endurance sports who had a 2nd, a 4th, and a 5th in the Ironman, said what still excites the imagination of elite athletes who tackle the Ironman is its speed. "The title 'world's greatest endurance athlete' some writers have given to the Ironman champion is wrong," she said. "I don't want to sound egotistical, but it is not that hard a race to finish. I have done the Western States 100-mile run and the Iditasport, 100 miles on snowshoes in the Alaskan wilderness. Both of those involve much less intensity for a much longer time. The thing that is truly difficult about the Ironman is the intensity. The Ironman distance demands a lot, but what sets it apart is how fast they go. No other race gets that good an athlete on that kind of course. You add the fatigue from the swim, the fatigue on the bike, and the fatigue on the run, and what results is a huge fatigue, an exponential multiplier of fatigue."

Greg Welch of Australia, who won the race in 1994, agreed. "It's so hard because it's no longer a pace; it's no longer take-your-time-to-change-your-clothes. It's swim 2.4 miles in world-class time, get out and change in a minute and a half, and bike for four and a half hours at Tour de France pace with your heartbeat at 170 beats per minute, and then run as hard as you possibly can without putting yourself in the hospital, without dehydrating, without losing all your salt, without running out of glycogen, trying to do it not only in record time but first. Because it gets faster every year. It is the ultimate test for a triathlete."

It is no accident, either, that in a world where many sports have gone mad with fame, money, drugs, violence, and power struggles, triathlon has remained largely immune. Most professionals make less than the amateurs who hammer themselves every weekend for the fun of it. Few speak ill of one another. There is little jealousy for those who do prosper, however modest those fortunes may be when compared to those of Shaq or Michael or Montana or Tiger. It's because when it comes down to race day, there is no lying. It is your body and the work you have put in. There are very few upsets, especially when it comes to the Ironman. There are no shortcuts, and, unlike in cycling, track and field, and swimming, there is a remarkably low percentage of cheating. Their God-given talent is just the tip of a huge pyramid of work done over years. The pros and amateurs alike often feel part of a common mission, a quest for the Holy Grail. And nowhere is it more clear than along the finish line on Ali'i Drive at the Ironman. That's where the elite athletes return after their trials and cheer all the others who are finishing up to 9 hours later. "As a professional, I feel honored by the average people on the course with me," said Mark Allen. "Of course, no one who does the Ironman is an average person."

And that is precisely why they do it. It is an occasion for finding out if you have the capacity to be a hero, and it requires the inner strength and physical discipline to be one. And it carries over into the rest of the athletes' lives. The Ironman has value because it demands value. It cannot be done in one blast of self-destruction or prodigal effort. What sets it apart from bungee jumping or other dares is that it cannot be done on a whim. And it is so hard that you cannot simply do it and risk damaging your body as a cheap price to pay. It demands a long-term physical and mental discipline, a careful accumulation of hard work, and control over the mind and emotions to allocate your energy to the last drop.

When you have asked that much of yourself and delivered, you see that your potential is unlimited. For everyone who gets to run toward the lights within the cutoff time of 17 hours, the feeling is ecstatic. As most come in, it is dark, and they run toward a bright light down a long canal warm with cheering on either side. "It is like what I imagined being born is like," said one Ironman.

"Why do I smile?" said a Japanese man as he finished. Pointing back across the line, he said, "It is because back there is hell, and on this side is heaven."

—*Timothy Carlson*

ONE | JULIE MOSS

"Winning means reaching the finish—reaching the finish means winning."

ASK ANYONE FAMILIAR with the early days of Ironman about the race's signature image, and they will all mention the same thing. Not winners in flowered leis. Not swimmers churning through Kailua Bay. Not cyclists bent over their bikes like insects moving across the sun-baked lava fields. The image in everyone's head is that of Julie Moss crawling to the finish line. Moss's never-give-up determination to reach the ribbon embodied the defining ethos of the endurance athlete, and in her Ironman debut she was immediately embraced as a full-fledged member of the tri pantheon. Surprisingly, though, Moss was only an accidental triathlete. At heart she was a surfer.

In 1981 Julie Moss was studying physical education at California Polytechnic State University at San Luis Obispo when she met lifeguard Reed Gregerson at a Carlsbad beach. Gregerson had caught the bug of the new sport of triathlon, which had originated in nearby San Diego, and he was talking about competing at the Ironman Hawaii, then three years old.

Her curiosity piqued, Moss tuned in to the ABC broadcast of the 1981 event, which had just moved from Oahu to the lava fields on the Big Island of Hawaii. As she watched triathletes struggle in the heat and wind, she was intrigued. "I remember Scott Molina collapsed, and Olympic cyclist John Howard looked strong on the bike but awkward on the run as he won the thing. But I do not remember seeing a woman. I thought it was both compelling and ridiculous at the same time. And it had parts I could relate to, like the swim in the ocean and the marathon. Afterward Reed contacted a friend and started training for it, and all of a sudden it looked like a doable thing."

Moss had been a desultory high school athlete. "I liked being part of the basketball and volleyball teams for social reasons," she said, "but I didn't want anybody to throw me the ball. I didn't like the pressure!"

Although she disliked the spotlight in team sports, her surfing played a crucial role in the development of her self-reliance and courage. "When I was in college I paddled out at a secret break in central California near a spot called Killers. There were really big sets, and as I tried to push through I was thinking, *I may get washed up on the rocks, and I might not get out of this one.* This was a situation where I had to rely completely on myself, and I managed to survive."

And so, with her new boyfriend, Gregerson, Moss was drawn into long bike rides and running to go with her surf-honed swim. Ever practical, Moss decided to kill two birds and write her senior thesis on training for and competing in the Ironman, then held in February each year. A self-described "born procrastinator," she put off the start of a training regimen until the clock was about to burst, relying on her belief that "you do your best work under pressure." So it wasn't until September 1981, with the February 1982 race a scant five months off, that her training got seriously under way with a half-iron-distance triathlon in Santa Barbara. The triathlon went well, but she received a dose of reality in December when at mile 20 of the Oakland Marathon she experienced the phenomenon that marathoners refer to as hitting the wall and dropped well off her sub-3:30 pace. With her self-confidence hurting, she penciled in a second marathon just three weeks later in Mission Bay.

But first, less than two months before the Ironman—on Christmas Eve, no less—Gregerson broke up with her. "I was devastated and would not have done the event if I didn't have to finish my thesis to graduate," said Moss. "My mom was single and raised us on a teacher's salary. She had paid for my college, and I owed that much to her to finish." Cornered by her commitment to graduate, she decided she was doing the race for herself and plunged ahead.

At Mission Bay she covered the 26.2 miles in an encouraging 3 hours 33 minutes. Then, to polish her bike training, she drove to

Santa Barbara, planning to ride 200 miles back to Carlsbad with a midway overnight stop at her grandfather's house. She cut the ride short at 150 miles.

With two weeks to go, she traveled to Kona, planning to put in some long bike training sessions. Those rides were intended to give her a final boost of confidence leading up to the event. But there was a catch: She was staying about 35 miles outside Kailua-Kona, where the course started and finished and most athletes began their training rides. Indomitable, she added her commute to the distance and ended up riding over 135 miles one day. Combined with some shorter rides back and forth to swim training in Kailua Bay, she pedaled more than 340 miles in the week before the race—a disaster in waiting from a scientific training standpoint.

But as she faced the awesome challenge of her first Ironman, her most important preparation was attitude. She had no ambition to do anything more than finish and certainly did not anticipate any attention except from friends and family. "I didn't have a concept that I actually would be seen," recalled Moss. "Nor did I care about what you wear. So on race day I wore a ridiculous bubble-shaped bike helmet and a huge John Deere–style hat with the Ironman logo on it that came with the race-day schwag. And I wasn't as lean as I would become, so my face was round, and I looked like this big-eyed kid with freckles playing dress-up with a grown-up's hat."

She had also planned to wear regular bike shorts and a tank top signed by Olympic skating hero Eric Heiden. But she was rescued by a man she met on a pre-race ride in Kona who found a more modern Lycra skinsuit for her to wear during the ride.

While most of the attention was focused on the coming duel between Scott Tinley and Dave Scott, the women's field had two competitors of note: professional cyclist Pat Hines and Kathleen McCartney, a member of the first professional triathlon squad, Team J David. Moss was a rookie—a college student writing her thesis on training for the event and the ultimate dark horse. "Starting this thing, I never pictured myself as any kind of good athlete," she said. "I gave myself a pat on the back for being gutsy enough to go out and do it. But I never thought of myself as a top-level athlete. So it was actually good to not have that burden of seeing myself in any particular way. All I asked of myself was to find a way to finish."

Moss now sees that her unknown status was a plus. "I was really unburdened by any sense of being competitive or preconception of being good at this," she said. "My own personal reason I was there was to find myself. The importance came from sticking with it, and finishing. And the challenge of Hawaii allowed me to melt away expectations."

On February 6, 1982, seconds before 7 a.m., she was treading water along with 579 other athletes in anticipation of the start that would get the fifth edition of Ironman Hawaii under way. When the starting gun fired, it was a release. She was wearing race number 393 and held her own much better than she had expected. After 1 hour 11 minutes she emerged from the water as one of the leading women, with a 21-minute lead on McCartney. Five hours 53 minutes later she finished the 112-mile bike trailing only Hines. She also had an 8-minute advantage over 1981 third-place finisher Lyn Brooks and retained an 18-minute 39-second lead over McCartney, who was weakened by food poisoning suffered two days before the race.

As Moss came into the bike-to-run transition, her bra strap broke, and she persuaded a volunteer to surrender her bra. "When it broke, that diffused any tendency I might have developed to approach the run with too much competitiveness," she said. "Which was a help because I knew I had a long way to go." Just a few miles into the run, Hines quit with cramps, and from then on Moss had two escorts—the ABC camera van and helicopter. Still, she said, "I didn't know I was in first place until we reached the turnaround, about 8 miles from the finish."

When McCartney hit the run turnaround, she was 8 minutes behind Moss. "I was so stoked," said McCartney, "but I also knew

I couldn't go any faster." Soon McCartney was trailed by her own media helicopter. "I noticed Julie's helicopter and mine were coming closer together," she said.

About two miles later Moss's competitive instinct had fully awakened. But with every step in the heat of the lava fields, her stride became more labored. Over the final 6 miles she sensed that she was losing strength. She struggled from aid station to aid station, from drinking cup to drinking cup. Again and again she found small reserves of energy in her ever-weakening body that got her closer to the finish. "How far is she behind me?" Moss asked spectators and the camera crew who accompanied her. Each time her voice sounded less confident.

Moss had never expected to win the race, but now that victory was within reach, she was no longer willing to let anyone take it from her. When she reached the top of Palani Road, about a mile from the finish, she still had a 6-minute lead. No one who stood on the side of the road and cheered for her doubted that she would be the first to reach the finish line. But that last mile did not go as expected.

After the steep downhill on Palani Road, she quickly realized that something was wrong. As quickly as night falls in winter, Moss lost control of her body. Her knees buckled, and she stumbled and fell for the first of many times. In that last mile Moss's ignorance of the heavy demands of Ironman race-day nutrition hit her hard. Although she had run a good 3:30 marathon on bananas and sports drinks, her total time on the Ironman course was approaching 11 hours. She was running on empty.

Moss fell four times yet still held her lead. "I kept trying to not give in, but various parts of my body shut down and failed me while I was still running," recalled Moss. "Near the end I kept falling, not because I was near death or hurting. I was simply out of fuel and was too weak to hold myself upright while running."

The last few times she fell, she looked like a doe slipping and falling on ice. Retreating into a tunnel of concentration in which she ignored the crowd and the cameras, she struggled to think of a way to raise herself back up. "I had more strength in my arms, so I formed a tripod with my arms and legs and pushed off and rolled up," she said. "The first time I tried it I almost got up, but my legs didn't hold. I fell and rolled over on my back again. I tried again, and I was up and moving."

As she turned onto Ali'i Drive, there was a quarter mile to go; she could see the lights at the finish near the pier. "I was aware of the competition, and I thought, *Oh man, I am so close! C'mon, c'mon, c'mon!*" Unable to contain herself, she began to run again. But 200 feet from the finish line, where the big banyan tree arches over Ali'i, it took only the slight curvature of the road to throw Moss off track, and she fell hard.

Moss's body was out of her control, but her mind was clear and focused on race director Valerie Silk's warning that competitors receiving outside assistance would be disqualified. Ingrained in every marathoner was the sad story of Dorando Pietri of Italy, who led the 1908 Olympic marathon into the stadium, where he collapsed and fell several times. He was revived and held upright by well-meaning officials who helped him stagger to the end. Though he crossed the finish line first, he was disqualified.

"I made a point of shooing away people who wanted to pick me up and help me because the last thing I wanted was to be disqualified for outside help," said Moss. "At one point I started to fall back, and I thought if somebody held me up I couldn't acknowledge I wanted that. I had to show it was all against my will."

Moss got up again and was walking shakily just 100 feet from the line. She saw the lights and, thrilled by the sight, tried to run once again. Just yards from the finish her mother tried to give her a celebratory lei, but Moss weakly waved away the sweet gesture. Thrown off-kilter by the effort, she fell again 10 yards from the finish.

Again volunteers rushed to her side. One of them pointed a finger forward as if to say, "There's the finish. You can do it." It was at that moment that, out of the corner of her eye, she noticed a pair of legs run past her.

They were Kathleen McCartney's legs.

Moss could rise no more. She couldn't stand or walk, much less run. But she was determined to finish. With her last bit of strength she began to drag herself across the asphalt on all fours, yard by yard, inch by inch, crawling her way to the end. After a total of 11 hours 10 minutes 9 seconds—only 29 seconds after the winner—she collapsed over the finish line.

"I realized later I had enough of a lead and could have walked and won," said Moss. "But near the end I got the idea that I needed to respect the effort I had put in and what I had learned about myself that day. And so I could only envision myself running across the line."

Naturally she was disappointed with the outcome. But, as she wrote in an account on the World Triathlon Corporation web site, "I was forced to dig so deep within myself that I was able to see what I was really made of."

Ironically, ABC's *Wide World of Sports* on-site producer, Bryce Weisman, had been so discouraged and bored by the taped footage of most of the race that he had told Silk, "I don't know if I have anything I can use" for the broadcast. Just as he said he did not know if ABC would pay Silk the contracted $5,000 license fee, all hell broke loose at the finish line. "All of a sudden I hear just this incredible noise and applause and shouting and cheering at the finish line," recalled Silk. "The crowd was going nuts! Then all of a sudden one of the cameramen came to the van and said, 'Bryce, you gotta get out here! You won't believe what's going on!'"

When the delayed segment aired the next weekend on *Wide World of Sports*, complete with a heart-tugging flute accompaniment that underlined the passion of Moss's struggle to the finish, it struck a nerve with viewers. ABC Sports called her struggle to finish a defining moment in sport. The word of the race's drama spread like wildfire, so ABC flew Moss and McCartney to New York for studio interviews to accompany the segment, which was repeated on Mother's Day.

Many thousands of people swear that watching Julie Moss's crawl inspired them to take up the sport, notably including San Diego lifeguard Mark Allen, who ultimately married Moss and became a six-time champion of Ironman Hawaii.

Since that fateful day in February 1982, Moss has participated in many races, including other Ironman events. She proved she was a world-class athlete by winning Ironman Japan in 1985, with a time of 10 hours 4 minutes, and improving her best finish at the distance to 10 hours 13 seconds as an age grouper at the 1997 Ironman Australia. In that same decade she made the qualifying standard for the U.S. Olympic Women's Marathon trials with a time of 2 hours 47 minutes in Boston.

Still, her lasting legacy will always be that inspiring first finish in Hawaii. Again and again she hears from other athletes how her effort and unconquerable determination in 1982 was the reason they were taking part in the world championships. Even today that epic battle motivates thousands of enthusiasts. The Olympic message that participation is everything has nothing on Moss's credo: "Winning means reaching the finish—reaching the finish means winning."

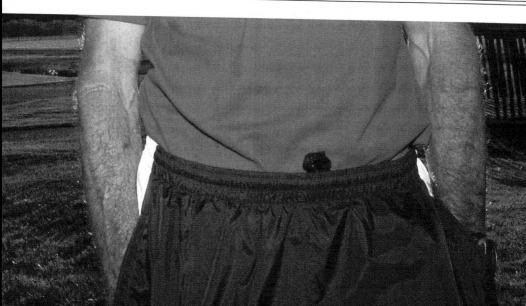

TWO | **MARK ALLEN**

"Trust in yourself and never give up!"

BEFORE A RACE his eyes had the remote, cool look of an eagle's, set deep behind a blade-sharp nose with a small notch in it. While others were warming up with the pent-up energy of boxers, his 6-foot, 155-pound, elegantly angular frame was still. His smooth, supple muscles expended no energy. He was calm, alone, and (frightening to his competitors) had no nerves or anxiety to burn off. All of his energy was saved for the battle. This was Mark Allen at the peak of his Ironman career.

They called him the Grip because once he got hold of a race, he held on with the grip of death. They called him the Zen Master because his mind seemed to have the focus of a trained Buddhist philosopher. And yet, during his first seven tries at the Holy Grail of the sport, Allen was gripped by insecurity and haunted by failure. Despite all the laurels he ultimately won in Hawaii, despite the aura of invincibility that threw all of his rivals (except Dave Scott) into some version of panic, his greatest victory was over his own fears.

The son of a physician, he grew up in an affluent home in Palo Alto, California, and took up swimming as a kid. He became a swimmer at the University of California–San Diego but described himself as "not national class." He took up lifeguarding after college in 1980 and took surfing trips to Mexico before he passed the medical boards. He assumed he would either follow his father into the cramped indoor world of medicine or would pursue a career in marine biology.

The spark that lit the Ironman fire in Allen came the same way it did for countless others: watching television coverage of the February 1982 Ironman Hawaii. "I was in a limbo at the time," recalled Allen. "For some reason in February 1982, I was sitting on a couch watching *Wide World of Sports* when I saw Julie [Moss] in her dramatic finish at Ironman. Tears were streaming down my face. From where I sat, I thought she stood 9 feet tall."

He couldn't get the race out of his head. "I had just gotten out of college and didn't know what to do with my life," he said. If he spent the next six months getting ready for the race, he thought, at least he wouldn't need to think about his future.

So he bagged medical school, spent $1,000 on a bike, and targeted the next Ironman, newly changed from its original February date to October, seven months away. Totally new to cycling and running, he managed a remarkable fourth place in his first event, the June 12, 1982, U.S. Triathlon Series (USTS) San Diego race, finishing behind Dave Scott, Scott Molina, and Scott Tinley. Together these men would be called the Big Four and would dominate triathlon in its first decade. Remarkably, Allen won his third event, the half-Ironman-distance Horny Toad Triathlon in San Diego.

In Hawaii in October 1982, Allen emerged from the Pacific right behind Dave Scott, who had finished second in February. Allen shadowed the leader through the transition area to his bike, and together they powered north over the rolling Queen Ka'ahumanu Highway and through the microwave heat of the lava fields. They left everyone behind, even Tinley, who had beaten Scott in February. More amazing was the fact that Ironman rookie Allen matched Scott's speed. At the bike course turnaround in the small town of Hawi, Allen was still hanging tough. By the time the two were rocketing back downhill, they could see their adversaries still climbing and knew they had a healthy lead. Just a few miles later, however, Allen's derailleur broke and ended his day. He wasn't discouraged. "I thought if I trained more, maybe I could even win this race," he recalled.

Easier said than done. Despite the talent to win every other triathlon, Allen's true greatness came in his unremitting struggle to win in Hawaii. In 1983 he was just barely outrun by Scott and Tinley. In 1984 he blasted to a course bike record on the hottest day in Ironman history, fried himself in the process, and ended up staggering across the line in fifth place and into the medical tent for IVs. In 1986 he came off the bike equal to Scott but was outrun by 6 minutes and finished second, 8 minutes behind. It was another ray of hope, so he thought 1987 would be his year to finally beat The Man.

From the swim to the halfway point of the marathon in 1987, Allen and Scott fought side by side, leaving the other competitors far behind. For the first time, Allen was feeling strong late in the race. He pushed the pace and banked time ahead of the reigning hero. With 9 miles left to run, Allen had a lead of almost 5 minutes.

What happened next was not easy to explain, even to himself. He didn't know whether he had overexerted himself or his mind was playing tricks on him. "As soon as I thought, *That's it, I've done it,* I found myself by the side of the road, unable to do more than walk." Allen's stomach had shut down near the end of the run, and Scott once again left him behind. Allen staggered in second—again. Adding injury to insult, that night he was hospitalized with internal bleeding. Doctors stuck tubes up his nose and down his throat and pumped ice water into his stomach to stop the bleeding. A week later he saw a snapshot of himself on a vacation cruise in Kauai and thought it might be time to quit his Ironman quest. "I looked like a death camp survivor," recalled Allen. "My body started consuming my muscles for fuel in the race when my stomach shut down."

In retrospect, said Allen, "It looks to me like I was on a classic warrior's journey. For seven years I faced the irrevocable, implacable force of Dave in Hawaii. It was a supreme test to go there thinking I was deserving and prepared to win. Then, every time, in absolute black and white, I could see I was on some level not ready—physically, emotionally, spiritually, and mentally. I was basically intimidated by the race, the conditions, and Dave. Dave became very strong when he stepped on that island. I was the opposite. For a long time I didn't know how to deal with Hawaii. It was a very powerful place, and I needed to find a way to gain strength from its intensity instead of becoming scared by it.

"At the time I asked myself if I could ever really win this race," he continued. Ironically, he had already beaten his competitors in other races all over the world; it was only in Hawaii that victory proved so elusive.

In 1988 Scott had to withdraw a day before the start due to a knee problem. "Now I'll do it," Allen thought. His and Scott's superiority had been too stark in previous years for him to be overly concerned about any of the other challengers. But once again things didn't go according to plan. Not one but two flat tires on the bike course dropped him to fifth place, despite posting the fastest marathon split. Scott Molina, who had had even more trouble than Allen with the heat in Kona, persevered for the win. "Even when all the stars seemed lined up, another bizarre thing happened to me," said Allen. "I was on the verge of giving up and never coming back to Hawaii."

Allen was perplexed. "What needs to happen? What do I need to do to win in Hawaii?" he asked himself.

Inspired by Molina not to quit, Allen and his soon-to-be-wife, Julie Moss, visited Molina and Erin Baker in New Zealand and had an epic, uninterrupted six weeks of long-distance training. "That time was magical," said Allen. "It showed me what volume of work was necessary to win and set me up for my best year ever."

It was normal for these athletes to train over thirty hours each week. But Allen suspected that his struggles were less physical than psychological. "I was afraid of this race and afraid of this island," he explained. "Every time I came to the Big Island, I fell apart mentally."

There were other pieces missing in his quest that were physical, objective. "As a kid, I loved solving puzzles, and the Ironman was the grandest puzzle of them all," said Allen. One key piece was scientific analysis of his salt loss. "Dr. Doug Hiller analyzed my blood after '87, and he said my salt levels were just one step above athletes who had gone into convulsions." In the summer of '89, he volunteered for an 8-hour Ironman-scope endurance workout at a Duke University lab in simulated 95-degree Hawaiian heat. "It may seem extreme, but I wanted to do whatever it took to understand what I had to do to win that race," said Allen. The answer: Allen's sweat loss was not great, but his percentage of salt loss was high. The solution: salt pills and salt added to his electrolyte replacement drinks.

Later that summer he won the first Olympic-distance world championships in Avignon, France, and wondered if his future would be better served by sticking to shorter distances. Ironman Hawaii 1989, he decided, would be his final attempt. If he couldn't pull it off that time, he vowed never to return to the island.

When Allen flew to Kona and was driving into town from the airport, he had a premonition and an inspiration. "As I drove up that last long uphill before Palani, the thought occurred to me, *This might be the place to make a move because this is the last long uphill, and it's very late in the race. I thought, If I show any weakness against Dave once we crest the hill and start the downhill, I will not have a chance because he is a fantastic downhill runner.* That close to the finish line, he has never completely blown up. He has struggled, but he never blew up. You can count on him to hold it together somehow. This was a foreshadowing, the first time I noticed how dramatic that hill was. I put myself into the mind-set of the marathon, how to break up on that hill. As it played out, that was where it happened."

But Allen needed something more. The moment Allen calls "the turning point of my life" occurred in Kona in the days preceding the 1989 duel with Scott. For his first six tries at Kona, Allen had relied upon his own superior endurance, hard work, and science to beat the man they called the Man on the lava fields. Always he'd lost, thwarted by broken equipment, heat exhaustion, even internal bleeding. On this, his seventh attempt to topple Scott, Allen needed a psychological transformation.

In his condominium he noticed a copy of *Yoga Journal* with a cover photo of Brant Secunda and Don José Matsuwa, two shamans of Mexico's Huichol Indians. "Those two faces drew me in because they had this look—so peaceful and happy to be alive."

Allen had always been wracked by doubts in Hawaii. "When you're under pressure, you see all the things that might or are or will go wrong," he said. "Just the opposite of that 'I'm happy to be alive' look. Then I realized I had spent so many years trying to get that feeling by winning this race. But those two shamans were just beaming without effort, and I realized that it was a powerful place to start from. I can see this so clearly in retrospect, but then it was happening in my subconscious. I just knew that picture had bright light and color and those beaming, easy smiles."

Seeing Scott draw strength from the island, Allen also felt that he needed to get in sync with Hawaii's powerful spirits. A few days before the 1989 race, he visited the tiny St.-Peter-by-the-Sea chapel on Ali'i Drive, 4.5 miles south of Kailua Pier. "As I sat in the church, I saw all the healers of the island, the kahunas," he said. "They told me, yes, I could race the way I hoped, but first I must show courage. When you are out there racing in the heat, a lot of doubts come into your head. The kahunas were telling me I had to have the courage to go through the race and win. But first I must be brave."

Allen also thought a lot about strategy. He had tried surging to the front on the bike and the run but always blew up and cracked under the stress. In 1989 he decided to stop wasting physical and mental energy coming up with an aggressive strategy and simply shadow the man who had already figured out the mysteries of pacing. "My single strategy was to stick with him and shadow him all the way," said Allen. "To let him set the pace because I knew I had not known how to pace correctly. I had either gone too hard in the beginning of the bike and run and blew up [1984], or I had gone too hard at the beginning of the run and blew up [1987]. My goal was simply to stay within sight of Dave and let him set the pace. At whatever point the feeling struck, it would be time to go."

On the swim and all the way through the bike, Allen and Scott stayed together a few minutes behind swim-bike specialist Wolfgang Dittrich. "The bike was pretty much the pace I'd picked," recalled

Allen. "Easy to stick with." The first big test arrived coming out of Kona Surf to start the run. "Turn left, and for the first 10 km Dave set an otherworldly pace [5:48 per mile]," Allen recalled. "It was so fast that sticking to my strategy was really hard. I thought, *Well, this is way too fast to start out the Ironman marathon. It is probably a death sentence, and we will blow up in the lava field and reenter the realm of reality.* But I made the move and stuck."

Scott remembers that the race really started on the run. "When I got off the bike, I pushed the pace by myself," he said. "We were aware that Wolfgang was ahead, but we knew his run was no threat. Mark responded to that higher push. Ultimately we knew what was happening. After the first 8 miles, my spotter, Pat Feeney, a math man, said, 'You are running a 5:48 pace.' Now I had a chance to see Mark side by side. I wanted to get a sense of his stride, his breathing and rhythm. We were really racing now. The shadow was next to me now. And so throughout the run, I never questioned whether we had gone out too fast or wondered if we would blow up. I knew I could hold that pace. I could set a ferocious pace at the beginning and hope that this would possibly make Mark ache a little more than I did on the bike."

Side by side, shoulder to shoulder, the two strongest Ironman triathletes of the previous several years matched one another step for step. Neither gave the other an inch. At the halfway point of the marathon, after 127 miles of racing, they were still running in sync. Then Scott surged again.

Allen recalled that push as his big test of will and resolve. "Dave really started to put it on, and I had a very hard time matching his pace," he said. "I thought, *I can't keep up with him. He's too fast. This is too demanding. This is way too hard for me.* I felt like I was losing it. My energy started to go, my legs started to fatigue and I thought, *Oh, no! Not again!*"

Allen said he started to wallow in his situation. "It got so hard to keep up, it took all I had to focus. And the only way I could do that was for my mind to go quiet. And when it did, over on my right side, floating over the lava, I saw the face of Don José. Of course my Western mind immediately had to go, *Real? Not real?* I went back to zoning out, letting my mind be quiet, and I got this huge surge of life force or energy from my vision of the face of that ancient shaman."

As Scott ran faster, Allen recalled the expression on the face of the older shaman in the *Yoga Journal*, the expression that didn't need an Ironman victory to find fulfillment. It became clear to Allen that he was putting a lot of pressure on himself for nothing. "I should be happy because I'm here, and because I'm running side by side with the best triathlete at the world's most important race," he said, explaining his thoughts at the time. It was in those seconds that the pressure from his six ill-fated showings in Kailua-Kona fell from his shoulders. "From then on I felt stronger and stronger, and I thought I could win this time if I just kept running," he recalled. At that point his legs hurt beyond description, but he remained calm, driving negative thoughts from his mind.

The final moment came with 2 miles to go, at the 24-mile mark of the marathon. Scott was anticipating his move a little farther up the road.

"I knew at the top of Palani Hill I can run a 5:10 pace or below going down the hill," said Scott. "At that point your legs are pretty fragile. I knew it would hurt his legs. I looked at what my strengths or weaknesses were at the time, and I'd say that because my form was not as smooth as Mark's, and I have more upper-body movement, going uphill more so, Mark might have been stronger than I on a long, steep grade. At that point of the race, I was trying to hold my rhythm and not extend myself. I knew it's going to be very difficult for him coming downhill."

As they started up the grade, Allen saw his opportunity. A voice inside him yelled, "Now! Go now!" When Scott looked up from his cup of water, he saw his rival on the attack 5 meters up the road. Now Scott was under the kind of pressure that Allen had so often dealt with, and he wasn't prepared for it. He raised his shoulders, cramping, not able to match Allen's pace.

"He made his move before I anticipated it," said Scott. "When I saw him going away, I was thinking, *Hey! This is too early. Wait for me!* Going up the hill, I just could not respond."

Allen ran the marathon in a still-standing race record time of 2 hours 40 minutes 4 seconds. His 8:09:15 finishing time smashed Scott's old course record by 19 minutes 22 seconds. But the accomplishment was a product of both men's brilliance: Just 58 seconds separated the two at the finish, the second-smallest margin of victory that a male winner had ever recorded.

The new champion was overcome with emotion when he crossed the finish line. "As soon as I was sure I wouldn't get any more cramps, that I wouldn't fall, that Dave wouldn't catch up to me, the pent-up emotions from seven Ironmans came to the surface. It was incredibly beautiful," he recounted.

"As I look back, it could not have been scripted better," said Allen. "If I had won in '88, it would have been without Dave. Instead I beat the guy who defined the sport in its early years in his best and fastest race ever." He celebrated that winter by marrying Julie Moss and maintaining his famous twenty-win streak. Once at the pinnacle, Allen had seven years of abundant good fortune, but they were filled with tests as well.

Allen won Hawaii the next four years straight, but his win in 1989 was the most important of his career until his last trial by fire in Kona, his 1995 farewell to Ironman.

Coming after his 1994 year off from the rigors of Kona, when he tried and failed to break 2 hours 20 minutes in the Berlin Marathon and 8 hours in Ironman Europe, Allen knew he had only a slender chance to hold off the onslaught of hungry challengers led by newcomer Thomas Hellriegel. After his Hawaii hiatus, and perhaps driven by pride to try to equal Scott's six victories, he went for a comeback in Kailua-Kona.

For much of the race, things did not look promising. Hellriegel, a young German, rode away from everyone on the bike and entered the transition area with a 13-minute lead. "If I hadn't been working with Brant Secunda—the younger of the two shamans—for quite a while, my predicament in that race probably would have seemed hopeless," recounted the veteran. After his win in 1989 he had traveled to Mexico. Since the 110-year-old Don José had recently died, Allen explained, he was tutored by Don José's disciple Secunda, who taught him how to free his spirit and be at peace.

"Thirteen minutes behind Thomas, I would have thought, *The gap is too big! I can't make that up! He is much younger than I am! I'm too old! I've already won five times; why am I here? I don't need all this.*" But his instruction had taught him to clear his mind of his opponents and to focus only on himself. It could seem in one moment that there was no way out, but the next moment the world could look a lot different. "You have to trust in yourself," Allen said. "You have to trust in yourself and you never give up!"

Allen calculated he had to make up 30 seconds a mile, and it was too much to dwell on. "So I just dedicated myself to make up time every single step of the marathon," he said. "A quarter of a second at a time, no time to catch my breath. All of a sudden a door of possibility opened up, and I knew I would finish, and I continued to race on another level."

Allen passed the fried Hellriegel at mile 23 and cruised in with a 2:42:09 run, 2 minutes 25 seconds ahead of the German. "It was probably the best I ever felt," Allen said. "Usually near the end I feel like I am breaking down. But biomechanically my body was on fire that day." Still, Allen prevailed by a razor's edge. "I got through the NBC interviews all right," he recalled. "But as soon as I stepped away, I had our son Mats on my shoulders and I started to shake. I told Julie to take Mats because I was going to drop him. Then I just hurled." It was a great green gallon of Gatorade, and Allen retired to the IV tent. "It was a very thin thread, an absolute gift to have that kind of race," he said. "And the door of opportunity in my body opened just for a brief time; then a few minutes after I finished, it shut down."

This was now his most important victory, he would later explain. The first victory laid the foundation for his career, but he would take the energy from his final race in Hawaii with him for the rest of his life.

Like Michael Jordan, Allen had written a classic farewell. But unlike Jordan with his serial retirements, Allen had the discipline to refuse to return to the well. His knockout punch of Hellriegel was every bit the equivalent of Jordan's last jump shot that sent the Utah Jazz to perdition in 1998. "I could have eked out another year or two from my body, but I thought it might do permanent damage," Allen said. He quit on an unbeaten streak at Kona, physically undamaged. "I vowed when I got into the sport I would quit before I did anything that would leave me unable to live to a healthy old age."

After a farewell tour with the well-paid short-course International Triathlon Grand Prix (ITGP) series and a few shorter races, Allen retired as a professional triathlete in 1997. Unlike Scott, who looks forward to another Ironman Hawaii reprise every few years, Allen is content to run a few miles a few times a week, work out, and enjoy the acclaim that comes to *Outside* magazine's 1997 "Fittest Man on the Planet." He works as a commentator for NBC's Ironman coverage every year, does corporate appearances and motivational speaking, holds seminars on shamanism and fitness with Secunda, and has built a highly successful online coaching business that has led hundreds of age-group athletes to competitive success. When he looks at the future, he looks at his son, Mats, and smiles. "I just hope he has a clean world to live in," said Allen. "So many of the places in San Diego where we biked and ran are overrun with people. That was a golden time. Now, we hope we bring him up to have passion for health and life, fitness, and sharing with other people what it is all about."

THREE | **TEAM HOYT**

"Every individual should have the opportunity to take part in daily life."

WHAT HAD ALWAYS been a fundamental attitude of Judy and Dick Hoyt became their life motto when their first son, Rick, came into the world under dramatic circumstances on January 10, 1962. He was strangled by his own umbilical cord during birth, and his brain didn't get enough oxygen. When the Hoyts held him in their arms, it was determined that the child suffered from cerebral palsy.

The doctors believed there was no hope the child would develop normally. They were sure he would remain in a more or less vegetative state for his entire life. Function on his own? Impossible. Communicate? Unthinkable. They advised the Hoyts to put him in a nursing home.

For Judy and Dick, that was out of the question. With all of their energy, they did their best to integrate the boy into a full, rich life. In 1964 and 1967 Rick gained two healthy brothers, Robert and Russell. Like any other family, the Hoyts wanted to enjoy life with their children.

All of the activities the family was involved in over the next several years included Rick. Swimming, cross-country skiing, hockey, hiking—the Hoyts found a way to pursue them together. Once, when passersby were amazed that the family wanted to bring Rick on a hike, Dick lifted his son onto his shoulders and said, "It's just a mountain."

Even though Rick didn't miss out when it came to family life, he was denied entry into public life, especially the opportunity to attend school. No one outside his family could understand him. His inability to speak was misinterpreted as a lack of intelligence.

It wasn't until a visit to Tufts University in New England that the family obtained the help of some faculty members to prove to the outside world what it had known all along: Rick is smart. "Tell him a joke," the boy's father prompted the university staff. Rick's reaction to punch lines and his hearty laughter convinced the academics, who committed to building a machine that would allow Rick to express himself.

Several years and several prototypes later, they successfully constructed a communication device that would allow Rick, then 12 years old, to make his thoughts known. The Hoyts called it the "Hope Machine"; the apparatus displayed on a monitor single letters that their son could choose by moving his knee.

As Rick began using it for the first time, everyone crowded around to see what his first words would be. They made enthusiastic guesses such as "Hi, Mom," "Hi, Dad," "How are you, Rob?" and "What's up, Russell?" But no one got it right. Letter by letter Rick composed his message. First a "g," then an "o" followed by a space, and then a "b." No one could figure out what he wanted to say until he finished all the letters and they saw "Go Bruins!" displayed on the screen—a cheer for his favorite professional hockey team in nearby Boston. At that point they realized that Rick was a sports fan. It was a realization that, along with Rick's new high-tech tool, would change the family's life.

Three years later Rick was attending middle school. One night he went with his gym teacher, who coached the Westfield State College basketball team, to one of the team's games. At halftime Rick heard an announcement that one of the lacrosse players at the college had been paralyzed in an accident, and a charity 8K road race was being held to help pay his medical bills. That night Rick wrote on his computer, "Dad, I want to run in that race."

"At the time I was 40 and was not a runner," said Dick. "I used to run a mile three times a week to keep my weight down, but I hadn't done anything more since high school. But I told Rick we would try it. Rick had an old Mulholland wheelchair form-fitted to his body, and it was heavy and hard to control because the crowns of the road made it want to head straight out into the woods."

They started the race with 00 as their number. Some family members predicted that Dick would turn around after the very first curve, but Dick and Rick would not give up that easily. Encouraged by the cheers of the spectators, they were next to last, but they made it. "We had a picture of Rick that day, and he had the biggest smile you ever saw," said Dick. When they got home that night, Rick wrote on his computer, "When I am running, it feels like I am not handicapped."

"I couldn't walk normally for days," Dick Hoyt recalled. But his son's joy trumped any physical discomfort.

The race made it clear that they needed a better wheelchair. Hoyt and an engineer in Greenfield, New Hampshire, designed one with a special seat fitted to Rick's body. They got some pipe and welded it together with one wheel in front, two in back. It was a big improvement.

At the same time Dick Hoyt intensified his training, and father and son participated in more running events. In 1979 they entered their first official race, a 5 miler in Springfield, Massachusetts. "Before the race nobody came near us," said Dick. "I think they didn't want us in the race. But when we finished 150th of 300 runners in the race, that opened up a lot of eyes." Every weekend after that they went to road races, and people started talking to them. "They could see that Rick had a personality, and he loved to be involved and meet people and be in the middle of them," said Dick. "He just loved people."

In 1981 Team Hoyt planned for its biggest challenge yet: the Boston Marathon. To that point the Boston Athletic Association (BAA) hadn't foreseen the need for a category for people like Dick and Rick Hoyt, and they turned down the Hoyts' request. Father and son were disappointed. They didn't really feel that they could blame the organizers. A lot of people simply didn't understand that even someone who couldn't walk or talk might have a passion for participating in sport.

Although the Hoyts hadn't obtained formal approval, the lure of starting the world's oldest annual marathon became irresistible.

Dick once again ramped up his training. While his son was in school, he loaded up the wheelchair with bags of dry cement and pushed it mile after mile.

On the third Monday of April, Patriots' Day in New England, the time came. Along with thousands of other runners, the Hoyts worked their way to the staging area. At noon, when the starting gun fired, there was no turning back. Their goal was to finish under 3 hours, a time many runners who didn't have to push someone in a wheelchair could only dream of.

Everything went well that day. Dick wanted to show the BAA that he and his son belonged there, and he ran hard. But while Rick was enjoying the applause of the spectators, his father came face to face with the dreaded wall that haunts every marathoner. Dick's chest felt like it was caving in, his legs were cramping, and his arms felt like rubber. Nothing helped; he had to take a break and walk. But the spectators' cheers left no room for a breather. After just a few yards, he regrouped and began running again. It wasn't much farther. Before he knew it, they had arrived on Boylston Street, and Team Hoyt crossed the finish line of its first marathon. Even though it wasn't official, their time of 3 hours 16 minutes was within the qualifying standard for a man Dick's age. People asked Dick if he would run the marathon alone. "I don't run that way. Rick started me out. He asked me out running. We started out running this way, and that is the way we run," he answered, explaining that he also ran with Rick to raise awareness about the need to integrate the handicapped into everyday society. How could he ask that of others if he failed to do it with his own son?

In fact, Dick Hoyt was beginning to demonstrate that, given his load, he was a world-class runner for his age group, and that he and Rick belonged with the thousands of excellent athletes in one of America's great running races.

Despite their enormous accomplishment, in 1981 the Hoyts were once again unable to obtain official permission to start the

Boston Marathon. They again had to sneak in, and like the year before, they put on an amazing performance. With a time of 2:59, they made it under the magic 3-hour barrier. In 1982 they ran unofficially again and did it in 2:58.

Several media outlets were now covering Dick and Rick Hoyt. Perhaps the best indicator of why the Hoyts truly belonged in the race came with some questions reporters asked. "People would ask me if I derived any advantage from pushing the chair, much as the wheelchair athletes have surpassed the runner's times," said Dick. "I think it is harder pushing the chair. I weighed 172, and Rick weighed 100, and our first chair weighed 58 pounds. Your legs are still pumping, but I don't get the advantage of using my arms. Actually, they get real tired and sore."

In 1983 the Hoyts took the start in Boston, again without a race number. But this time they had been invited by the organizers to participate in an unofficial capacity. It took Dick and Rick Hoyt 2 hours 57 minutes that year. The ever-growing media exposure finally led to a compromise by the BAA. The official stance was that if the Hoyts could qualify for Boston at another marathon, then they were welcome to participate. It sounded good at first, but there was a catch. The qualifying time for a 42-year-old man (Dick's age) was 3 hours 10 minutes. But the Boston organizers were stipulating that Team Hoyt meet the 2:50 requirement for a 21-year-old man (Rick's age).

"If you're willing, you can handle anything," Dick would say. They chose the Marine Corps Marathon in Washington, D.C., as their qualifying race. They'd heard that the course in the nation's capital was fast, but would it be possible to beat their own best time by 7 minutes? Everything had to go well on that day: Dick's fitness, Rick's morale, the weather, the wheelchair, the tires. . . .

From the gun, Dick Hoyt began running his fastest pace to date. Everything went perfectly, and at mile 20 they burst through the infamous wall as if it were made of paper. Nevertheless, Dick was nervous. With 1.24 miles to go, he was already trying to read the race clock at the finish. How fast would they be? Would they make it under 2:50? Would they ever! When Dick and Rick Hoyt completed the course, the clock read 2:45. They were in for Boston.

On Patriots' Day in 1984 the Hoyts started the eighty-eighth Boston Marathon with a race number for the first time. It took them 2 hours 57 minutes. The resulting media interest was huge; everyone wanted an interview and a photo. And the organizers, who for years hadn't wanted to include them in the race, were now asking for their help in publicizing the event.

Later in 1984 promoter Dave McGillivray walked up to Dick Hoyt at the Falmouth road race and invited him to try his Bay State Triathlon. "Yeah, but only if I can do it with Rick," said Dick. McGillivray, seemingly stunned, walked away speechless. The next year they talked again, and McGillivray told Dick to build some equipment so he and Rick could compete together in the triathlon. "At the time I didn't know how to swim and hadn't been on a bike since I was four years old," said Dick. The Hoyts moved to Holland, Massachusetts, where they bought a house on a lake so Dick could practice swimming. "I jumped in, and I sank!" said Dick. "I couldn't believe it. Jesus, I can run marathons, and I can't swim! But I was committed to do a triathlon in eight months. When I got tired I did the sidestroke and swam on my back. I just went a little farther every day."

He tried to set up a new running chair so he could take off the front wheel and attach the chair to the bike to tow Rick. He got a Boston Whaler 9-foot inflatable raft with a wooden floor and seated Rick in a beanbag chair with a life vest. He then tied a rope around his chest to swim and tow.

"The run was easiest, the swim was tough, and the bike was hardest," said Hoyt. "We push a total of 345 pounds on the bike, which is built for two with a special seat in the front for Rick. Most triathletes are fortunate, but I gotta think of accidents."

On Father's Day in 1986 they finished a 1-mile swim, a 40-mile bike, and a 10-mile run, coming in next to last. "That was close, but we have never finished last in any of the events we were in," said Dick. It was the beginning of a new era.

"When we crossed the line, it was quite a celebration," Dick said. "We really loved it. We loved the triathletes, and Dave had us make a speech, and the crowd was great, and we were triathlon freaks from then on. Ricky loves triathlons. He always loved to swim, and he loved the water, and he sits in the boat and is part of it. He gets wet and it rains and he is in the sun and the wind and all of that. In the ocean it is a bumpy ride. On the bike the winds blew me back, and him, too. He said he loved all three sports."

Later that year the Hoyts were invited to Ironman Canada in Penticton, British Columbia, which was held in late August. They hesitated only briefly. It was true that they had never set their sights on such a long course before, but the challenge proved enticing. They accepted the offer.

On August 31, 1986, the starting gun fired at 7 in the morning on Lake Okanagan. Everything went smoothly at first, but then Dick began cramping. An escort boat came over to ask if they wanted to quit. But to this day the word "quit" does not exist in the Hoyt family vocabulary. Dick fought on and reached the shore. The swimming was not the hardest test of the day, however. On the bike course he still had to contend with Richter Pass, which peaked at 5,000 feet in elevation.

Even though they were riding a new cycling rig that positioned Rick in front of the handlebars, it took the Hoyts 10 hours to complete the 112-mile bike, which put them over the cutoff for an official finish. Dick asked Rick at one point if he wanted to stop, and his son said no. It was already September 1, according to the calendar, when the Hoyts reached the finish line in 17 hours 53 minutes. Even though it was the most demanding event they had done so far, they were both ecstatic.

A year later father and son put in a masterful performance at the Hyannis Endurance Ironman in Cape Cod, Massachusetts. They covered the entire course in 13 hours 45 minutes—4 hours faster than their time in Canada the year before! The ultimate goal had now become Ironman Hawaii.

Just as their first requests to start the Boston Marathon had been declined in the early '80s, so was the Hoyts' request to participate in the famed Ironman in Kailua-Kona. "Too dangerous" went the reasoning. The swim crossed open ocean instead of a lake, and rough water was the order of the day. Officials were concerned that waves could put the boat and therefore Rick Hoyt at risk.

But the Hoyts wouldn't give up. They even asked a U.S. senator to intervene on their behalf. And it worked. In October 1988 the Hoyts took their rightful place at the start of the Ironman world championships. The entire family traveled to Kailua: Rick, Dick, Judy, and Robert and Russell as well as their young families.

Race day didn't go as planned. In the intense heat, Dick decided he needed to drink a lot before the race, so he loaded up on an electrolyte replacement fluid, Exceed. "I drank it the night before, but I learned later you don't drink it until you've started competing. It stayed heavy in my stomach all that night." The next day the Hoyts were sailing along in the swim, well within the 2 hour 15 minute cutoff time, when that Exceed became a big anchor in his stomach. "We just had a half mile to go and all of a sudden I couldn't move my arms, and I couldn't move my legs," recalled Dick, who experienced stomach cramps after the swim turnaround. He tried to change from his customary breaststroke to a sidestroke. But the Pacific swells crashed over him, and he swallowed saltwater.

An escort boat was quick to offer help that he declined. He knew if he accepted help at that point, the race would be over for him and his son. Only when the race officials told him that he would no longer make the swim time cut did he allow them to help him and his son back to shore.

It was the first race the Hoyts hadn't finished. Dick felt dejected, as if he had let everyone down. He said he would have liked nothing more than to jump right back in the water and swim all the way back to Massachusetts.

Despite the team's disappointment, the race organizers were impressed. They extended an invitation to the following year's race right then and there. Twelve months later the Hoyts set out to prove that they hadn't bitten off more than they could chew.

Things went much better the next time around. Dick and Rick finished the 2.4-mile swim in 1 hour and 54 minutes. Gone were the ghosts of the previous year, along with any lingering doubts. They finished the 112-mile bike just 8 hours later. By the time the Hoyts set off to run the marathon, they were half an hour ahead of the cutoff, and the run was their ace in the hole. But what was normally their specialty event became an all-out struggle. The swells in the morning and the heat in the afternoon had taken a lot out of both of them. Dick was digging deep in order to keep from tripping so he wouldn't lose control of the wheelchair and his son. What motivated him were the hopes and wishes of family members who had once again made the trip, as well as the dreams of his son Rick, who had been just as disappointed as he the year before.

Shortly after 9 p.m. the Hoyts reached the city limits.

Just a few hundred meters from the finish, they heard the cheers from the finish area. Only the steep descent down Palani Road remained. One left turn around the corner, then two right turns. And then they were there, just yards away from the ribbon. Dick ran the final mile at a 5:30 pace, faster than overall winner Mark Allen had run to drop Dave Scott in their epic clash. As they sprinted down Ali'i Drive, the fatigue seemed to melt away. Dick passed a few more competitors while Rick waved ecstatically to the crowd. Flowers and leis flew through the air as they crossed the finish line together. And before the wheels of Rick's chair came to a stop, he and his father were being smothered by their family's kisses. The clock read 14 hours 24 minutes. It wasn't the Hoyts' fastest time, but they agreed that no other finishing straight was comparable to this one; no other had inspired such a deep feeling of joy.

Dick and Rick Hoyt proved how much can be accomplished with perseverance, determination, and love. They challenged conventional wisdom and prejudice in sports as well as in everyday life. In 1993 Rick obtained a degree from Boston University and began work in the computer department at Boston College, where he was involved in the development of a device that could be steered by the eye movements of a disabled person.

In 1999, 10 years after their first personal triumph in Kailua-Kona, the Hoyts once again finished Ironman Hawaii, this time in 16 hours 14 minutes. In 2000 they finished Ironman Germany with a time of 16 hours 9 minutes. They tried three more times to finish in Hawaii, but unfortunately without success. In 2003 they crashed on the bike. In 2004 the wind was so strong along the bike course that they didn't make it to the second transition zone before the time cutoff. And in 2006 Dick wasn't able to overcome the strong ocean currents.

Now that Dick is 66 and Rick is 45, they are probably not planning to tackle any more Ironman events. But they will continue to compete in half-iron-distance (Ironman 70.3) events. And they competed in their twenty-fifth Boston Marathon a few years ago; they have long served as icons of that classic footrace.

The Hoyts have inspired thousands of people. "In Hawaii athletes are always talking to us during the race, telling us that they are only there because they saw us do it," said Dick, betraying some pride. They would often get asked which of the two contributed more to their accomplishments, and each would inevitably give the other credit. Rick says his father is the perfect role model, while his father has always considered Rick to be the driving force. "Before Rick asked me over 30 years ago if we could do that charity run, I was lazy, a couch potato," he explained. But now he was in the best shape of his life. Rick, on the other hand, had always loved sports and been a true athlete. Dick just lent Rick his hands and legs so his son could measure himself against other athletes and have fun.

The extent of Rick's gratitude to his father became clear when he answered a question for his biographer, Sam Nall, who wanted to know what Rick would do if he weren't confined to a wheelchair. "I'm not exactly sure. I love sports and would maybe want to play hockey, baseball, or basketball. But when I really think about it, the first thing I would do is ask my father to sit in the wheelchair so I could push him for a while."

FOUR | **PAULA NEWBY-FRASER**

"It's not so easy."

THE GREATEST IRONMAN triathlete of all time was born in Salisbury, Southern Rhodesia (now Harare, Zimbabwe), and raised in Durban, South Africa. "I was a good girl growing up. A very good girl," Paula Newby-Fraser told writer TJ Murphy about her childhood. Her father was a wealthy industrialist who owned a paint factory. Her mother was a university lecturer in psychology and social sciences. Newby-Fraser studied hard, got good grades, and excelled at ballet and swimming.

Her government-controlled all-girls school was strict. "The choices were limited. You did what you were told. You just did," she recalled. At school the girls lined up every week for inspection, shortest to tallest. No talking, no earrings, no makeup. Lengths of skirts and fingernails were checked.

The outlet she found was sports. "Because there were no boys around, we didn't have the social dimension to think about, to take up our energy," she said. "Instead we focused on things like sports." Girls who performed well at games were praised at assemblies and cheered by the crowd. But a career in sports was unthinkable. Proper girls married well or became teachers.

Ever practical, she embraced the discipline of her early schooling and studied social sciences at the University of Natal in Durban. After graduating in 1984, she ditched academic life and embraced the town's active party scene. When a friend said she was getting fat, they started running together and lifting weights. Sparked by her increasing fitness, Newby-Fraser checked out a local triathlon with her boyfriend. Though she thought the challenge was slightly ridiculous, her boyfriend convinced her to give the event a try the following year, and they bought bicycles and began training. Only 8 weeks after buying the bike Newby-Fraser won her first triathlon, setting a new women's record for the course. She also finished 4th among the men, giving a hint of her power to come. Three months later she won the women's division of the South African Triathlon and won a free trip to Hawaii to compete in the famed Ironman Triathlon.

There, in 1985, virtually unknown and relying on raw talent (she had never swum 2.4 miles, biked 112 miles, or run a marathon), she placed 3rd. Moreover, she finished just 5 minutes 42 seconds behind the women's winner, Joanne Ernst. That performance, along with what she had learned in preparation for the race, convinced Newby-Fraser that additional training could give her the tools to win.

On her way to Hawaii Newby-Fraser had stopped in San Diego—triathlon's original mecca—and found a collective passion for the sport among the pioneers. In a story in *Encinitas* magazine, she said, "I planned to visit San Diego because of the great athletes that were there, like Scott Tinley, Mark Montgomery, and Colleen Cannon. I stayed at a friend's in Leucadia and started doing all the famous workouts: the Tuesday run in Rancho Santa Fe, the Wednesday bike ride, swimming and track workouts at UCSD."

When Newby-Fraser returned to South Africa she couldn't shake Encinitas from her mind. "All I could think of was that I had to get back," she said. After talking it over with her parents, she flew back to America with $1,000 in her pocket and moved into an apartment with fellow triathletes Linda Janelli and Maggie Smeal. During those first months she met the man who would become the lasting love of her life, Paul Huddle, an elite triathlete now recognized as one of the best triathlon coaches in the world.

In her second Hawaii Ironman in 1986 she eased into history when 1st-place finisher Patricia Puntous was disqualified for drafting and Newby-Fraser, who crossed the line 2 minutes later, inherited the victory. She was awarded the $10,000-plus top prize, the first year the event offered a pro purse. When she heard that she had won, Newby-Fraser seemed stunned. "I just feel that I have no control over the situation," she told journalist Mike Plant. "I feel for her, but I have no control. I'm pleased that I've won now, but that's just the way it goes."

While her victory may have felt anticlimactic, Newby-Fraser's winning time was a clap of thunder announcing the arrival of professional women to the sport. Her 9:49:14 mark broke the previous record by 36 minutes, and she was the first woman to break the Ironman 10-hour mark. Her finish would have won the men's division in the first two Ironman contests and would have placed 2nd to the top man in the 1980 and 1981 events.

In 1987 Newby-Fraser started strong, holding the lead for 21 miles of the marathon, but then faded in the brutal heat. Two-time winner Sylviane Puntous of Canada, Patricia Puntous's twin, was stalking her all day, and New Zealand star Erin Baker, a superb 2:36 marathoner and excellent short- and long-course triathlon star, caught both of them at mile 22. Newby-Fraser was tapped and could not fight back. Puntous, as was her habit in the early years of the sport, walked through the aid stations while the fierce newcomer Baker, shocked at the Canadian's lack of warrior ethic, stormed past to a new record time of 9:35:25, with Puntous 1:32 back. Although she had broken her own 1986 course record by 9 minutes, Newby-Fraser fell to 3rd.

Afterward, Plant wrote, Newby-Fraser realized that winning the Ironman would demand her full attention. For her part, Baker said, "I had to concentrate like hell to get to the finish. I didn't have anything left. I couldn't smile." From that point forward, every woman knew she would have to run every mile of the marathon to prevail.

———————

Newby-Fraser's remarkable Ironman finish in 1988 was the shot heard 'round the world of sport. Rival Erin Baker upped the ante tremendously, topping her year-old record by 23 minutes with a 9:12:14 finish. But Newby-Fraser slaughtered Baker by 11 minutes and her old standard by 34 minutes with a 9:01:01 finish. Indeed, Newby-Fraser appeared to be in a league of her own; her greatest rivals were men. She finished 11th overall, just a breath over 30 minutes behind the men's overall winner, Scott Molina, and along the way she bested a string of certified men's stars, including her boyfriend, Paul Huddle, by 3:45; Greg Welch by 6:13; Jeff Devlin by 9:53; and Peter Kropko by an amazing 20:36.

For all Joan Benoit Samuelson's greatness, she never finished near the top 11 at Boston or in the Olympics. Florence Griffith Joyner would not have qualified for the men's Olympic team. Only Ann Trason, who finished the 1995 Western States 100-mile trail run just 5 minutes behind the men's winner, was in the same area code as Newby-Fraser in women's remarkable push toward equality in endurance sports.

But Newby-Fraser, who maintained a highly disciplined, scientific approach to the sport throughout her career, was never carried away by the hype over her 1988 feat. "That year I had a good performance, and the men lagged," she remembered. "The next year I went just a little bit quicker, but I was 51 minutes back of [men's winner] Mark Allen. Had Mark been winning the race in 1988, the gap would not have been as small as it was."

Over the next three editions of Ironman Hawaii, Newby-Fraser racked up similarly impressive results. In 1989 she topped women's runner-up Puntous by 21 minutes. The next year, on a hot day, she proved she was human and lost another duel to Erin Baker, 9:13:42 to 9:20:01. She came back in 1991 to beat Baker by nearly 16 minutes, giving her four wins in six years—a record that many an athlete might happily call a career. Yet all of these performances were but a buildup to one of the most remarkable years recorded by any athlete in triathlon.

Newby-Fraser started her 1992 campaign by winning the three-quarters-Ironman-distance Nice International Triathlon. Two weeks later she won her fourth Ironman Japan in 9:16:13. Just a few days later she told Huddle she felt surprisingly good. As recounted by writer Ken McAlpine, Huddle replied, "Are you saying what I think you're saying?" Indeed, Newby-Fraser thought she could win

Ironman Europe at Roth, Germany. Thirteen days later she did, in a then-world-record time of 8:55:00. While even the best triathletes take weeks to recover from the pounding and the energy-sapping dehydration of just one Ironman, Newby-Fraser had just won three Ironman-proportion events in five weeks, recording perhaps the greatest high-intensity stretch in Ironman history.

A mere 13 weeks after the European Ironman, she stepped across the finish line in Kona to take her fifth Ironman Hawaii title, setting an 8:55:28 course record that stood until 2009 and winning the women's title by the biggest margin of the modern era, 26 minutes 12 seconds, the triathlon equivalent of Secretariat's 31-length Belmont Stakes win.

By this time Newby-Fraser, working with superagent Murphy Reinschreiber, had built an empire of sponsorships, appearance fees, and business deals that was estimated by *Inside Triathlon* to bring in half a million dollars a year. It was peanuts by the standards of pro golf, tennis, and running superstars but groundbreaking in terms of the tiny niche occupied by the still emerging sport of triathlon. And in contrast to the pampered rich of mainstream sports, Newby-Fraser remained modest, utterly approachable, and without a shred of arrogance.

The following year's preparation for Ironman Hawaii did not begin auspiciously. Newby-Fraser suffered an overtraining injury to her ankle, and the women's field began to believe an upset was in the cards. "This year I was forced to take three months off from running and a month and a half from the bike," said Newby-Fraser before the race, displaying a small wrap on her ankle. "This is the least prepared I have ever been for the Ironman. I just hope my years in the sport and my strength can carry me through."

Erin Baker, the 1987 and 1990 Ironman women's champ, wasn't buying the "poor Paula" routine. "It would be stupid to think Paula won't be tough," said Baker. "But," she added, "I expect a much better run out of myself."

Baker herself had seemed like a prohibitive long shot, as in May she had given birth to a child. A few months later she had started training again and felt her strength return. Then Reebok offered her a three-year contract she couldn't turn down—her husband, 1988 Ironman champion Scott Molina, was out of commission with a bad back, and Baker felt the need to take the sponsorship to support her family. She got retired Ironman champ Dave Scott to design a new training program for her Ironman. "I used to come to this race just feeling wasted," said Baker. "But now Dave has me running shorter distances and faster times. I don't just go out for 4-hour bike rides anymore. I run and ride shorter, faster intervals. And I feel fresher."

Baker claimed she was stronger and more flexible since the birth of her son, Miguel, and said she was now blessed with a higher red-blood-cell count. "The birth has had the same effect as training at altitude," she said. "All mothers get that at birth, and the increased red-blood count typically lasts nine months. And this is soon enough so it's still true for me." Baker added, "The most important thing is I am running harder at a lower heart rate in training. I am readier than I have ever been."

Baker was kicked in the head right at the swim start and fell 5 minutes behind Newby-Fraser's 53:29 swim. On the bike Newby-Fraser set a still-standing record of 4:48:30, topping Baker's bike split by 1:36 and her own bike-split record set the previous year by 8 minutes. On the run, fighting exhaustion and lack of training mileage due to her injured ankle, Newby-Fraser held on grimly for a 3:16:54 marathon, which rewarded her with her second sub-9-hour Ironman and a final 3-2 edge in head-to-head Kona encounters with her not-so-friendly rival Baker.

In the race, Newby-Fraser had intrigued 1993 Ironman rookie Karen Smyers, the 1990 International Triathlon Union (ITU) short-course world champion from Massachusetts who had tested the waters of the Ironman with some trepidation and a touch of naive optimism. After finishing 4th, Smyers emerged with a deep appreciation of Newby-Fraser's skills and toughness. "Paula? Geez. I know it was irrational, but part of me said if I can beat her by 2 minutes in a short race, in a long race I could beat her by 10 minutes," said Smyers. "I had never done a long course, so I did not know what the times meant. So Paula blowing away the competition there didn't mean much to me until I saw her beat Erin Baker, who had won the first ITU World Championship and was nearly unbeatable in short course. I have the utmost respect for Erin Baker. Erin went undefeated one year at all distances. That gave Paula's Ironman record the most credibility with me."

Afterward Newby-Fraser let down her guard a little about just how tough it had been. "I lost a part of myself, a part of my soul, out there on the run," she said. "I think it's still out there."

Lost in the excitement that accompanied the Greg Welch duel with Dave Scott coming back after 40, Newby-Fraser won another predictable dull-from-the-outside, gutsy-from-the-inside race in Hawaii in 1994. With Baker gone forever from Kona, Newby-Fraser's closest challenger was now Karen Smyers, one year wiser about the demands of Ironman.

From the beginning Newby-Fraser's 54:19 swim gave her an unexpectedly large lead over Smyers's 58:22. On the bike Newby-Fraser's 5:02:25 added another 8:30 to her lead. Starting with 12 minutes in hand, Newby-Fraser showed she was hurting with a 3:23:30 run, 18 minutes off her best time. Nevertheless, that subpar performance gave back only 4:37 to runner-up Smyers.

"I don't know why it was such a tough day," Newby-Fraser told Bob Babbitt of *Competitor* after the race. "I worked hard on the swim, and I had a terrific swim and bike ride. But I paid for it on the run." She felt terrible starting the run and stopped 12 miles into the marathon. "When I got out of town, I stopped at an aid station on the highway and had a talk with myself," she said.

"Come on. Get it together. I'm having a hard day. Everyone has a hard day," she told herself.

Then, foreshadowing the next year's race, she said, "It's not fun to have someone like Karen Smyers coming up from behind." With 4 miles to go, Smyers was 7 minutes back. But, talking to herself all the way, Newby-Fraser ended up maintaining the 8-minute lead she had on the bike to take her seventh win.

When asked if she would come back in 1995, Newby-Fraser was ambivalent. "Mentally, I don't know if I can make those kinds of sacrifices. I have to put so much of my life on hold for this race. I'd like to come back and do this race again. But I don't know if I'll make the same kind of commitment."

Newby-Fraser was 36 years old, and the expectations that she could continue to lead the sport were gnawing at her. Despite achieving a degree of dominance that prompted ABC Sports to call her "the premier woman endurance athlete of the century," Newby-Fraser did not enjoy an emotional bond with her fans, largely because she played her cards close to the vest. After the fact, her victories often seemed too easy. In truth, though, those wins had come harder than the hype suggested. Baker had taken her down in 1987 and 1990, and in 1993 Newby-Fraser had to dig so deep in the heat to fend off Baker that she said, "I don't know if I can do this again."

And yet, of course, she did. At the start of her 1995 season, Newby-Fraser was on form once again with big-margin wins at Wildflower, Ironman Lanzarote, and Ironman Germany. "During the past couple of years it was hard work—not very exciting, but winning was everything," she told *Inside Triathlon*. "The result was all important. I didn't want to put myself through training and not win." But always seeking to come closer to perfection, she soon found herself flying too close to the sun.

In midsummer she journeyed to Boulder, Colorado, triathlon's new center of gravity, where she began training with Mark Allen. "I did things I thought I'd never do," she told Deborah Crooks at

Inside Triathlon as she embraced a new training blueprint incorporating high mileage and high intensity. "I thought if I wanted to race like the men, I was going to train like the men. If Mark was going to ride 500 miles a week, I'd ride 500 miles a week. I'd go with Mark on a 150-mile ride. I was doing long runs at altitude, at 8,000 feet. I was getting stronger. I was breaking new ground in training. The journey there was an accomplishment."

Coming into Ironman Hawaii, the greatest Ironman triathlete of all time set the stage for a grand exit by announcing that she would retire from serious competition after this race, her eleventh Kona assault. She was confident, having arrived rested, trained, and without injury for the first time in several years. "There will be no excuses," she said. "This will be their last shot at me."

Just 20 miles into the bike, Karen Smyers was shadowing Newby-Fraser when the riders were blasted with the opening salvo from some of the most brutal headwinds in Kona history. When 1991 and 1994 men's podium finisher Jeff Devlin and some other contenders came along, Smyers recalled, "These guys beat me on the bike by 45 minutes, so I thought, *I'll just back off and I'll let them go.* Then Paula followed and just tore into the wind like an arrow. Before I knew it there was a huge gap I could not make up."

Newby-Fraser had followed her 53:45 swim with a 5:06:04 bike—phenomenal in the terrible winds—and was in command of an 11-minute, 30-second lead on Smyers at the second transition. Her charge looked unstoppable. In fact, by the end of the bike leg Newby-Fraser's seemingly insurmountable lead prompted Huddle, calling the race on local television, to break tradition and predict victory. "In the Ironman, it's never over till it's over," he intoned. "But with a lead like that, with Paula and her history, it's over."

But it wasn't. Inexplicably Newby-Fraser had stopped refueling. In her book *Peak Fitness for Women,* Newby-Fraser had laid out her winning strategy: "When I am racing, I am constantly checking every technical aspect of my performance. The efficiency of my swim stroke, my rpms during cycling, my leg turnover on the run. My nutritional requirements. I am constantly checking energy levels and monitoring fluid and solid food intake." Yet that was not the case now.

The first outward sign that Newby-Fraser had abandoned her usual discipline came when she threw away her special-needs bag at the bike turnaround at Hawi. "I thought I was stretching myself on the bike, but as I started the run I thought I was well within myself," said Newby-Fraser later. "I felt comfortable, and when I started running I actually felt pretty good. And you know the bottom line was that Karen had a spectacular run. She was bearing down on me the whole way. Logically she still shouldn't have caught me but by the time I got out of the Energy Lab, I realized I was suffering from some heat exhaustion. So I ate a banana and felt better and thought I would be able to make it."

Smyers, headed to a near-record Kona marathon of 3:05:20, was chipping away and had whittled the margin to 3 minutes leaving the Energy Lab. There were 6.5 miles to go. With her half-mile lead, Newby-Fraser thought she had the race under control, but her seamless facade was crumbling, and her nerves were frayed under Smyers's charge. Newby-Fraser blew past the last few aid stations, dancing on the edge of meltdown. A crash into a careless aid-station volunteer with 3 miles to go—she fell hard and popped back up immediately—was another sign that she was running on empty.

With less than a mile left, Newby-Fraser had carefully doled out her energy cards and now held a 1-minute lead. "I knew if I stayed on my feet, I could still win, although it might be cut down to 10 or 15 seconds," she recalled.

Then the improbable became the impossible.

"I could feel it coming on, and I think it was the pressure of being in front," she said. "Everybody was going, 'Just put one foot in front of the other.' I thought I would arrive at the finish line with a few seconds in hand. But I was just blowing through the last three or four aid stations, and when I came down the hill on Palani Road, I was weaving all over the road."

Once she turned left on Kuakini, with a half mile to go, it got worse. "I stopped at one point and said, 'I can't finish.' I was starting to lose consciousness. I know it looked like something out of a movie. I couldn't believe it. Even now, as I look back on it, I think, *Why couldn't I have kept going another 300 yards?* But there was no way."

After turning right on Hualalai Road, Newby-Fraser said she was not really conscious of Smyers going by. Smyers said she only saw Newby-Fraser when she turned the corner onto Hualalai. When she saw that she was just 50 yards behind, Smyers accelerated as if she had been hit with a jolt of electricity.

As Smyers caught her, Newby-Fraser wobbled into her rival, and the challenger half caught her and prevented her from falling. "I was running very fast as I came up to her," said Smyers, "and she stopped a couple steps before I got there and kind of fell into me. So I had to catch her and straighten her up. And to be honest I had been in this mode of 'Go! Go! Go!' getting 30 seconds on her here and there. So I could not get out of that mode of 'Run fast and pass her!'"

Even 200 meters later, Smyers looked back to see if Newby-Fraser was coming back at her. "I had no idea she was feeling that bad," said Smyers. "I knew she was struggling, but I thought for sure she would at least be able to jog it in. So I waited at the finish line for 5 or 10 minutes for her to come across and congratulate her. I didn't know how bad she was."

On the same spot a quarter mile from the finish where Julie Moss had fallen in February 1982, Queen Paula sank to the curb near Uncle Billy's Kona Bay Hotel. And Newby-Fraser, who for a decade had been the cool, composed assassin of everyone else's hopes, wondered aloud, "Am I dying?"

"When I sat down on the curb, I said to myself, 'Just take another step,'" said Newby-Fraser. "But there was no way. I couldn't move. I actually thought I had given my life to that race and I was going to die. I felt like I was going into seizure. There was a moment when I thought I was going to be taken away to a hospital, but even if I had to wait until midnight I wanted to finish."

Huddle ran out to Newby-Fraser. "My gut instinct was, let's call 911, call a doctor, get her to the hospital. But then I talked to her and I realized she was coherent," he said. "She just wanted people to get away from her. But she was really dazed and told people to stop touching her and leave. It was like a car crash and everyone wants to see, saying, 'Jesus is with you.' Right then she didn't need Jesus; she needed a doctor and some breathing room. She said, 'I just wanted to get to the finish line. I may take until midnight and cross with [295-pound former NFL tackle] Darryl [Haley, whom Newby-Fraser had coached that summer], but I will do it on my own."

Then Huddle got a laugh out of Paula. "I joked, 'You've always dreamed about being able to stop and sit down by the side of the road at an Ironman,'" said Huddle. "She laughed and said, 'That's right. I just want to sit down here for a while.' Then I knew she was okay."

Twenty minutes later Newby-Fraser gathered herself and walked to a 4th-place finish, offering no resistance when Brazilian Fernanda Keller nipped her at the line for 3rd place. Her sole worry was that her dramatic meltdown didn't "take away from what an awesome race Karen had."

Smyers cried when she saw Newby-Fraser walk across the line. "After the joy and the ecstasy, I got a sort of a weird feeling; it was heart-wrenching to see her that broken down. Yet I felt proud for her in how she battled through. I don't think I would have the mental power to endure so much." Smyers took tremendous satisfaction from the victory nonetheless. "I know how important it was, not only for me but for all future Ironwomen champions to come, that Paula did get beat before she retired. If she had retired undefeated, it would have been hard for anyone who came later to be viewed as a true champion. Now there won't have to be an asterisk on anyone's win A.P.—After Paula."

Afterward Mark Allen said, "Now you can see how daring she was all those years, how close to the edge she raced, how much of herself she gave to the race." Indeed, the race revealed, perhaps for the first time, the true measure of Newby-Fraser's intensity and grit. For years Newby-Fraser had been triathlon's Joe DiMaggio—the classic performer who worked relentlessly in training to make it all look effortless on game day. She was so smart and planned so well, that surely many fans thought it *was* easy. Other competitors may have become beloved icons for stepping over the line and suffering the consequences. But this breakdown was, for Newby-Fraser, an inexplicable exception, and for her fans a telling—and perhaps endearing—one.

Typically, Newby-Fraser would accept the fact of it, but she would not brook praise for it. "It was just idiotic," she said some years later. "There was no reason to lose the race other than rookie error. It was not a hard day, just stupid. There was nothing courageous about it. There was nothing anxious about it other than the excitement of the race. As a professional I didn't tend to my nutrition and dehydration, and it was just a very, very stupid lack of concentrating on things I needed to take care of. That is all there was to it. Anybody who reads more into it and sees anything courageous about it is looking at it wrong."

But in an interview with Crooks three months after the 1995 Ironman, Newby-Fraser opened a window into what might have been going on in her mind, exploring what roots might lie at the bottom of this mystery.

"In retrospect, I think a lot of what happened was mentally motivated," she told Crooks. "On some subconscious level, I think I decided to do something stupid. People got the impression that it was easy for me to come there and win. In some very obnoxious way, I think I was saying, 'Hey, it's not so easy.'"

After 10 years in the United States, Paula Newby-Fraser became a U.S. citizen in July 1996, which, along with her solid relationship with Huddle, seemed to lend some permanence to her idyllic existence in Encinitas. With a few months' distance from her disaster, Newby-Fraser regained equilibrium and a renewed mastery over the emotional and mental side of her sport as she approached Ironman Hawaii 1996.

By this time Newby-Fraser had adopted Buddhist principles and gained peace of mind by, as she described it, "living in the moment." Early in the year she withdrew her declaration of retirement from the sport and vowed to make one more charge on Kona. Nevertheless, she vowed, "I have no expectations" about Hawaii. She didn't want the pressure of being the favorite, and she didn't want to feed the expectations to lead. Instead, she said, "I just want to mix it up with the girls." She had won Kona seven times and did not want to put the weight back on her psyche.

During the year Newby-Fraser won Ironmans in Australia in April and Canada in August despite throwing up and staving off a collapse in Penticton. If she had allowed triathlon success to remain an obsession, she might have fretted over her coming clash with two fast-rising rivals, Karen Smyers and Natascha Badmann. Defending Kona champion Smyers was coming off a rare double, as she had wrapped up 1995 with a win at the ITU short-course World Championship and then, in mid-1996, won the ITU long-course World Championship. She had also become faster in all three sports at the Ironman distance.

Badmann, meanwhile, was a late-blooming Swiss star who had won the prestigious Powerman Zofingen long-distance duathlon world championship with a devastating bike. Badmann and her New Age coach and partner Toni Hasler's philosophy was tied to nature, and their attitude toward her Kona debut mirrored Newby-Fraser's in its deflation of expectations. "I just want to finish it and enjoy it," said Badmann.

Newby-Fraser's attitude adjustment came to the test midway through the 1996 encounter in Kona.

At the start, Smyers's 54:11 swim led Newby-Fraser by 79 seconds and Badmann by 6:30. On the bike Smyers took the lead from Wendy Ingraham and held off Newby-Fraser until mile 70 and Badmann until mile 90. At that point, Smyers recalled, "Natascha blew by me like a rocket and looked so fresh I was shocked."

Newby-Fraser beat Badmann (who clocked a stunning 4:53:47 bike) into T2 by only 18 seconds but had to serve a 3-minute drafting penalty. Newby-Fraser didn't mind. "To be honest, I didn't want to be leading out on the run," she said. "I stretched, put my feet up, did an interview." Newby-Fraser felt even more at ease when she saw Smyers come in fatigued 2.5 minutes later. "I knew Karen had pushed herself and I'd get her on the run."

At the Hot Corner in downtown Kona, where runners turn right on Palani Road for the steep uphill to the Queen K, Newby-Fraser had regained the lead from the Swiss rookie and was looking relaxed. She was 45 seconds up on Badmann, whom she had passed 15 minutes before at mile 6. And, in the surprise of the day, she was 4 minutes up on Smyers.

Smyers had made up a minute on Badmann in the first 3 miles and said, "I was desperately trying to regain the feeling I had last year, which lasted the entire race." But after mile 3, when her feet got sluggish and slow, "I knew it wasn't my day."

While Smyers came unraveled for good by mile 4 of the run, Badmann's race was full of surprises, which the newly calm Newby-Fraser handled with equanimity. "I passed Natascha at mile 6 of the run, but coming up on mile 13 she blazed by me going maybe 6:30 pace, some 30 seconds per mile faster," Newby-Fraser later recalled. "I was surprised because I didn't know she was closing. I just let her go. I didn't panic. I didn't say, 'I need to go with her.' It was a big rookie mistake, and I knew it wouldn't last."

Sure enough, on the Energy Lab Road the gap slowly shrank. Newby-Fraser caught Badmann in the first mile past the Energy Lab and then played cat-and-mouse with her in a duel. "I pulled in by her side, but she didn't like that, so she tucked in behind me because it was a bit of a headwind. So I swerved to the middle of the highway, and she swerved with me. That gave me the sense that she was trying to hang on to my energy. So I thought, *Let's see how bad it is*. I knocked off and started to run an extremely comfortable pace. She still didn't come up and run with me. She allowed me to lead."

By then the aid stations started to play a role. "I led through the aid stations and it was difficult for her because by that time most volunteers are looking the other way, and after the first runner goes through it is difficult to get enough water," said Newby-Fraser. "She wasn't getting the water she needed. We ran like that for a good two or three miles with all the motorcycles around us."

As they approached the hill at mile 24, made famous as the spot where Mark Allen broke away from Dave Scott in their epic 1989 race-long duel, Newby-Fraser stepped up the pace and steadily pulled away to the finish. Her time of 9:06:49 was the sixth-fastest for women on the course. Badmann, obviously suffering from lack of water at the aid stations, struggled in 4.5 minutes behind Newby-Fraser despite having been virtually tied with 2 miles to go. Newby-Fraser's 3:09:45 marathon had closed the deal.

―――――――――――

That 1996 race marked the end of Newby-Fraser's Hawaii wins and presaged the beginning, two years later, of Badmann's reign as Kona's queen. It also marked the true winding-down of one of the most impressive records in sports history.

In 1997 Newby-Fraser started the race but, feeling cooked in some of the toughest conditions in memory, dropped out 16 miles into the run. "I was going backward, and after what happened to me in 1995, I knew what lay ahead," she said. "It would be a death march; I would be entering a place where I would be subjecting myself to serious injury." Most impressively, Newby-Fraser admitted, "I was finally free of the ego or the fears that people would say

I was a quitter. I was quite comfortable retiring out on the Queen K because that was the place where I had left so many pieces of myself in the past. I didn't need that again."

Now, more than a decade after her long good-bye from a fully dedicated professional triathlon career, Newby-Fraser's accomplishments loom over the sport like a comet whose bright aura cannot be dimmed even by the arrival of the sensational Chrissie Wellington. In a professional career that extended from 1986 to 2004, she won 24 Ironman races; the next closest, her friend Heather Fuhr, won 15. Newby-Fraser took the crown jewel at Ironman Hawaii eight times; the next best—Mark Allen, Dave Scott, and Natascha Badmann—have won six each. In 1988 Newby-Fraser's 11th overall finish against the men was labeled "the greatest performance in endurance sports history" by the *Los Angeles Times*.

On the way she was named "Greatest All Around Female Endurance Athlete in the World" by ABC Sports and the *Los Angeles Times* and named as one of the top five professional female athletes in the world from 1972 to 1997 by the United States Sports Academy. *Sports Illustrated* listed her as number 60 among the greatest female athletes of the twentieth century. Until Wellington broke her course record at Kona in 2008, Newby-Fraser held the top six times in the history of Ironman Hawaii. By 1999 she had won 21 of the 26 Ironman races she entered around the globe.

And yet if you simply look at the numbers and the résumé and accepted her apparent invincibility without seeing the human heart and soul behind it, you would be missing the essence of her greatness.

In 1998, when Newby-Fraser crossed the Kona line in 11th place in a humbling 10:03:44, she was bathed in loving applause. "I realized today that people cared about me for who I am and did not care where I finished, only that I was OK and happy," she said.

And just to remind the sport of her prodigious talent, Newby-Fraser had one more impressive result to log at Kona: a 4th-place finish in 2001.

FIVE | **GREG WELCH**

"Yes! It's mine!"

AT THE PEAK of his career, Greg Welch was the Puck of triathlon, a clever and mischievous sprite with a raft of nicknames. His Aussie friends called him "Plucky." Paula Newby-Fraser called him "Pipsqueak, this naughty little thing you never knew what he was going to get into." Agent Murphy Reinschreiber called him "an adult Mickey Mouse." Paul Huddle fondly called Welch "Little Weasel."

Look fast, and you'd see Welch before an Ironman Hawaii press conference, running madly to get his propeller beanie up to speed. When asked by a fan to autograph his T-shirt after winning Ironman Japan, Welch took the magic marker and drew nipples, chest hair, and belly button, then went to the man's face and drew a mustache as the man and nearby fans laughed with astonished delight. While rivals might watch their diets like monks and avoid fat like the devil, young Welch favored late nights at the pubs, hamburgers, and his mom's Gummi Bears.

After Welch exploded into prominence with his 3rd-place finish in the 1989 Hawaiian Ironman, everyone wondered when he would fulfill his enormous promise. Was he the true successor to the 1989 Iron War leading men, Dave Scott and Mark Allen? Welch had won a few other world titles, but could he win the big one?

———

Greg Welch was born in Sydney and raised in the small coastal suburb of Bangor. His father, Pat, was a Rugby League player with a major league team called St. George, which won 11 straight titles in the 1960s. His mother, Noelene, was a tennis and squash player. Since this was Australia, water sports were also on the menu. His dad surfed, and his grandfather bought 5-year-old Greg his first surfboard, a Midget Farrelly foam model with a rubber fin and Greg's own special signature. "The way I could always tell my surfboard from my brother's was I used to stick my fingernails underneath to carry it and left my mark," said Welch. At age 12 he played Rugby League ball but found he was more competitive during the warm-up runs. "It turned into a bit of a race, and I won all the time, so I took up cross-country in high school," said Welch. From 14 to 19 he opted for the pleasures of squash and surfing. But at 19 he got back to running, joined the Sutherland Running Club, and qualified for the Australian cross-country nationals, where he finished 9th and was an alternate for the World Cross Country team.

When he turned 21 Welch was lured into triathlons by a good friend. Richie Walker was a lifeguard in Cronulla, a beach just down the way from where Welch grew up. "Richie's mom, Elizabeth Fraser, was a member of the 4 x 100 gold-medal swimming relay team in the 1956 Olympics, and Richie was a fantastic swimmer," said Welch. "We were in the same surf club and were friends from the beach. He told me, 'Welchy, you've gotta do these triathlons! It's a great sport!' I'd say, 'Nawww. Y'know I can't swim.'"

Welch had never ridden a bike in his life, so he went to watch Walker tackle a local triathlon. Walker got a 4th that weekend, and Welch was amazed: "They rode a big loop in the park where I live, 42 kilometers around and full of these nasty hills."

Welch went home, bought a 12-speed Clermont bike, and started training. "The first day I went to swim in the pool, I could barely make 50 meters before I had to stop and get a breath," recalled Welch. But Welch soon jumped into the fastest workout lanes because that was the quickest way to get better.

Late in 1986 Welch and Walker started training for the Australian Ironman scheduled for early 1987. Walker turned 21 on October 29. "We were supposed to go race at a place near Sydney that weekend, but Richie decided to go to a triathlon at Tamworth because there was less competition and he thought he might win it," said Welch. "I said, 'Aw, Richie, just chill out. Come with me and we'll have fun.'" But Walker stuck to his plan. At the Sydney race where he competed, Welch heard over the loudspeaker that Richie Walker had collapsed with a cardiac arrest at Tamworth. "The radio reported that he was taken away in an ambulance, but he was all right," said Welch. "It turns out they revived him, but he died on the way to the hospital, three days after he turned 21."

Welch came away from that tragedy with good memories and motivation. "Me and Peter Brunker, Richie's other best friend, kept up the tradition, and we both did the '87 Australian Ironman," said Welch. "I finished 3rd and qualified for Hawaii in '87. So I was following Richie's dream, trying to win Hawaii. Richie said his dream was to do well in Hawaii. But I know Richie better than that. It would have been his dream to *win* it. That's how competitive he was."

Welch carried Walker's ambition with him but vowed he would never put his life on hold, either. If anything was worth doing, do it *now*.

Welch played his first Hawaiian Ironman conservatively, finishing 45th overall with a time of 9 hours 45 minutes in 1987. In 1988 he improved to 19th place in 9 hours 7 minutes, not bad for a blue-collar amateur who worked days full time as a carpenter and nights full time as a pub crawler.

In July 1989 he was selected for the Australian national triathlon team and got an expenses-paid, two-month whirlwind tour of seven shorter races against world-class competition that put his fitness over the top. He won in Macombe, France, the first week and again in Cucoron, in the Alps, in a sprint finish with one of his idols, Rob Barel of Holland. In the third race, the first ITU World Championships in France, "I got smashed in the face by Rick Wells at the start and lost my goggles," said Welch. "I'm absolutely blind without them." Welch finished 45th in the race, which was won by Mark Allen. He finished the next race 3rd in a sprint finish with American stars Mike Pigg and Ken Glah. In the final race he finished 3rd to Pigg and Wells. "Those races were my breakthrough," said Welch.

Welch returned to his carpenter's job and managed to log the minimum long-distance workouts over the next five weeks to get ready for Hawaii. "It was a blessing in disguise," said Welch. "I didn't have time to do much more than a 90-mile bike ride and a few 15-mile runs and never swam over 2 miles. So I never got burned out, and I was fresh."

In a sign that he was headed for greatness, he ran a 2:56:53 marathon, a time previously bettered only by six-time winner Dave Scott, first-time champion Mark Allen, and Aussie Greg Stewart.

In 1990 Welch slipped back to 5th in the second-hottest Ironman Hawaii ever. But the next year he was ready for an assault on the summit. Welch, the man who had gasped and hung on the pool edge in his first attempt to swim 50 meters, came out of the water in the 1991 Ironman within a minute of former college All-American swimmer Mark Allen. Riding on pace with Allen through the whole bike leg, Welch also stuck with him for the first 8 miles of the run until he hit a steep incline known as Pay 'n' Save Hill, which leaves the town behind. "Mark and I were neck and neck, and all of a sudden I got this stomach cramp, and it lasted 5 or 6 minutes where I had to ease off the pace a bit and stop," recalled Welch.

Welch never made up the time, since Allen managed a 2:42 marathon and Welch's best proved to be 2:48 that day. But Welch made a crucial breakthrough, useful for his future competitive confidence. "I managed to run that last 10 kilometers in under 36 minutes, which was fantastic," said Welch. "And I brought Mark's lead back from 7 minutes to 5:50. Mark later told me I was the only one who ever came back at him on the run, the only person he was worried about in the last three years."

Allen had served a painful apprenticeship while learning how to win in Hawaii—six years of nosebleeds, internal bleeding, heat exhaustion, and spectacular physical breakdowns—and Welch had some dues to pay as well. The next year NBC set up a big Allen-Welch rivalry in the television coverage, and a triathlon magazine arranged a photo shoot promoting the race as a duel between the Grip and the little Joker, with Welch donning a court jester's outfit.

Welch's careless attitude was starting to harm him. Training in Boulder, Colorado, in the summer of '92, Welch made a more serious miscalculation. "I was training really hard," he said. "It is really dry in Boulder, and you need to drink a lot of water while working out. I would go out for a long ride and drink only one bottle of water."

In fact Welch gained some notoriety among training partners for his sparing thirst—they called him "Camel"—but it was no compliment. "It turns out I was so dehydrated I was bleeding internally," said Welch. "Twelve days before the race I needed an operation to remove hemorrhoids, and they patched up some holes in my colon."

When Welch arrived in Kona, he recalled, "My heart was telling me to race flat out, but my head was telling me to be sensible. I knew I could swim and bike hard. But I had to be really careful when it came to running." On a hot day the bill came due 15 miles into the marathon at the Natural Energy Lab Road, which he entered in 4th place. "I had a bit of a cramp coming on, and I had to relieve my stomach and got down on all fours," said Welch. "I just crouched down in the bending position and stretched and breathed properly to get rid of it."

At that moment two top Germans, Wolfgang Dittrich and Jürgen Zäck, cruised up. Normally in the Ironman, the focus is so commanding that competitors pass each other with slight or no acknowledgment. But Dittrich and Zäck loved the irrepressible Welch and stopped to give him a pep talk. "Velchy! Get up! Run vit us! Come on! Start running," they yelled.

Welch was encouraged. "I got up and kept those two in sight the whole way in. I was really happy to finish 6th that day," said Welch. "I found I could race, but 12 days after surgery was a bit tough."

Welch had one more hard lesson to learn. After recovering from a broken collarbone suffered in the 1993 Ironman Japan, he was on a roll aimed at Hawaii. In September he won the World Duathlon

Championships in Dallas. Then, after the last swim workout before Ironman, he rode home on his bike.

"This was my last ride, and the next day I would be on a plane for Hawaii," said Welch. "I should have been going easy, but I was absolutely rocketing. I was down on the handlebars and riding as hard as I possibly could on a slightly downhill section when a car cut in front of me. It was too late to avoid, and I tore up the medial collateral ligament in my knee. But I was lucky. My career could have been over."

Welch arrived in Hawaii with a cast and his customary good humor: "Tell my friends if they see me on the pier Saturday morning to chain me to a pole or I'll take off after them."

The next year, 1994, Welch decided to go to Japan for the Ironman in late June. Although his doctor advised against it, "I felt I had to go to Japan to have the confidence to go to Hawaii and know I could win," said Welch. "My goal was to know whether or not my knee could handle it." In Japan's 90-degree heat and 90 percent humidity, a sauna that made Hawaii almost feel air conditioned, Welch led by 10 minutes off the bike and held on in the run for the win. With the victory came an unexpected bonus, a shocking defeat of the Hawaii pre-race cofavorite, Pauli Kiuru, who had placed 4th, 3rd, and 2nd the previous three years in Kona.

Before his 1994 appointment with destiny in Kona, Welch said ITU world titles were not enough. "The Ironman is my Everest," he said. "I want to win it at least once. If I never win it again, I'll still feel satisfied with my career. But if I never do it, that will always be a disappointment."

Welch had a brilliant 50:22 swim, took off fast on the bike, and was comfortably in the lead pack by mile 25. He showed he had studied well the year before by letting Jürgen Zäck and Ken Glah go ahead and expend energy on the bike. But even Welch was a bit shocked when Dave Scott arrived at the front. "I was on the bike in the lead, and the camera car came up, and he said to his driver, 'OK, make way! Make way! Let Scott through.' I thought, *Dave Scott? Gee, what's he doing here so early? Wow, he's on!* I looked at him, and his muscles were rippling and everything looked good. He was calm and relaxed, and I thought, *He's the guy to beat today*."

The odd thing about the 1994 Gatorade Ironman was that the fearsome field of pre-race favorites seemed to fold like a stack of cards in a breeze in the days before the race. Cristian Bustos withdrew when he was almost killed by a Jeep on the bike leg of a triathlon in Argentina. Wolfgang Dittrich fell prey to a knee infection, and Mark Allen was taking his sabbatical. Without those men in the field, Welch's Ironman win might have lacked the resonance of the great victories over great rivals until Dave Scott showed up in better form and moving faster than all six of his victories on the third-hottest day in Ironman history. Ultimately it was Welch's battle with Scott, under the watchful eyes of Allen in the NBC truck, that made this one for the ages.

Dave Scott had the best seat in the house. "Going into the Energy Lab I did not see it as it had been built up—as the moment of truth, or the most difficult section of the race," Scott recalled. "To me it was just a nondescript part of the course with fewer people and a little downhill going in. I run very well downhill, so I told myself to close the margin a little bit. But on the way back up I started to feel fatigued. I thought, *Damnit. Why am I tired now? I've never been tired at mile 18.* For one fleeting moment I thought, *Geez, maybe it's because I'm 40.* By the time I got back to the highway I was 52 seconds down.

"In that whole time I never saw his eyes," Scott continued. "Greg was very focused, and part of that focus is being able to relax and stay calm within himself, no matter who was next to him, because he knew he was running a good pace. By the time he got back to the highway, his allies let him know that he was 50 seconds up. That knowledge is like an extra fuel pack."

Welch didn't see it that way. "At the Energy Lab, that is the time Dave made his move and it sort of backfired on him at the same time," Welch said. Venturing a guess at Scott's thoughts, Welch said, "[Scott] said to himself, 'OK. The Energy Lab. This is the most energy-zapping part of the course, and I am going to have to make my move now because I know how well Greg runs that last 10 km.' He knew he had to make the move there to win the race. The first downhill mile he got within 8 seconds, one story said. But by the time I got to the turnaround I clicked my watch and it was 20 seconds. Halfway back to town, someone on a camera car yelled, 'Two thirty! Two thirty!' I thought, *That can't be right! He was just behind me*. So I took a sneak peek over my shoulder and I couldn't see him. I thought, *Yes! It's mine!*"

Mark Allen, serving as an NBC analyst at Kona that year in the midst of his one-year racing sabbatical, had the next-best seat in the house. "I was not emotionally caught up until they got out on the lava fields, when I noticed Greg's head was bobbing, and at that point Dave looked great!" Allen said. "I thought, *My God!* It was so intense. That's because I know how strong Dave is. If you show any weakness, he will run to it like a shark smelling a trace of blood."

Once he reached the line, Welch launched his signature jump at the tape, leaping high and full of pent-up joy. That exultation, the product of his seven years of struggle to the summit of Ironman's greatest race, gave him an adrenaline boost that fueled him well into the night. In fact, he was photographed dancing on Ali'i Drive with his wife, Sian, on his shoulders—no mean feat after his ultimate effort. After all the businesslike focus and discipline that had finally harnessed his talent, it was time to let the old pub crawler out of confinement.

━━━━━━━━━━━━━━━

Of course Welch always had too much of everything: too much fun, too much to drink, too much speed, too much talent for triathlon at every distance, and too many visits to the emergency room. Finally, Greg Welch had too much heart.

Heart*beat*, that is. Leave it to Welch to develop a condition that revved up his heart rate to 300 beats per minute during the body's own drum solos brought on by haywire electrical impulses to the heart.

On the heels of his shocking retirement from triathlon on January 11, 2000, at age 35, while still possessing the speed to be one of the favorites for the inaugural Olympic triathlon in his hometown of Sydney, Welch said he was at peace with his decision to quit the sport. Although he was a man who seemed to have a charge card at emergency rooms worldwide, it had taken Welch and his doctors a long time to determine that he had a career- and life-threatening heart condition called ventricular tachycardia.

Welch's medical perils were legion. There was the internal bleeding and hemorrhoids owing to dehydration while training for Kona in 1992; the broken clavicle and ribs in the pre-Kona bike crash in 1993; the broken collarbone and ribs in his post-Kona victory revels in 1994; and another detached clavicle in the 1996 ITGP event in Oceanside, California. Then, in 1997, Welch was diagnosed with hereditary hemachromatosis, a disease in which the patient produces too much iron in the blood. Welch found that draining a pint of blood every six months kept the condition under control. But the disease was enough to make Welch swear off Ironman-distance events in 1997, after finishing 4th in 1995 and 3rd in 1996.

Ventricular tachycardia was something else. Cardiologist Kenneth Carr of Tri-City Medical Center in Oceanside, who treated Welch later, said that episodes of viral infection can precede incidents of cardiomyopathy. "Such weakening of the heart is often the cause of episodes of ventricular tachycardia," said Dr. Carr. Sian also caught the virus, but she was spared its serious effects. "Such viruses are very common, but there are a small percentage of people whose hearts are affected," said Carr. "Greg was one of the unlucky ones."

In the 1999 Ironman Hawaii, Welch was holding 3rd in the 2.4-mile swim, feeling strong. "Life was looking very good when, whammo, it happened," said Welch. "My heart rate went through the roof." He began breathing irregularly and gasping for air. He was concerned but unshaken. "I figured it was a severe asthma attack, and so I literally stopped in the water several times to rest and catch my breath," he said.

He ran into more trouble on the 112-mile ride. "Again, I could not get a breath and felt my heart rate was incredibly high," he said. Welch continued the race, stopping several times on the bike to try to lower the drumbeat of his runaway heart.

Welch paused several times during the run but finished the race, though he didn't know how he managed it. "It was really proof of what the human body can be forced to do when the mind wills it," he said. "But I was taking my life into my hands."

After an exhaustive battery of tests, Welch's doctors made the diagnosis. They added that if Welch had not been in such superb physical shape, he would probably have died.

Amid his usual optimism, Welch admitted, "My body was kind of in shock. It was very traumatic. My heart was inflamed after the ordeal, and there is a substantial recovery period. I must say it is hard to sort of sit through this problem knowing what I used to do was so physical."

After two years spent in search of a less invasive solution to the ventricular tachycardia, Welch finally had a defibrillator implanted underneath his left pectoral muscle in February 2002 at Cedars Sinai Medical Center in Los Angeles. Welch explained that his new device would not solve the problem of sudden increases in his heart rate, but it would provide a safety net against heart failure. "In the end, we could not stop it," he said. "My doctor really felt there was nothing else we could do and told me, 'It's not safe to be tempting fate like this anymore.'"

The disease changed Welch's lifestyle dramatically. His once marvelously sculpted body has rounder edges now because he cannot risk even a modest run or a moderately swift bike. "I am very limited as far as exercise," he says. "I have diet restrictions and have to keep my stress level very low." The highlights of his activity became walks with his daughters, Annie May and Emma Rose, in a double stroller. He can play a little golf as long as he rides a cart. He explained to IronmanLive.com how he made peace with his plight. "Acceptance," he said. "I have a potentially fatal condition, and I feel lucky to have survived. I just have to remind myself how much I have accomplished in my life and be grateful for that."

Welch now works as a technical adviser for the World Triathlon Corporation and acts as host and commentator for its Ironman events and many major international triathlon events. He did commentary for the 2000 Olympic Games and works for Tri-California, which puts on the Wildflower and the Escape from Alcatraz triathlons. He also serves as a triathlon coach for Multisports.com. "It helps me because I feel like I am giving back to the sport," he said. "I do it because I love the sport and it's very rewarding to help someone realize his or her goal."

Careful as he is with his health, Welch's instincts remain generous. At the 2002 Ironman Utah, when a wild windstorm threw the scheduled swim into chaos and the waves drove competitors well off course and many were panicking, Welch instinctively dove into the fray. With no regard for his medical condition or his own safety, Plucky Welchy waded into the water and pulled swimmers to safety on the rocks.

SIX | SISTER MADONNA BUDER

"What have you got against me and the Ironman, Lord?"

SISTER MADONNA BUDER says each race is a prayer, an act of devotion you offer up to your Creator. If so, she has offered her Master Coach a mountain of aerobic hosannas. By now the totals are well over 40 marathons; 325 triathlons and duathlons; and three dozen or more of the grandest of them all, Ironman finishes. She began all these miles of pain and devotion, while shrugging off enough broken bones to match X-rays with Evel Knievel, at age 46 after a quarter century spent in a quiet order whose chief work was counseling fallen women of the street.

If each prayer is an arrow aimed at heaven, Sister Madonna has refined her instrument to the max, removing all nonessential matter. When last measured, she had 7 percent body fat, and her tanned limbs and smiling face appeared 20 years younger than her 79 years. She has a marathon best time of 3:16. Her age-group Ironman world record of 13:19 at age 62 once seemed soft to her. In her athletic prime—in her early 60s—she sensed she might break 13 hours in Hawaii, a time that would have put her in a tight duel with the 1979 women's *overall* winner, Lyn Lemaire (12:55:38). Now, as she approaches 80, she may well be working toward her greatest athletic miracle: beating the 17-hour deadline for an official Ironman finish. But all these numbers and clockings miss the point of her higher purpose, which she finds in a verse in Saint Paul's Epistle to the Philippians: "I strain to reach the end of the race and receive the prize for which God is calling us up to heaven."

Dorothy Marie Buder was born July 24, 1930, in a 105-degree St. Louis heat wave that arrived long before air conditioning. Ironman weather. "My mother immediately put me out in a bassinet in the sun," said Sister Madonna. "I think that is why I have more tolerance for heat and sun exposure than most people. And genetically,

I was blessed." Her father, Gustavus Buder, was a champion oarsman and rowed single sculls until the Century Boat House in St. Louis burned down when he was 35. "My father was of German extraction," she said. "He was very physical and practical. My mother was French, and she was very much in the ethereal realm, idealistic and spiritual. Somehow I am a balance of the two: I have that endurance quality and also mental, emotional, and spiritual motivation that can put me through very trying circumstances."

Growing up, she excelled on the occasional field day when the girls would do the standing broad jump and the high jump. She hiked, played tennis, and became a champion equestrian, riding with her mother in Forest Park in St. Louis. And she loved to swim.

"When we flew in a plane, I always wanted to be the first to spot Lake Michigan," she said. "I thought, *I am going to marry somebody and live on Lake Michigan.*"

When she was in sixth grade, her parents became alarmed at boy-girl parties in the public schools and decided to move her to an all-girls school. "It was my choice to either go to the Sisters of the Visitation, which was like a dungeon, a medieval castle with long dark corridors, or to attend this school for girls I felt were snobs. I chose the dungeon over the snobs."

Because her father was not a Catholic, her baptism and confirmation had been delayed until she was 10, which made the impact greater. "Because I was older when I received instruction into the faith, I was more able to experience the feeling of being a child of God," she said. "As an adolescent I was really taken by the lifestyle of the sisters, and I decided this was the way I wanted to live my life, to dedicate myself to giving."

Buder was considered smart and pretty, quite a catch in postwar St. Louis society. She fended off proposals from several suitors and spent a year teaching before she surprised nearly everyone with her first big career choice: In October 1953 she joined the Sisters of the Good Shepherd. Usually that would be the end of the story in the semicloistered order whose mission included helping prostitutes get off the streets. But Sister Madonna was fated to hit the streets in quite another way.

After celebrating her silver jubilee with the Sisters of the Good Shepherd in 1978, she went to a psychology workshop on the Oregon coast. A young priest, Father John Tope, preached the value of running. "He said it harmonizes the mind, body, and soul, helps counter depression, helps the heart and diabetes," Sister Madonna remembered with a laugh. "He built it up as the panacea for everything. I thought it was unreal. I told him I had been active all my life, but I couldn't see running for no reason. I had to have a goal. He said, 'Go out to the beach and run between two eddies.' So one night I went out to the beach and ran. When I came back, he told me, 'Keep doing this. You'll feel different.' I couldn't stop."

When she got back to her order she ran around a small ball field, seven times to the mile, for 4 miles a day. "I got sick of running in circles, and I started wheezing from pollen. So I headed for the streets." An award-winning photographer, she saw some pictures of Spokane's famous Bloomsday Run on the wall of a local photo lab. "I thought, *My God, it's hard enough to run, period, without going elbow to elbow in a herd like that!* It repulsed me." But when she got home she got a call from her mother warning her that the marriage of one of her brothers was headed for divorce due to an alcohol problem.

"I said, 'I'm going to run that blooming Bloomsday with the hope that God will transfer my will to endure to my brother's will to give up dependency on alcohol,'" said Buder. "I dedicated that 8.2 miles of the Bloomsday as a living Way of the Cross." At that point she had been running only a few weeks, and her longest run had been 4 miles.

Four weeks before the race she was warming up for her daily run by doing yoga in the library when she was overcome by pain. "I said, 'Oh, Lord, I can't do this.' My knees were so enlarged I could scarcely bend 'em back. My calves were so tight, I was in a tizzy. I couldn't muster the strength that day to go out and run. I fell apart. 'I can't do this,' I sobbed."

But she did. She finished Bloomsday and started dedicating every race to a cause. And she was having an effect. In May 1981 she ran a marathon at Coeur d'Alene, Idaho, in 3:29:18 and qualified for the 1982 Boston Marathon. She went to the bishop and asked permission to enter the race. "He said he had no problems with it," said Sister Madonna, who dedicated her Boston Marathon to a fund to help children with multiple sclerosis and collected $4,000 for the cause. She ran a 3:31. Later that year she borrowed a child's oversized 10-speed bike and did the Spokane Troika half-Ironman triathlon. "At first I thought, *Oh my God!* But the more I thought about it, I remembered I loved to swim as a kid and I liked to bicycle. So I did it."

But her new avocation, however beneficial for those to whom she dedicated her races, did not please the head of her order. In a period of one year, beginning in early 1983, she ran 7 marathons, 3 triathlons, and 20 lesser events, and her entry was accepted for the 1984 Hawaiian Ironman. She dedicated each of the three legs in the race to the victims of a tragedy. Then, as she trained, her own life seemed to come apart with a series of catastrophes. On June 11, 1984, five days after she went to St. Louis to help celebrate her parents' fifty-fifth wedding anniversary, she borrowed a bike with balky brakes from some in-laws to train, and she flew over the handlebars. The toll: a broken jaw, fractured scapula, compound fractured elbows, and multiple abrasions.

Three weeks later she traveled to New York, having qualified for the Diet Pepsi championship 10K run. "By that time I had the original cast modified, so the doctor gave me travel permission, not running permission," said Sister Madonna. "Someone suggested, 'Why don't you put a sign on your back?' So I did. 'Beware Injured Runner! No Passing on Right, Please!' Only a few hassled her, and she was 4th in her age group. Then she returned to Spokane and did the half-Ironman Troika Triathlon again. "It took all the psychological strength I had just to straddle a bike again. I did it and thought, *OK. I can do the Ironman in October.*" But a second bike crash that September in Spokane changed the plan. "I was crossing a four–lane, and the light changed and everyone stopped because they saw me," said Sister Madonna. "But one guy went right in front of me. It looked like a head-on collision, and I thought, *Oh Lord! Not again! What can I do? Oh, swerve!*" She cleared the car by four inches and came down hard. "I felt something in my hip slide. I knew there goes Ironman." Her hip was broken in two places.

"Before the operation, there were no assurances I would walk again for a whole year," she said. "The doctor went into the surgery with apprehension and came out elated. He said the femur was broken, but it went down the shank, and the break was not as long as he thought. He put in five pins and a metal plate. The bones were strong, and he thought it would hold."

At that point the provincial leader of the Good Shepherd forbade Sister Madonna to continue with her training for Hawaii. "While I was laid up, I had a lot of time to think and examine my walk of life," said Sister Madonna. "I came to the conclusion that I really didn't have to be under a power play of the wills. That wasn't what religious life is all about." She was reading a book called *A Sudden Spring*, written by a former nun of the Holy Name, which spelled out a new type of religious life more in keeping with Vatican II in which more responsibility is left to the individual. "I began to realize I had been living in a cocoon where the order is like a mother which takes care of me," she said.

In the midst of this crisis, her father was dying. "I was losing my father and my religious family, and that created quite an emotional strain," said Sister Madonna. "I don't know how I ever got through it except with divine guidance." She decided she would break with the Sisters of the Good Shepherd and transferred to a new order, the Sisters of the Christian Community, founded for nuns leaving traditional orders who chose their own ministry and their own lifestyle. It is a noncanonical order with no injunction from the Holy See.

"It was scary," she said. "I almost had to start from scratch, pick up from where I left off at 23, and I was being met with challenges one after another, and they all kind of met at one juncture. It really threw me on complete dependence on the Lord."

In August 1985 her rehabilitation was progressing well when she went to Australia at the invitation of a fellow nun. She kept training hard. Just a week before she was ready to leave, she was biking into the sun in Rockingham, near Perth. "All of a sudden I am flying through the air with the greatest of ease and I come down in a five-point landing. Before I hit, I thought, *What have you got against me and the Ironman, Lord?* Then I checked myself and thought, *No broken bones? I am still in the Ironman!*"

She *had* chipped her heelbone and broken some ribs, and she sported a wicked hematoma on her leg. "The doctors told me I simply could not run a step for six weeks. I saw a doctor in Hawaii who gave me a cortisone shot three days before the race, and fortunately, he was able to hit the right spot."

At Ironman orientation, race director Kay Rhead told the competitors that a hurricane was scheduled to hit the island on race day. "She said it so offhandedly, half of us thought she was joking," said Sister Madonna. "It finally veered away but churned up the water with swells two to four feet high. With my broken ribs, I had a hard time and missed the 2-hour, 15-minute cutoff time by 4 minutes." But unlike many others who retreat into a cocoon of pain and concentration during and after the rigors of Ironman, Sister Madonna has never abandoned her first calling: to help others. Broken ribs and all, she hopped on her bike and went out looking for athletes who needed encouragement. In an ecumenical gesture, she found Episcopal Rev. Jim Curtis, who had just missed the bike cutoff in 1984. "I made myself the carrot on a string and reeled in the Rev. Curtis and helped him make the bike cutoff by 5 minutes. He finished the Ironman with 6.5 minutes to spare, and it was his privilege to be the last legitimate finisher."

In the 1986 Ironman she was clear of major injuries going in, but her bike shoes were too tight and her toe straps were cutting off her circulation. Just before the last tough hill on the bike course, she could hardly stand, and she hobbled out on the marathon, able to run only a third of the way. "My feet were dead, and I could hardly run," she said. "Near the end I amused myself by creating haiku verses about the moon casting a shadow out on the Queen K Highway. That preoccupation helped me get through." She got 2nd in her age group in a little over 14 hours. She had done one Ironman, but she was hardly finished with it.

She came to Hawaii in 1987 with a stress fracture in her foot and a sense of foreboding. Her intuition proved true. She wrote in her book, *I Have Finished the Race,* "This particular island, more than any other, is Mother Nature in the raw. The locale is under the spell of unpredictable heat and testy trade winds, all the more reason to be attuned to the Creator for anger. But this year [1987] I feel He went deeper. My intuitive nature was under a premonition of sorts." Pat Griskus, a one-legged marine who had finished the Ironman several times before, was killed when he was hit by a cement truck while riding the course nine days before the Ironman. She dedicated her race to him.

That fall Sister Madonna wore a nursing shoe with Velcro straps that made her transitions faster, but the shoe hurt her foot. In the middle of the Ironman marathon, while hobbling in excruciating pain, she stopped to minister to a middle-aged man who was "heaving his guts out." She ran a mile to get to the turnaround to get him some aspirin in the dark and stayed with him until medical workers took over. Then she started running again and felt she could easily surpass her goal of finishing under 14 hours. But the pain in her foot kept increasing, and she tried to adjust. She tried to stick a cut-off sponge under the ball of her foot to alleviate pressure, but nothing worked. She was walking with 8 miles to go. By the time she crested the last hill, she wrote, "I found a one-legged hop goes a lot faster than a hobble." With a half mile to go, fellow Spokane age grouper

Roy Allen, himself badly blistered and hobbling, came up on Sister Madonna. They had 7 minutes left to break 15 hours and thus qualify for the race the next year. They made a bet, and Sister Madonna said, "I dunno, let's give it a try." They made it with 1 minute 45 seconds to spare. Afterward X-rays showed that she had run the Ironman with a stress fracture.

Sister Madonna said she has had moments of doubt during the past 15 years about whether she should continue her extraordinary long-distance quests. Even though she has grown a little more aware and become a little less accident-prone than in her early days, she has still encountered accidents and injuries that might drive a competitor of lesser faith into retirement.

At Ironman Hawaii in 2000 Sister Madonna had perhaps her closest brush with mortality. Hit by fierce, gusting side winds that forced many pros to hold on to their handlebars for dear life, Sister Madonna suffered a crash that left her with a broken scapular, multiple abrasions, and bruises and cuts on her face that required 20 stitches. Perhaps the karma of her many good works and generous acts of charity in the middle of her own Ironman struggles were returned by two passersby.

"I am so lucky to be alive," she said afterward. "I have some angels to thank for that, including the two competitors who sacrificed their race to stop and make sure I got medical attention." Nancy Taubner of Edmonton, Canada, and Bill Hoon, a dentist from Pennsylvania, stopped and found the multiple age-group record-holder facedown on the road "in a pool of blood," as Sister Madonna described her plight. "I was just whizzing down from Hawi for all I was worth, having the race of my life, plowing through the headwinds, chasing after [her age group rival] Ethel Autorino. All of a sudden I was airborne. I came down on my head, and I am sure my helmet and my glasses saved my life."

At age 76 Sister Madonna broke through to another level of physical achievement by finishing the 2006 edition of Ironman Hawaii in a time of 16:59:03—with just 57 seconds to spare to beat the deadline for an official finish under 17 hours. While this time was 65 minutes slower than the 75–79 age-group record she'd set just the year before, the achievement pushed the previous limits of gender and aging back by a quantum leap.

With that nail-bitingly close official finish, Sister Madonna could have sailed into the sunset, winning more age-group national and world titles at more modest distances. But in 2009 Sister Madonna demonstrated the truth of the legendary Michael Jordan's Basketball Hall of Fame induction speech: "One day you might look and see me playing the game at 50," said Jordan. "Don't laugh. Never say never. Because limits like fears are often illusions."

Fifty? That's nothing, Sister Madonna seemed to say as she showed up at the starting line at Ironman Canada in 2009 and finished in 16:54:30. By doing so, she qualified for the 2009 edition of Ironman Hawaii. Given the proven standard gender differences of 10 percent for world-record performances in endurance sports, Sister Madonna's finishing Ironman before the regulation cutoff at age 79 stands as one of the great athletic performances in history.

Despite the wear and tear, Sister Madonna told reporters at Penticton that she plans to be back at Penticton the next year at age 80—which, if she finished, would match Robert McKeague's mark as the oldest person, man or woman, to finish an Ironman. And that would serve as a landmark of gender equality in human history.

When asked whether her pursuit of ultimate endurance sports finishes might not be a selfish, obsessive pursuit contrary to her spiritual goals, Sister Madonna answered with a bit of humor in her first book: "You can idealize it or condemn it, depending on your mood. Or accept it for what it is. But what is it? This Ironman is an exhibit of physical endurance, either designed by fools for heroes, or designed by heroes for fools."

SEVEN | **KAREN SMYERS**

"Where there's a will there's a way."

SIMPLY COMPLETING AN Ironman demands a tremendous amount of dedication, discipline, and desire to overcome the pain and suffering on the long road to the starting line. For a genetically gifted few, it is possible to win triathlon's most sacred event with remarkable focus, great training, and cool nerves under pressure along with a serious dose of luck. It is very rare, however, in this modern age of increasing athletic specialization, to find an athlete who is able to win both triathlon's short-course world championship and the four-times-longer Ironman World Championship once in a career. So far only five people have done so. The only competitor to do it in the same year—within a two-month span, in fact—is a remarkable woman from New England.

If the double win of the short-course and Ironman were Karen Smyers's only claim to fame, she would remain a remarkable athlete. But what makes her an icon in a sport that celebrates and makes its trademark overcoming the odds is what she has endured, survived, and transcended on top of the rigors of her sport. At the peak of her career, Smyers gave birth to her first child, suffered a sliced hamstring, got smashed on a training ride by a semi, broke a collarbone in a crash in a race, placed 2nd at Ironman Hawaii, and made a valiant attempt to qualify for the Olympics while fighting and beating thyroid cancer. In fact, Karen Smyers is one of the best athletes the sport of triathlon has ever generated—not only despite the many setbacks she overcame in her life but in no small part because of them.

Karen Smyers was raised in Weathersfield, Connecticut, the middle child of seven. Her father, Bill, was an engineer. Her mother, Mary Anne, was a full-time overloaded mom until the children all finally left the home, after which she worked as a computer programmer. Both Bill and Mary Anne were athletic, but they were not heavily into sports; that was for their children. When Smyers was growing up, her mom ferried her brood to endless swim workouts and meets. Smyers also did gymnastics in the winter and tennis in the spring and worked out in the pool mornings and evenings. "I could not imagine a time of year with no sport to focus on," she said.

Smyers went to Princeton and swam on the team that won the Eastern Relays three of her four years. In running with the swimmers, she was the fastest, so she asked the track coach if she could work out with his team. "Like most swimmers, my heart was way ahead of my legs," recalled Smyers. "When I started running, my lower legs and my ankles gave out on me. So the coach said, 'Why don't you come back when you can run a full hour without stopping?' I never did make it to that point. Then I had all these hip problems, so I had to back off and run shorter. But I had a huge aerobic capacity to run half miles and miles." She got her mile time down to 4:42, but running remained an amusing diversion.

When she graduated in 1983, Smyers was disconsolate that her swimming career was over. She moved to Boston with a Princeton swim teammate and started running for fun with the Irish-American Track Club. "You didn't have to be Irish, and I liked that it had a strong social component," said Smyers.

She also kept swimming and commuted on her bike. In June 1984, at the age of 23, she tried a minitriathlon put on by the Harvard women's swim team. "It was very, very short and didn't do justice to what a real triathlon was like," she said of the half-mile swim, 8-mile bike, and 3-mile run. "But it was good encouragement. I won." In her next triathlon she came out of the water in great shape, but, riding her old clunker bike, she got passed by virtually everyone.

By the end of '84 she was ready. "I signed up for the Boston Bud Light triathlon as an amateur and was 2nd overall," she said. "I would have won $500 as a pro, so after that I always signed up as a pro."

By 1985 her job with a small Cambridge, Massachusetts, computer consulting firm gave her the flexibility to train harder, and she got better. She also met a man and a great workout partner, Michael King, an accomplished local road runner and triathlete who worked as manager and part owner of the Boston runners' pub of choice, the Eliot Lounge.

That year she won the Bay State Triathlon, beating national triathlon champion Colleen Cannon and passing marathon star Allison Roe on the run. She was still working full time, and her results plateaued for the next three seasons; she became a regular in the lower half of the top 10. In summer 1988, Smyers's company went bankrupt; she transitioned to half-time work and was able to devote herself to bike training. By 1989 the training paid off. Smyers made the national team and beat United States Triathlon Series star Jan Ripple in a big duathlon in Columbus, Ohio. After that breakthrough, Smyers said she thought she could make a pretty good living at the sport "if I went all out. So I gave it a go."

Until then her stubborn modesty and ingrained thrift had stood in her way. "Up to that point I never used aerodynamic disc wheels," she said. "I had a thing against equipment advantages. I got that philosophy from New England and my parents. They would always make do with what they had. It was all hard work in the pool. I didn't feel I had earned the right to the equipment."

At the 1989 world championships in Avignon, France, she had her breakthrough. "I was 4th to Erin Baker, Jan Ripple, and Laurie Samuelson, but I beat the Puntous twins and a lot of other people," she said. "I had a terrible swim, the worst of my life, and when I got out of the water, Michael thought, *Poor Karen; she is having a really terrible day.* I was the last American out of the water, and then, with my new wheels, I started passing 'em all, and I thought, *C'mon, c'mon! Why are you all going so slow?*"

A year later she triumphed at the world championships in Orlando. It was during this time that she swore never to take the start at an Ironman event. She dismissed the long-distance competitions as survival races, not true tests of speed.

Coincidentally, she became friends with fellow Massachusetts triathletes Dick and Ricky Hoyt the year that Dick towed, rode, and pushed his disabled son, Rick, through the Ironman. "I had run side by side with them at a lot of road races, and I saw them do the Boston Marathon," said Smyers. "I thought Dick was in incredible shape, and it was a great show of love and devotion on his part. But it looked pretty hard on Rick, and I suspected that Dick was a lot more into it than his son. But then I went to a party in their honor after they did the Ironman and heard Rick's professor read a speech that he wrote. Then I realized how much Rick wanted it, and that's why Dick did it. I am a pretty cynical person, but when I heard that I was crying."

In 1990 Smyers was the world champion short-course triathlete after defeating a tough field of sprint specialists in central Florida at a distance approximately one-fourth of the Ironman. The only similarity was the weather. Orlando in July is every bit as hot and humid as Kona in October. So the matter-of-fact New Englander could handle heat. That opened a glimmer of possibility. Another clue to her Ironman potential was her marathon. In 1988 Smyers qualified for the U.S. Olympic women's marathon trial with a time of 2:42. That put her in fast Ironman company; perhaps five women in the field could beat that.

Such inspirational deeds did not fuel Smyers's Ironman ambition. "People with one leg run across Canada," she said. "People do amazing physical feats every day. I always knew I *could* do it. I knew it would come down to finding a reason I *wanted* to do the Ironman." In 1991 the triathlon World Championships were in Australia, and on their way back Smyers and King stopped in Hawaii and saw the Ironman. "It was a blast to watch it," said Smyers. "It was really exciting, and I gained a new appreciation for what people go through. It also made me see it as a race, not just a question of survival. For me that was a critical distinction. I did not want to see if I could go out and endure the most hardship. But when I saw Mark Allen run a 2:40 marathon, I knew this was a race!"

Smyers laughed when she recalled the reason she finally decided to lift her personal Ironman embargo. "My husband and I train with a group we call Team Psycho, and a lot of them were trying to qualify for the Hawaiian Ironman, and some got in on the lottery," she said. "I said to Michael, 'Well, if you qualify for the Ironman, I will do it.' He said he would hold me to that. So he finished 3rd in his age group in the Bay State Triathlon, and he qualified. I agreed to do it as an experiment for one year, to find out once what it is all about."

As the swim began in Kailua Bay in 1994, Smyers kept getting hit. "I could not get clear of people to swim my own stroke more than one-tenth of the race," she said. "I had had a little taste of that at the start of other races or at buoy corners, but never the entire race. I tried to stay relaxed, so I turned over and rolled on my back a dozen times to clear my head. I know I am not a good competitor when I am stressed out, and I made myself relax when things got out of control. In the grand scheme of things, during a 9.5-hour race, I thought it would not matter." On the bike her chain fell off once, and she took a minute to put it back on. "At the time I thought, *What is a minute?*"

When she reached the bleak lava fields on the Queen K Highway on the run, the desolation started to work on her mind. "Three words occurred to me: *daunting, stark, unforgiving,*" said Smyers. "Once you are out of town, it is *very* lonely. There is no shade. I was scared and felt left alone with the monumental task of finishing 18 more miles. I realized the accumulated fatigue had left me emotionally and physically down. Also, I had taken in no calories for the first 8 miles of the run. I thought I could get by with nothing but water, but I started to fade badly at 5 miles. I was plodding along, and people I'd passed were passing me back. I was discouraged and desperate and afraid I'd drop out."

Around mile 12 she took a gulp of Coca-Cola, and it revived her. "I didn't care about my minimum daily vitamin requirements;

my craving was sugar and calories," said Smyers. "Then I had to make sure I took Coke at every stop after that to avoid a counter-bonk worse than the first."

At the run turnaround at mile 17, Paula Newby-Fraser was out of sight, her sixth Ironman Hawaii win safely in her grasp. But Smyers saw the rest of the field during the out-and-back at the Energy Lab and realized she had just passed two competitors and was in 5th place. "With the Coca-Cola, I was back. I was running at a respectable pace, and I knew I was gaining on Wendy Ingraham and Sue Latshaw. That was a definite morale booster, and it gave me focus. By mile 18 I stopped taking breaks at the water stops."

Smyers passed Ingraham before the last long incline outside town and relaxed to enjoy the finish. "I made myself aware of the people cheering and ran and smiled and waved and took it all in because I was not sure if I would ever do this again." Smyers finished 4th in 9 hours 21 minutes 12 seconds—32 seconds behind distance specialist Latshaw. Smyers's was a stunning first effort, the eleventh-fastest time by a woman in Ironman history to that point.

―――――――――

At the start of her most spectacular year in the sport—perhaps as spectacular a year as anyone has had in triathlon—Smyers spent the first half of the year recovering from a debilitating bout with giardia that left her weakened and walking home dispiritedly from a dozen training runs. "I guess if I have any New England traits, it would have to be perseverance and patience," said Smyers. "I am determined and do not give up easily, and this year I was rewarded for that."

The year was 1995, and she was coming off a 4th-place finish in the 1994 edition of Ironman Hawaii. She followed that with a discouraging 17th place at the ITU World Championship in New Zealand.

"After Ironman 1994, I faded at worlds, and people told me, 'You can't race that hard right after Ironman. You'll just have to focus on one thing or another.' But I thought I had enough in me to do both."

If she was healthy.

Early in 1995 she pinched a nerve in her neck lifting weights and lost a few weeks. Then, right after her Pan Am Games win in March, where she soldiered through despite flu symptoms, she was diagnosed with giardia and spent many weeks flat on her back, her stomach unable to absorb crucial nutrients. She managed to recover enough for the Chicago Powerman Duathlon victory in June, but her endurance had suffered. "When I began to train long days for Hawaii in August, I would have one good ride, and then the next time I would end up feeling so dead I couldn't even stand up to eat," said Smyers. "If I didn't listen to my body, I could have knocked myself completely out, but I realized I had to take it easy until the body was ready." Finally it was.

In Hawaii Smyers had the chutzpah to plan to stay with Newby-Fraser, not only on the swim but for every mile of the bike, Newby-Fraser's strength. That was what led to Smyers's worst doubts as she struggled into the howling *mumuku* winds 25 miles into the ride. "When Paula rode away from me, I stood up and tried to crank it into a higher gear and got nowhere," said Smyers. "I was surprised and panicked and desperate as I watched her bore into the wind like an arrow and disappear. I kept losing minutes, and I would curse and stupidly stand up on the pedals into the wind, and say to myself, 'C'mon! Accelerate!' Finally I realized I had to relax and keep the faith in my run." Down by 12 minutes after the bike for the second straight year, Smyers was mad but did not surrender.

Newby-Fraser had worked hard to put that 12-minute lead off the bike in the bank, and she paid for it with every step of the run. On her way to a 3:05:20 marathon—4 seconds better than Newby-Fraser's best—Smyers kept getting reports of her rival's dwindling lead. So did Newby-Fraser, who had perhaps unintentionally put more pressure on herself to win because she had announced before the race that this would be her last Ironman. In apparent desperation as Smyers cut her lead to under 5 minutes coming out of the

Energy Lab, Newby-Fraser made a rookie mistake, failing to take water and nutrition at every aid station. With 3 miles to go, a dazed Newby-Fraser was bonking; she ran into an aid-station worker, fell to the ground, and popped right back up. Smyers was now only 2.5 minutes down.

Finally, with a 1-minute lead in hand, Newby-Fraser came off the downhill at Palani Road with about three-quarters of a mile to go. By the time Smyers rounded the corner at Hualalai, just under half a mile from the finish, she could see Newby-Fraser wobbling precariously. As if hit by a jolt of electricity, Smyers accelerated, only to be shocked when Newby-Fraser staggered into her path. In full stride, Smyers gently caught the elbow of the greatest Ironman competitor who ever lived to prevent her from falling, then raced ahead to the line, a winner in 9 hours 16 minutes 46 seconds.

After the pass, Newby-Fraser sat down on a curb near Uncle Billy's Kona Bay Hotel, suffering from extreme dehydration. Ironically, that precise spot was one of the places where Julie Moss had fallen and struggled to get back up during her heroic finish in February 1982. Newby-Fraser sat for 15 minutes to recover as spectators poured water over her head to cool her off. Finally the great champion slowly walked to the finish in 4th place.

Smyers cried when she saw Newby-Fraser walk across the line. "After the joy and the ecstasy, I got a sort of weird feeling—it was sad and heart-wrenching to see her that broken down. Yet I was proud of how she battled through. I don't think I would have the mental power to endure so much."

Coming into the ITU World Championship at Cancun, Mexico, a month later, Smyers felt comfortable with her underdog role. "I felt I had nothing to lose," said Smyers. "Because it was the ITU's first year of draft-legal biking, it was a runners' race, and there were maybe a dozen women with better pure 10K times than I had [34:40]."

Plus she had a secret weapon. "It was also real hot there, and I had been acclimatized to the heat for six weeks, from before Ironman and including a visit to Thailand." Although she was opposed to the rules change that allowed drafting on the bike, Smyers played the new game well and arrived in T2 with a large pack of contenders. She took off running in the lead with fellow American Joy Hansen, surrendered temporarily to 1994 ITU world champion Emma Carney, then fought back when future ITU world champion Jackie Gallagher took over. "I had to make a decision to dig a little deeper than I wanted to, and finally at 7 km, I sensed Jackie weakening and made a break and she let me go," said Smyers.

Afterward Smyers felt just plain lucky. "I did not expect the Ironman win, but I had been working for it the whole year, so I felt I deserved it. But with conditions at worlds, it was more of a crap-shoot. I dug deep on the run, and I felt that was very rewarding. But the bike was inconsequential. And to be honest, Michellie Jones [her greatest rival] wasn't there."

Smyers's sensational historic double—winning Ironman Hawaii and the short-course world championships—made the then-34-year-old the only athlete in the world ever to have won both in the same year.

A year after a very good race and 3rd place at Kona in 1996, she experienced her first serious setback. While she was working in her kitchen, a window in her house broke and a big piece of glass sliced through her thigh muscle above the knee. "Since I was home alone, at first I worried about bleeding to death," she recounted. Fortunately, the razor-sharp shard missed a main artery. Smyers was taken to the hospital, and doctors immediately operated. When she emerged from the anesthesia hours later, she found a big cast on her leg.

With her participation in the 1997 Ironman Hawaii canceled, she and husband King made the most of the time off. In May 1998 their daughter, Jenna, was born. For Karen Smyers, raising a child and competing as a pro athlete did not present a conflict. "Where there's a will, there's a way!" she explained.

It didn't take her long to get back into shape. But in August 1998 she experienced her next fateful setback. While training on her bike on a road near her Lincoln, Massachusetts, home, she was hit by a truck and knocked into a ditch. She ended up back in the hospital with six broken ribs, a punctured lung, and a dislocated shoulder. "Aside from the physical injuries, I was completely in shock; I realized that my little Jenna had almost lost her mother," she said with a trace of guilt. But, determined to be more careful in her training, she got back on the bike. "Training is neither a luxury nor a burden for me; it's part of my life," Smyers explained. In fact, every setback made her realize how much she missed training and racing.

In the fall of 1999, while she was again preparing for Ironman Hawaii, she suffered her most serious setback. When she went to a doctor to treat a recurring sore throat, what at first appeared to be tonsillitis turned out to be an enlarged thyroid and swollen lymph nodes. A biopsy revealed she had thyroid cancer.

Compared to the previous accidents, the cancer hit with a higher order of magnitude. "It took away the confidence I had in my body," she said. "The fact that those cells were growing inside me without my knowing gave me the feeling I was losing control." But instead of resisting fate, Smyers asked if her operation could wait a few weeks. She was feeling fit and wanted to start in Hawaii no matter what. The doctor gave his permission for the trip since it appeared that the tumor was growing very slowly. A few weeks later Smyers reached the finish in Kailua-Kona in 2nd place at 9 hours 20 minutes, just 7 minutes behind winner Lori Bowden.

She told her doctor afterward that she felt great and quickly left for Mexico to compete in a World Cup race before undergoing surgery. The race in Central America didn't go as she had hoped, however. On the bike course a competitor crashed right in front of her and took Smyers down to the pavement. The impact broke her collarbone.

When she got home her thyroid and six lymph nodes on the left side were removed. She had hardly gotten back on her feet when she tried to qualify for the U.S. Olympic team. "I didn't quite make it, but the goal really helped keep me from thinking about my cancer the whole time," she recalled.

After failing to make the team at the final 2000 U.S. Olympic Trials in late May, she had more lymph nodes removed. The doctors also advised her to undergo chemotherapy. Through it all, Smyers continued to train. "Having a goal, a passion, motivated me to get healthy again as quickly as possible," she said. "I had no time for self-pity." As she worked tirelessly to regain her health and strength, she continued to live her credo: "Where there's a will, there's a way."

Journalists, competitors, and even her own family looked on incredulously as she reasserted her place among the world's best by finishing 5th at Ironman Hawaii in 2001 with a time of 9 hours 48 minutes. For Smyers, it wasn't a big surprise. "It was never a question of whether or not I would get back in top shape; it was only a question of when!"

She experienced her hardest and most emotional Ironman Hawaii the following year. Four weeks after celebrating her second pregnancy, she lost the unborn child a day before her departure for Kailua-Kona. At first she wanted to cancel her start on the island. Then she made the decision, together with her husband, that she would at least try. On race day everything was going according to plan as she swam 57:50 and biked a fine 5:09:08. But in the second half of the marathon she felt so weak and empty that she had to spend an hour in the medical tent. Finally the doctors gave her the green light, and after a few miles she got back into her rhythm and finished the run in 4 hours 43 minutes, crossing the line in 10 hours 53 minutes 10 seconds, behind her older sister, Donna, an age-group competitor. "It was the only time I cried at the finish," she recounted. "I think it was just that in that moment all of the pent-up feelings and the sadness about the miscarriage came out."

Better days were ahead. In 2003, at age 42, she became pregnant again, and in 2004 her son, Casey, came into the world. A few months later Smyers took 19th at Ironman Hawaii. She crossed the finish line as 9th-best woman in 2005, and in 2006, at age 45, she came in 12th with a time of 9 hours 39 minutes.

She couldn't decide whether to take a break from Ironman Hawaii in 2007. She claimed that she wouldn't mind doing the race every five years or so. "I'm less focused on my result at the event than how good I feel when I race," she explained. What was really important was having goals and preparing her body accordingly.

She advised those with a lack of motivation to "just get started!" She explained that many hold themselves back because they don't feel they know exactly what to do. Her long-term goals were clear: "One day I'm going to try to break the record for athletes over 80," she said.

"I need to be active!"

THOMAS HELLRIEGEL ACCOMPLISHED what no German had done before him: He won Ironman Hawaii in 1997. In the buildup to that victory, his legendary appetite for training likely pushed him to cover more miles than any triathlete before or since. And on that long road he lost two heroic duels that prompted two of the greatest wins in the race's history before his iron persistence rewarded him for his battles with disappointment, illness, and sacrifice.

Hellriegel was born in Bruchsal, Germany, a town of 30,000 people in the Rhine Valley in southwest Germany, about 30 kilometers from the French border. His father, Walter, was a nuclear engineer who worked at the Karlsruhe research institute studying superconducting devices for space technology and nuclear fusion as a potential source of energy. Walter and his wife, Ursula, had no idea that their son Thomas would become a spectacular one-man source of energy in the field of Ironman triathlon competition.

As a child, Thomas was already athletic. At age 6 he went to children's gymnastics, at 10 he played European handball as part of a local league, and he also played tennis and participated in track and field. "I was always active, riding my bike 10 kilometers to school while others rode the bus," he recounted. At 15 he also swam with the local club, not yet imagining that several of these individual sports would one day propel him toward stardom.

In 1988, when he was 17, a friend who was swimming with him in a summer camp program told Hellriegel about the sport of triathlon. His curiosity piqued, Thomas saw the 1988 Ironman on TV. He also bought a German triathlon magazine and read about Scott Molina, who won that race, and pioneer German Ironman athlete Dirk Ashmoneit, who was 7th.

"I started training that winter, and the next spring I ran a 10 km," said Hellriegel. "I had been running just three times a week for two or three months, and my time in the race was 33 minutes [5:20 per mile pace]. I didn't know whether it was fast or slow. My friend Christian said he couldn't believe it, so I decided I might be good and should train more seriously."

Hellriegel was 18 when he entered his first triathlon. He easily took 3rd place in the Baden-Württemberg youth and junior championships held in Fischbach along Lake Constance on July 1, 1989. One year later, at 19, he was already thinking about iron-distance events. "I always wanted to do Ironman, but since I was still so young, I had to slowly develop my body with short-distance events," he explained.

However, his outwardly reasonable attitude didn't stop him from quietly registering for Ironman Europe in Roth, Germany. "I didn't tell anyone about it," he recalled with a laugh. He borrowed his parents' car and set off without telling them where he was going. Purely by coincidence Walter noticed on his son's calendar that Ironman Europe in Roth would take place that weekend. He put two and two together and at the last minute took a train to meet up with his son. At 1 in the morning, Thomas Hellriegel picked up his father at the railway station in the Bavarian town. Since Walter Hellriegel was not able to find a hotel room on such short notice, they spent the night in his son's small tent.

Hellriegel's trainer, Gerhard Wachter, was as surprised as his father by the young man's appearance at the long-distance event. "Thomas, have you really thought about what you're doing?" he asked. When his protégé responded, "Nah, I'm gonna do it," the trainer protested that it was much too soon for such a young athlete, that he risked injury and might sabotage his athletic promise. But Hellriegel would not be deterred. The next morning the starting cannon signaled his first Ironman event.

Young and fearless, he pushed hard on the bike. During the marathon he started running with an experienced triathlete. "He was equipped with everything, from a water bottle to a timetable to a heart rate monitor," Hellriegel recalled. The teenager followed the lead of the veteran and was happy to finish in 9 hours 26 minutes. Taking 56th place in a world-class field at the age of 19 also gave him perspective. He realized that the best athletes were still 90 minutes faster, but he felt that getting to the top was within his reach.

After graduating from high school, Hellriegel attended a technical trade school, which allowed him enough time to train. The 500 deutschmarks in federal student assistance each month didn't hurt, either. After trade school he was so fit and strong that the military welcomed him into its athlete development program in Warendorf. He stayed with that program for four years, taking advantage of its rigorous training and advanced coaching.

He also proved that he had reached the elite level in short-course triathlon, finishing 2nd to world champion Simon Lessing in the 1992 European Elite short-course championship and taking 6th at the ITU World Championship that year with an impressive final 10-km run time of 33:15.

But 1995 was truly showtime. At 24, he was feeling strong enough and possessed the endurance to transition to the Ironman distance. The results came fast. He won Lanzarote in Spain's Canary Islands and came in 2nd behind long-distance triathlete Jürgen Zäck, the then best German, at Ironman Germany in Roth. His confidence high, Hellriegel felt ready to realize his long-nurtured dream of racing at Ironman Hawaii. He trained hard with his friend Holger Lorenz, who had finished 8th at Ironman Hawaii in 1993 and told Hellriegel that the bike course was custom-made for them both. As Hellriegel remembered, Lorenz assured him they would be able to "push meaty gears" over Hawaii's rolling hills.

On race day Hellriegel came out of the water just 3 minutes 27 seconds behind heavy favorite Mark Allen. Hellriegel went all out on the bike, he explained, and after 25 miles made it to the front of the race. But he didn't stay with the experienced contenders for long.

Before the race he'd had a discussion with fellow German überbiker Zäck about making a break, and he was ready to carry out their plan. "Jürgen said that Mark Allen is very strong this year on the bike, and if we make a break he will try to come with us," said Hellriegel. On race day headwinds were blowing 45 mph in gusts, giving the advantage to the strong cyclists. "When I came to the group with Mark Allen, Ken Glah, and some others, Jürgen tried to make a break, and I wanted to go with him to see what it was like my first time. I thought, *I will stay as long as possible with Jürgen; then I will see on the run.*"

At first the move unfolded as Zäck had predicted. "Mark Allen did try to come and rode also a little bit away from the group," recalled Hellriegel. "But then he didn't manage it, and he lost touch. Then Jürgen said he needed a little bit more water at this aid station just ahead. But I had enough, and I took off and just kept going. I thought, *Maybe he will have something to drink and then he will be coming with me.* But I was riding and riding and looked back and didn't see him. I asked the guy on the motorbike, 'Where is Jürgen? Is he coming or not?'

"'Oh, Jürgen, he is 2 to 3 minutes behind.'

"I said, 'What?'

"I was really surprised because I expected him to come and we would ride together. Then I thought, *I won't wait!*"

It didn't faze Hellriegel that he had just passed Allen, who was regarded by many as the best triathlete of all time. He just wanted to ride as fast as possible. "Mark Allen didn't want to push himself too hard on the bike because he knew he would have the guys under his thumb on the run," said Hellriegel. "I thought they would probably catch up. I was never scared much about the run. I know if I am dying, I still can run 3:10 or 3:20. But if I have a good bike, maybe I will be top 15 no matter what."

At the turnaround, 52 miles into the bike, Hellriegel and his pursuers took stock of his daring move. "At Hawi I saw the others, and Jürgen was in between. They were looking at me and I was looking at them. My lead was already about 4 to 5 minutes and I was very motivated. Still, the whole time I was thinking, *It's too fast! It's too fast! It's too fast! I will die here.*"

Hellriegel explained that part of the fuel for his colossal talent on the bike was an insecurity bordering on a phobia about what might happen if he ran out of energy on the bike leg. "When I raced Ironman races I was always scared to die on the bike," he explained. "For example, in January in Lanzarote, I was doing my first long mileage training, and after 120 km I was just dying because I didn't train enough. It is such a bad feeling. There is nothing worse. And maybe that's why I train hard on the bike—it makes me stronger."

No one caught him on the bike leg. Hellriegel was riding as if from another planet. His competitors would refer to him thereafter as "Hell on Wheels." He entered the final transition zone 13 minutes 31 seconds ahead of Allen. His 4:29:37 ride on a brutally tough day had put him 11 minutes ahead of Zäck and was an astounding 17 minutes faster than Allen's ride.

For the 37-year-old master Allen, the race was coming down to the wire. He was already a five-time winner on the Big Island, and this was to be his last race in Kona. For him a farewell as runner-up would be tantamount to a farewell as the last-place finisher.

Hellriegel, who was quite capable of running a marathon in under 3 hours at the end of an Ironman, was now hopeful. "I knew that if Allen, the strongest runner there, was going to catch me, he would have to work very hard," he explained. "If he only ran 2:50, then it would be all over for him."

Hellriegel was misunderstood and underestimated by the U.S. Ironman media. The experts thought Hellriegel fit the usual profile of a powerful German überbiker—like Zäck—who really could not run well in Hawaii. But under the coaching of old school East German Stefan Grosse, in various triathlon races at short and long distances, Hellriegel had outrun every other top German triathlete at the time. Hellriegel said he had the capability of running a sub-31-minute open 10K, just 30 seconds or so slower than Mark Allen himself.

With the growing prospect of an upset driving him, Hellriegel ran well. But he had devoted so much effort to the bike that the gap he had established over Allen was melting away. Allen, in one of the greatest come-from-behind campaigns of his career, calculated that he had to make up 30 seconds per mile to overcome the 13-minute deficit. On his way to a sizzling 2:42 marathon, Allen had cut the margin to 4 minutes as Hellriegel entered the Energy Lab. Soon Hellriegel's lead dropped to 3 and then 2 minutes, and Allen was running like a man possessed. On the final 5-mile stretch along the Queen K Highway before arriving back in town, Hellriegel was increasingly surrounded by motorcycles carrying journalists and photographers not wanting to miss the moment of the kill.

Just before the last hill before Kailua-Kona, only 3 miles from the finish, the jig was up. Mark Allen passed his adversary, who responded with one last surge a few meters past the famous American. When Allen once again upped the pace, Hellriegel knew he was beaten.

But he wasn't too disappointed. "If someone had told me the day before the race that at 24 I would finish 2nd, I would have laughed until I cried," he explained later. He was happy about his exciting debut in Hawaii and was more than pleased with 2nd place.

"I never thought about winning," he said. "Maybe that was a mistake. I was not cool enough. Maybe if I had slowed down and biked 2 to 3 minutes slower I could have run 5 minutes faster, and I might have won. But I never thought about it then. I just thought, *Okay, make a big gap. Then maybe you will be 5 or 10 km in the lead or something.* But I never thought before the race that I could be leading the race."

Things looked different a year later. In 1996, victory was his clearly defined goal. "Mark Allen had retired; now it was my turn," said Hellriegel.

With a firm resolve to be ready for battle, he dialed up his training. "I was a little asocial back then," explained Hellriegel. "Aside from training, eating, and sleeping, I didn't do much."

His immune system didn't take too well to the massive training volume, and he was tormented by shingles for several weeks. Despite it all, his training for Kona included 13,700 miles on his bike—up to 840 miles in his longest weeks early in the year, when he built a huge aerobic base by riding 50 hours a week in Tenerife in the Canary Islands. That year he also logged 3,000 miles of running and 500 miles of swimming.

When the shingles forced him to withdraw from Ironman Europe in Roth in early July, he was depressed, but the enforced rest was good for him. Seven weeks later he had recovered, and at Ironman Canada—his last test before Hawaii—Hellriegel was at the top of his game again. He won and set a new course record of 8 hours 9 minutes 53 seconds, smashing the previous record by about 20 minutes.

Bring on Hawaii.

The race in October 1996 unfolded much as it had the year before. Hellriegel trailed slightly after the swim, then stormed to the front on his bike. The last leader he passed was Belgian Luc Van Lierde, only two years his senior. "He was definitely a gifted athlete," the German acknowledged, a judgment obvious to anyone who knew of Van Lierde's silver medal at the 1995 ITU long-course World Championship at Nice and his silver medals at the 1996 ITU long-course World Championship at Muncie, Indiana, and the 1996 ITU short-course World Championship in Cleveland, Ohio, where he finished behind Simon Lessing

After receiving a 3-minute penalty for drafting, the Belgian sat it out in the transition area following the bike leg. Observing that Van Lierde appeared "flustered and frustrated," Hellriegel recalled that he wasn't immediately worried about him.

After setting a new Kona bike course record of 4 hours 24 minutes 50 seconds that would last for a decade, Hellriegel took off aggressively on the run at a much faster pace than the year before. He was feeling confident, having observed the Belgian vomiting on the bike. But Van Lierde was far from done.

At first everything looked good for Hellriegel. "I felt really strong, and I was not worried about him because I thought, *This is too fast for him and he will explode on the run.* I was very sure I could beat him. When I started running, my lead was 3 minutes. Then it grew to 4 minutes, and after 20 kilometers it was 4.5 minutes. I was running away from him; I felt very fresh and I was running really quick."

When Hellriegel entered the Natural Energy Lab, a 4-mile out-and-back, L-shaped segment of paved road that veered left from the Queen K Highway toward the ocean, he was 5 minutes ahead of Van Lierde. But when he left the Energy Lab, with only 7 miles left to run, his lead had dwindled. This did not concern him at first. "I was running less than 4 minutes per kilometer on my way to running 2:46," said Hellriegel. "So I felt very strong, and at that time I thought, *When he gets closer I can go harder.* I thought, *Oh, it is not so far to go.*"

But after he left the microwave heat of the Energy Lab, things looked different. "After the Energy Lab I was getting really tired," he recalled. "Just before the turnaround, they sent me to go the other way around the cones, which is stupid. I had to make a sharp move to get back on course, and that is where I cramped. You can see it on the video. Then leaving the Energy Lab, the cramps came back."

A spectator told him Van Lierde had radically closed the gap. "I thought, *That's not possible.* I was going pretty damn fast," he recalled. It was déjà vu, with only the name of the opponent changed. The gap was narrowing to only a 2-minute lead over his rampaging pursuer. Hellriegel was becoming increasingly surrounded; more and more motorcycles carrying journalists or photographers were riding next to him, once again not wanting to miss the moment in which he would be passed.

Despite the fact that it would only take Hellriegel 2 hours 46 minutes 55 seconds to complete the marathon, Van Lierde passed him with 2 miles to go, at the same place where Mark Allen had passed him the year before. "I was pretty ticked off, above all because it was on the same hill as in 1995," Hellriegel said.

Allen had closed with a 2:42:09 marathon and had beaten Hellriegel by 2 minutes 25 seconds. In 1996 Van Lierde ran 2:41:48 and beat Hellriegel to the line by 1:59. Buoyed by ideal conditions, Van Lierde's 8:04:08 finishing time was a record that surpassed all Mark Allen's race times and still stood 13 years later. Hellriegel's 8:06:07 also remains as the second-fastest time at Ironman Hawaii.

Discouragement can loom large. But giving up was not Hellriegel's style. For his 1997 Hawaii tune-up, Hellriegel again turned to Ironman Europe in Roth. The year before at Roth, Lothar Leder had become the first Ironman to break the 8-hour barrier. In 1997 Hellriegel also broke the magic 8-hour barrier but finished 4th behind Van Lierde, Zäck, and Leder. As at Kona in 1996, Van Lierde set a record time for the Ironman distance, 7:50:27.

"I felt very strong that day on the bike and rode 4:14 with Jürgen, and we led into the transition," said Hellriegel of Roth '97. "I never pushed too hard, and I thought I could beat Jürgen in the run and win the race because I ran so quick in Hawaii the year before. Luc was already so far behind, and so I was pretty sure to win. Then everything changed during the run."

When Zäck, much fresher on a cool Roth afternoon than in the heat of Hawaii, ran away, Hellriegel had to recalibrate. "I thought, *Oh man, this is too fast for me. I can't follow.*" When he heard that Van Lierde and Leder were also coming, Hellriegel recalled, "That was very tough mentally." At the end he crossed the line in 7:57 in 4th place. "It was crazy! After the finish I said, 'This can't be true.' But that is the sport. It doesn't depend only on you. It depends on the others, too. Everyone was just so strong that day."

Still, Hellriegel took comfort from one fact. No other German performed as well as he in the heat and winds of Hawaii. "When it is hot and humid, Jürgen suffers much more than I," he said. "Also

Lothar is very tall, and it is hard for him to ride against the wind. I am smaller, and it is easier for me to ride against the wind." He said he was not discouraged after Roth. "It made me even more motivated to train harder."

Hellriegel arrived in Hawaii optimistic as ever. Although he welcomed the best competitors, he also knew that one of the biggest requirements of a race like Hawaii is getting to the start healthy and ready. So he did not mourn when Van Lierde, who had a leg injury, did not show up in Kona.

Hellriegel made progress with his swimming, and his 53:08 opening split left him less than a minute behind all the serious contenders, his smallest deficit ever. The fierce *mumuku* winds returned that year along the Queen Ka'ahumanu Highway, and for the first time Hellriegel did not ride away from everyone on the bike. He knew that under those difficult circumstances he would need to carefully modulate his efforts.

For much of the ride Hellriegel and Zäck broke out to a modest lead. Near the end of the bike, both American Ken Glah and young Australian Chris Legh surged to join Hellriegel and Zäck. Then, with 12 miles left, Zäck made a surge and arrived at T2 with a 2-minute lead. Now a Hawaii veteran, Hellriegel did not panic.

"That time I knew there was no super runner like Luc," he said. "I knew I should beat Jürgen on the run in the heat. So I let him go because I knew he went very hard to get that lead, and I also knew his best marathon in Hawaii was about 3 hours and the year before I ran 2:46."

He transitioned from bike to run with three other athletes. While Glah and Legh were soon left behind, Zäck still hung tough. At mile 8, where the steep hill on Palani Road leads up to the highway, it got harder for Zäck. Two miles later Hellriegel increased his pace and returned the favor from Roth, leaving Zäck behind.

With just 7 miles remaining in the marathon, many spectators were already celebrating his victory. But Hellriegel, twice burned by late-race losses to Allen and Van Lierde, retained an understandable dose of paranoia. "After my experiences the past two years, I kept thinking that something was coming, that something would happen," he recounted. He remembered all too clearly the beginning of Mark and Dave Hill, at the 24-mile mark of the marathon where he had been caught twice on the verge of victory. When he was asked at what point he knew victory was his, he replied, "I was never sure. I kept turning around to make sure that no one was coming up behind me."

When a spectator gave Hellriegel a large German flag three-quarters of a mile from the finish, he reacted with anguish. "It seemed so incredibly heavy that I just wanted to set it down for fear that it would cost me my lead," he said. "I was completely uncertain. It was crazy, horrible!"

But after a total of 8 hours 33 minutes, it was a done deal. As he crossed the finish line, he turned around one last time, more symbolically than out of fear. Thomas Hellriegel became the first man of his nation, whose athletes' imaginations had been so captivated by this race, to win Ironman Hawaii.

Hellriegel's psychic wounds from his first two heartbreaking losses did not completely heal with the reception of the trophy in Hawaii. "A week later, I could not quite believe it," he recalled. "I was back in Germany, and it was cold and raining, and I thought, *Did I win Hawaii? Everything is so far away. Outside it is 10 degrees.*" In one of many celebrations, officials in Germany gave him a ring to celebrate his victory. "One morning after, I woke up and went to look in the cupboard for this ring. When I saw it, I thought, *Yeah, it's real. I have the ring.*"

The athlete from Bruchsal was now the trailblazer who opened the door for other German athletes to follow. He proved that there was no reason to be intimidated by the North American juggernaut. Two more Germans—Normann Stadler, who racked up wins in 2004 and 2006, and Faris Al-Sultan, who won in 2005—were inspired by his accomplishments, courage, and determination.

Thomas Hellriegel did not repeat his feat on the Big Island, but in 2001 he returned to form and took a respectable 3rd place and followed that with a 4th in 2002. The boy who began with an abiding love of outdoor activity and sport had become a man who retained that same unquenchable youthful spirit.

Nearing 20 years in the sport, he had competed in more than 30 iron-distance triathlons when he expressed his desire to compete two more years as a professional. Regardless of what awaited him, one thing was certain. "I will always participate in sports," he vowed. "When I don't train, I don't feel good. I need to be active!"

DAVID BAILEY & CARLOS MOLEDA

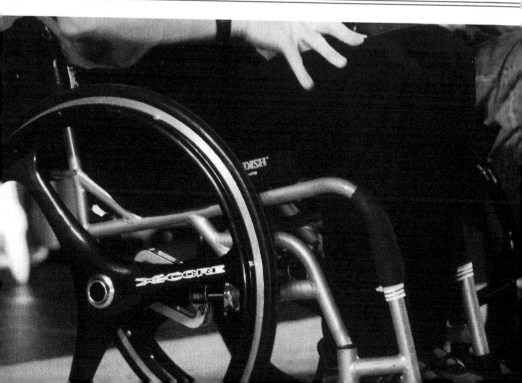

"We did this together."

THESE RIVALS HAD a three-year history, not seven. The final pass was made with 4 miles to go on the run, not 2. And once the final break was made, the margin at the line was 8 minutes, not 1. But in many ways the duel between David Bailey and Carlos Moleda at Ironman Hawaii 2000 compares well with the greatest previous clash ever: the Mark Allen–Dave Scott Iron War of 1989. Although the physics of physically challenged Ironman racing may be different from those of the usual Ironman competitors, the clash of wills and the courage to smash previous limits are the same.

The duel between Bailey and Moleda pitted a man who had been known as the world's fastest and smoothest motocrosser before a 1987 practice crash in northern California had snapped his spine against a former U.S. Navy SEAL who had been paralyzed by a bullet in the back during Operation Just Cause in Panama in 1990. It was the third clash between two proud, superior athletes who had incinerated any lingering pity and the shadow of their prior identities in the fire of their intense battle.

David Bailey took his first two losses to Carlos Moleda in Kona very hard. In 1998 Bailey, the media favorite who was featured on NBC's *Dateline,* on *Fox Sports News,* and in a write-up in *Competitor* magazine, was soundly beaten by Moleda and Randy Caddell. In 1999 Bailey arrived better prepared and led until painful catheter problems—he held off urinating until he stopped and then relieved himself for more than 4 straight minutes—short-circuited his race. He finished second in 11 hours 30 minutes while Moleda blasted in under the 11-hour mark.

On race day in 2000 Bailey arrived armed with an epic breakthrough September training day during which the Ironman warrior had pushed through pain for 110 miles, fighting off cramps by licking the salt encrusted on his arms. But Bailey's confidence was shaken

One of triathlon's most famous photos: Julie Moss crawling to the finish line in 1982.

TOP: In 1989 Dave Scott (left) and Mark Allen battled toe to toe for over 8 hours. Allen broke free on the final hill, winning the race with a spectacular 2:40:04 marathon.

LEFT: Allen took his fifth consecutive victory in 1993 in his best time of 8:07:45; he'd go on to win once more in 1995.

TOP: Dick and Rick Hoyt entered their first official running event in 1979; by 1986 they were competing in triathlons.

RIGHT: The Hoyts' fame has taken them around the world. At last count, they'd raced in 234 triathlons—including 6 Ironmans—and 27 Boston Marathons.

TOP: An absolute speed demon on the bike, Paula Newby-Fraser still tops the charts for the fastest women's bike split, a record she set in 1993.

LEFT: Newby-Fraser set a women's record of 8:55:28 in 1992, then followed it up a year later, shown here, with an 8:58:23 finish.

TOP: Always a strong runner, Greg Welch honed his skills to become a formidable competitor on the bike.

LEFT: In 1999 Welch's tachycardia hit hard. Though he finished the race, he nearly collapsed at the finish line and soon after was forced to announce his retirement.

RIGHT: At age 76, Sister Madonna Buder finished the 2006
Hawaii Ironman in 16:59:03, with 57 seconds to spare.

BELOW: Sister Madonna Buder took up running at age 48,
and from there triathlon was an easy step. "I remembered I
loved to swim as a kid, and I like to bicycle. So I did it."

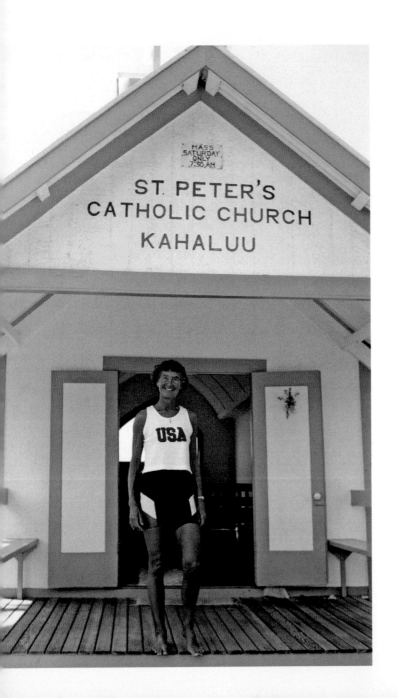

RIGHT: Karen Smyers was a swimmer who took up running to strengthen her legs.

BELOW: Smyers at first resisted the use of aerodynamic bike equipment but soon found greater speed with it on the Queen K highway.

LEFT: Thomas Hellriegel had a 13-minute lead over Mark Allen (right) in 1995, but bit by bit, Allen pulled it back. After two 2nd-place finishes, Hellriegel finally won the race in 1997.

BELOW: "Hell on Wheels" was Hellriegel's nickname, and for good reason: in 1996 he blasted to a 4:24:50 bike leg.

RIGHT: Carlos Moleda credited his U.S. Navy SEAL training for his endurance. "Most people don't know it, but they can do the impossible," he said.

BELOW: David Bailey had speed to spare in the run leg of his win in 2000 but credited Moleda for "pushing me to hell and back."

when Moleda screamed to a 6-minute 45-second lead after 70 terrifying miles on the windiest day in Ironman history.

"When I heard Carlos was that far ahead," recalled Bailey, "I said to myself: *This is the moment I knew was coming. The moment when you feel like you're puking your guts out and want to quit and you have to find the next gear or surrender.*" Right then Bailey forgot about the marathon to come. "All I thought was whoever gets off the bike first wins," said Bailey. His neck and arms encrusted with salt, Bailey ramped up the pain and the speed. "I used speed as a drug," he said. "I needed speed to propel me over the rises, and if I could maintain that speed, I could go faster on the downhills. If I could hit 24 mph, I saw no reason I couldn't hit 25. If I could maintain 25, I said to myself, *Carlos is probably already at 25, so if I want to make up the 6 minutes, I've got to go 25 and a half.* I didn't see the lava; I didn't see anything else but my cyclometer and a narrow tunnel of speed."

Finally Bailey could see Moleda, a former surfer and world-class skateboarder who had emigrated from São Paulo, Brazil, in 1980. Moleda was on the long climb up to a scenic viewpoint 10 miles before the Keahole airport. "I was cramping and feeling bad, and I'd nearly dug a deep hole for myself," said Bailey. "But when I saw him, all that went away. Carlos was 4 minutes ahead, and from that instant, all the pain and doubt left my body."

Bailey passed Moleda 2 miles past the airport. Then came a moment that revealed that the emotional Bailey was being fueled, at least at the moment, by pure, primitive aggression. "When I went by him, the wind was coming from the right, and in the corner of my eye Carlos seemed to position himself over to the left just a little too close, close enough to get an advantage. I thought, *C'mon Carlos! Stop drafting!*" Bailey recalled how Dave Scott had gotten mad at Mark Allen in 1987 for tickling his feet while drafting him on the swim (which is entirely legal). "Mark was in the hospital the next day with his internal bleeding and thinking, *C'mon dude. You won the race and I've got a tube down my stomach and you gotta bitch about that?*

That seemed harsh. But I found that when you're that close to each other and you want it so bad and this one guy is in the way of your dreams—if you so much as think that this guy is making it easier on himself by slightly cheating, you're pissed!"

Bailey admitted later that the dark passion of the moment unfairly cast Moleda as the villain. He tried to move past his frustration, seeing it as a sign of weakness. "I ignored it. I felt that mentally and physically I was in better shape than I had been before. I decided I'd drag him into the transition at the Kona Surf with me on my strength and let him see it. I thought whatever you do as a navy SEAL must be tough. You sit in cold water for a few weeks with nothing to eat and assemble bombs and hold your breath. I figured however long I was willing to match him, Carlos was ready to do it 10 seconds longer. I believed that however fast I went, Carlos would never give up. He was built to suffer, just like Lance Armstrong."

Indeed, Moleda recalled that after several of his 100-mile training rides, his wife, Sarah, looked at him and gasped, "You're dying!" "My face was pale and shrunken; my eyes were bloodshot and sunk back in my head," said Moleda. "You see, we only have half of the muscle mass available to able-bodied cyclists." For Bailey and Moleda, pushing through the 112-mile Ironman bike with their arms is like cycling 220 miles for men with legs.

In the wake of his two defeats, Bailey had read a chapter from Armstrong's book *It's Not About the Bike*. He focused on the day Armstrong scheduled a long ride and his team director, Johan Bruyneel, offered to let him take the day off because of spring sleet in the Alps. "Lance rode it anyway," said Bailey. "Lance was ready to go as hard and as fast as it takes to make the other guys surrender. Carlos is just like that. If he were to ride the Tour de France, he'd have to grab the yellow jersey from the start. So I prepared myself to do the same. However much it hurt today, it wouldn't hurt as much as the regrets I had for two years when I felt I had the opportunity to win and gave up."

If Bailey had an advantage over Moleda, it was that he had been in a similar titanic battle before during his motocross career. In January 1986, in front of 75,000 screaming fans in Anaheim Stadium during the opening round of the supercross championship, Honda teammates Bailey and Ricky Johnson had a duel most experts rank as the best in the history of the sport. In the high-adrenaline, aerial-circus world of supercross, riders usually fight until a pass is made and dominance is asserted. There is a mental release, and there is no fighting back. On that night Johnson and Bailey traded passes for 18 of the 20 laps, and the tension was unbearable. "After I'd passed him late, Ricky kept trying to get under and stuff it under me on the turns," recalls Bailey. "His plan was to wreck my momentum coming into this big double so he'd make the jump and I wouldn't. But I just had a smoother style and was using less energy and kept in front of the blocks. Finally he got exhausted, and he made four or five mistakes in a row and missed the jump."

The ironic outcome of this battle of classic, contrasting styles was that afterward Johnson always tried to emulate Bailey's flawless technique and smoother style, whereas Bailey saw something he yearned for in Johnson. "Ricky rode with his heart, and no one had a bigger one," said Bailey. "Ricky was always going over his head and putting himself over the edge and clawing back. Until the end I wanted to be more like him."

Carlos Moleda credited his navy SEAL training with teaching him that, as he put it, "I could do great things. Most people don't know it, but they can do the impossible. It takes something like surviving SEAL Hell Week or the Ironman to show ordinary people what they are capable of." Moleda needed that strength when he arrived in the Veterans Administration hospital in Seattle without the use of his legs. "SEAL training helped me," said Moleda. "I had a very brief period of shock. Then there was almost no grieving period. I immediately discarded the things I could no longer do and focused on doing the things I could [do] very, very well."

With the help of physical therapist Jennifer Young, who set successively more difficult challenges for him, Moleda doubled the other patients' number of pushups and was soon aboard a racing wheelchair. After nine months of intense rehab, Moleda and his friend Russ Walton completed a 1,200-mile wheelchair journey from Miami to Virginia Beach. The next year Moleda finished the grueling 367-mile Midnight Sun Ultra Challenge stage race in 21 hours, breaking the race record by seven hours. In 1993 he married Sarah Preston, and in 1994 their son, Spencer, was born.

Bailey's postparalysis recovery was a much longer journey, complicated by a period of emotional investment in the Miami Project, which offered hope for repair of the spinal cord. "I believed I would walk again," recalled Bailey, who went through severe depression when he finally faced medical reality.

Bailey's connection with triathlon had begun before his injury. "I was in Kona on my honeymoon with Gina and saw the 1986 Ironman," said Bailey. "I was so stoked, I told Gina I would do this one day, after my racing career. Afterward we met Dave Scott. He was by the pool at the King Kam and had a big, ugly-looking road rash, but he just ignored it. I shook his hand and told him I was honored to meet him. He knew about my racing career and said, 'No, I'm honored to meet *you*.'" Three years later, on the eve of the 1989 Iron War, Bailey was in Kona to watch the Ironman and got a call. "It was Dave Scott," recalled Bailey with wonder. "It was maybe 9 p.m. and he just wanted to chat, maybe to forget about the pressure. I kept saying: 'You ought to go to bed,' but he said no, he wanted to talk. Then, the next day, I saw him battle Mark Allen, and it was the most amazing thing I had ever seen."

Bailey raced chairs on the roads until 1997, when his friend, coach, and mentor Todd Jacobs, a former pro, convinced him to give triathlon a go. "I was scared witless of sharks, but Todd swam with me at Oceanside, and somehow we made it through. Funny thing, when he was carrying me out of the water, a woman who didn't know what was going on saw us—I looked exhausted—and yelled, 'Medical!' We still laugh about that."

Bailey and Moleda came to the sport in 1998, after pioneer Jon Franks broke the barrier for wheelchair athletes in 1994 and entered Ironman Hawaii and after John MacLean was the first wheelchair athlete to finish within the regulation cutoff time. Bailey and Moleda first met at the 1998 Lubbock half-Ironman qualifier; Bailey blasted past Moleda and everyone else on the run to a 12-minute overall win. The odd thing about the two men was that Bailey could now outswim the former SEAL. However, Moleda could outbike the former fastest man on two wheels. In their current incarnations, Moleda could outclimb and outsprint Bailey, the former master of the incredible terrain and sprint format of motocross, but Bailey, the former effortless technician, had become a grinder who wore down competitors with his heart and his endurance on the flats.

When they arrived in Kona in October 2000, Moleda was psychologically light as the two-time defending champion, the race and bike record-holder, the man who had Bailey's number the way Dave Scott had had Mark Allen's number for the first six years of their rivalry.

By contrast, the mercurial Bailey was blessed and cursed by a supercharged articulateness and a Dostoevskian consciousness of emotions, ego, and struggle. These qualities made him a great motocross analyst and journalist for ESPN, but the extra baggage associated with his self-reflection may have weighed him down in sporting combat.

"Before the race, Todd kept drilling into me how Mark and Dave, before their big race in 1989, did everything they could to stay away from each other, did not make eye contact, did not have any transfer of energy at the press conference," said Bailey. "So I was determined to stay away from Carlos until race day. I was sure nobody had prepared better than I, and by now nobody was tougher, but I still had that seed of doubt. I knew nobody got more out of himself in Hawaii than Carlos, and I knew that the difference could be small." He was startled when someone grabbed his arm from behind as he was checking into the hotel, not five minutes after he arrived in the lobby.

"What the hell? It was Carlos!" said Bailey. "I thought, *Dang it! Why's he grabbing me?* I was almost irritated. I thought, *I'm not supposed to even see him, much less touch him!* Right now I do not dislike him in any way, shape, or form. But at that moment I thought if I had to touch this guy, I would get something out of it. When we were shaking hands, I decided to suck all the energy out of the guy. At that moment he looked as he always looked, but he didn't look all that strong to me."

Bailey's assessment was partly correct. Although Moleda had had a strong spring racing bikes in Europe, he did not have his usual endurance base. "I hadn't trained specifically for Ironman in 2000," said Moleda. "But I felt that I had nothing to lose." Indeed, Moleda had written down 10 hours 30 minutes as his goal time. If he succeeded, Bailey would be outgunned once again.

For his part, Bailey was acutely aware of the strain on his family caused by Ironman training and had vowed that his third race in Kona would be his last. "I put the pressure on myself," said Bailey. "No exit. No excuses. I thought this was my last shot at Hawaii."

Bailey had made another crucial improvement in his preparation. "In my first two years, I had terrible problems with urinary tract infection and the catheter. Finally some wheelchair athlete friends of mine told me about the indwelling catheter. I said, 'What's that?' They couldn't believe I didn't know about it." The indwelling catheter works like a small balloon inserted into the bladder and filled with a saline solution that allows the bladder to stay snug inside yet still allows fluids to escape. Bailey would no longer face the horrible buildup of pressure and the necessity to stop to relieve himself. "Finally I could drink as much as I needed," said Bailey.

On Ironman morning Bailey was calmly trying to insert the indwelling catheter when the tip broke. "I had to try to hold on to the balloon and hope the solution stayed intact, but I didn't know if this would be a replay of '99," said Bailey. Then a security marshal refused to let Bailey's wife, Gina, onto the pier to assist as she had the first two years. Trying hard to remain cool, Bailey waved good-bye to Gina and proceeded to do all his preparations himself. He discovered that he had left his energy drink and Super GU gels in the hotel room and made an adrenaline-hemorrhaging dash in his chair through crowds to his room and back. "The elevator stopped at every floor—up and down," said Bailey. "I just made it back and pumped up my bike tires by myself and found myself jumping off the pier with Carlos."

When he was being carried out of the water after a 1:14 swim, Bailey saw liquid flowing out of the clear tube from the catheter. "Oh, my God, thank you, Madame Pele!" said Bailey. The catheter was working, and the race was on.

Bailey and Moleda started up the Palani hill together; Moleda, the hill-climbing charger, took off and led by 50 yards at the top. Todd Jacobs was at the top of the hill and yelled, "This is perfect! Just like Mark and Dave. Your race is right there in front of you!"

Moleda simply told himself, "Cool. We're together. No problem."

As Bailey wrestled with his demons, thinking dark thoughts about Moleda, they came together into the hot corner in downtown Kona, about 6 miles from the transition. "Carlos was right there on my butt, and I saw this official standing there in the middle of the intersection," said Bailey. "Once you're committed to the corner, you're on the brake and leaning; these things aren't maneuverable. So for a second, I went on two wheels and did a cool little saving act."

A motocrosser's sense of balance helped, no doubt. "I got a little out of shape, and Carlos went by me. I got irritated for a second, but then I jumped back and passed him back. I saw a look on his face and imagined him shaking his head and thinking, *Damn, there he goes again! What's with David today? I'm usually stronger on the bike.*"

Then came the moment that transformed Bailey's superheated psyche and shifted his competitive angst to a higher plane. Bailey heard his right tire start hissing at the valve stem. It was a slow leak at the rear and wasn't fatal—he only slowed from 21 mph to about 18—but it was a perfect opportunity for Moleda to lose him again. However, the Brazilian-born American did something remarkable: He waited.

"I told David, 'Don't worry; I won't pass you until we get to transition,'" said Moleda. "'Then it will be an even fight.' For me it wasn't worth it to drop him there. It would seem cheap. It's not like we were competing for $1 million."

Bailey remembered it well. "It wasn't like we came to a complete stop. We were still going pretty quick. But it was still a stunning act of sportsmanship, and it completely changed how I felt about Carlos. When we got to that last steep hill before the Kona Surf, Carlos took off again. That was more than fair. It was his strong suit to climb, and he was right to use it."

Bailey made a lightning transition and was only 90 seconds behind Moleda going up the heartbreakingly steep hill out of the Kona Surf in the racing chair. "It felt like it was 3,000 degrees in that changing tent and I came out all sweaty and slimy, and my hands slipped on the wheels," said Bailey. "For the first 100 yards, it felt like I had never pushed a chair before. But I got going and had a good run going up the hill, and I remember it was so steep that Carlos had shifted into reverse to use his biceps rather than his triceps. I thought, *This is a first. We are staring right at each other.* He was only 50 yards in front, and I started to push harder, but it was so steep I started to wheelie." Bailey tried to make a good show of strength dropping into the pit at the southern end of the run course, hoping to cut the margin, but Moleda had stretched his advantage to 2 minutes. "How can the guy go so fast?" wondered Bailey. "On my way back out of the pit, they told me 3 minutes. I started feeling lousy. My neck was in the wrong position. It was hurting. I was fighting doubt."

By the time he got to Palani Hill, 8 miles into the marathon, Moleda had stretched his lead to 5 minutes. "My family was all there," said Bailey. "Gina and my brother were trying to hide it, but I think they thought it was over. It was my mom's birthday; Darlene was 59. She told me, 'Don't give up!'"

Farther up the hill, Jacobs was almost beside himself. "Todd was shouting at me, 'Don't worry that Carlos has better abs! I don't want to hear it. Be a better person! Be a better athlete! Dig deeper! You can do it! Don't leave anything! Don't leave any doubts, or you'll swim home!'" Bailey, who had been drinking and saving energy for the turn onto the Queen K at mile 9, said, "Todd, trust me! I know what you're thinking. I will go harder. I will not crack. When I get to the top of the hill, it is on!"

For his part, Moleda was feeling good in the chair. "I just wanted to let it all hang out. I felt I had nothing to lose," he recalled.

But on the 5-mile stretch on the Queen K Highway to the Natural Energy Lab, Moleda's elbow began to hurt, and Bailey whittled Moleda's lead from 4 minutes to 90 seconds. Bailey ignored the splits being called out by spectators. "Dave Scott never raced with a watch," he said. "I was only conscious that I would either have the race of my life that I would remember forever or lose for the third time and regret it forever. So once again, I did not like this guy Carlos. He was the devil to me."

At the Energy Lab turnaround at mile 17, Bailey whittled the margin to 30 seconds but took more time to gobble some pretzels and pack in salt and water. "I didn't know if Carlos had more in him, whether he was just waiting for me and was going to dog me until the end and then win with his strength—climbing hills and the sprint. So I wanted to be ready when I came up on him. If need be I wouldn't need any more food or water. Until the finish."

By this time runners going by knew something epic was going on. Some stopped and stared with a kind of reverence, the way people had watched Julie Moss at the end of her February 1982 race or the crowds had followed Mark and Dave in 1989. Others cheered with the fervor of fans watching Lance Armstrong charge up Alpe d'Huez. Ironically, the pass came at exactly the spot where Bailey had gone by on the bike almost 3 hours before, at mile 22.

Once he was clear, Bailey knew he had the win, and tears began streaming down his face. Oddly enough to others but perfectly in character for him, Moleda had happy thoughts, too. "After I beat him last year, I knew how determined he was, and I thought it would hurt to lose to anyone else, but it was okay to be beaten by him," Moleda recalled. "I knew how much winning Ironman would do for him, not only as an athlete but as a person. It is true for me, and I think it is true for David. For the longest time he was known as the man who used to win at motocross. This win validates him as an athlete now. I could not hand it to him."

Moleda said he had no regrets for pausing to stay with Bailey when he had that flat. "No," said Moleda. "If I won that way, it would not be satisfying. I want the two of us to go hard and beat him in a fair race. If you get sick and can't pee, or vomit or get diarrhea because of the Ironman stress, that's racing. But at the end of the day, I wasn't bummed out by losing. To me it was win-win. He had a great race and was the better man on the day."

For Bailey the win was cathartic. "When he came in, Carlos was smiling as if he had won. He pointed at me and said, 'Man you were awesome today!' Then we hugged. Usually when I hug a guy, it feels like you are putting sunscreen on the guy's back; you don't really want to do it. This was different."

Bailey told Moleda, "We did this together. You still have the course record. You won twice. I just borrowed your crown. Thanks for pushing me to hell and back."

TEN | **ANDREAS NIEDRIG**

"You can do anything if you really want to."

AROUND THE TURN of the century, Andreas Niedrig was one of the best long-distance triathletes in the world. If anyone had met this man during the dark period when he was a heroin addict who paid for his habit with a life of crime and lies, they would not have believed he could emerge from that nightmare. Setting goals for himself, achieving them, and serving as a good example to others would have been unthinkable.

Born October 12, 1967, Niedrig grew up in the city of Oer-Erkenschwick in the middle of the industrial Ruhr area of Germany. It was a hardworking, blue-collar town of 30,000 where men, if they were lucky enough to survive their shift in the mines, would have a beer after work at the local bar, their eyelids still black from coal dust.

His father, Hans-Werner, learned the mining trade but then charted his own path in life as a police officer. Niedrig described his middle-class childhood as "good and exciting."

Like his sister, Conny, four years his senior, Niedrig joined the local swim team when he was 13. He had talent. With a time of 1 minute 6 seconds in the 100-meter backstroke, he was one of the best swimmers in West Germany.

Things didn't go as well in school. His grades dropped, and he had to switch schools. "I didn't know where I belonged and had a difficult time trying to find my place in society," he explained. The swim team represented a final chance. But when his trusted coach and some of his friends from the team left, he felt desolate and abandoned.

He was almost thankful to discover cigarettes when fellow students offered them to him at recess. Smoking was something he could hide behind, a distraction. Soon he smoked his first joint at school. He rarely went to swim practice anymore, dropping the only part of his life for which he had set goals.

The drugs soon roared into the vacuum and took control. At 15 he was using cocaine, speed, and LSD. After ninth grade Niedrig left secondary school for a trade school, but he soon dropped out. He had an internship to become an electrician but also abandoned that, dropping out right before the final exam. He considered signing on with the Foreign Legion but instead lucked into a position in the German military.

He was only 21 when his girlfriend Sabine became pregnant. She didn't know about his challenges with drugs, in part because he was able to resist them during their happy time together. But as Sabine's stomach grew, so did his doubts that he could support a family. He began smoking marijuana again, and not long before the birth of his daughter, Jana, he remembered looking into a glowing heroin pipe as it was passed around and feeling calm and reassured. Soon he was no longer able to resist.

He began buying his own heroin for the first time and soon exchanged the pipe for a syringe. After his stint in the military, he took a job as a truck driver. But when he was caught stealing from the company, he was fired. He didn't tell Sabine, who by then had become his wife. Every morning he would leave the house as if going to work. He needed money to support his family and also to support his drug habit, so he turned to crime. Under constant pressure to come up with big money, he avoided dealing small amounts of drugs on the street. Instead he traded in larger volumes and stole cars. At one point he carried a gun.

Eventually it all caught up with him; Sabine found out that he no longer worked at his old job and found him passed out in the bathroom from a heroin overdose. Despite her disappointment, she stood by him. She made him promise he would enter rehab, but he left therapy the very first day. He couldn't stand the pain of withdrawal and wanted to be home with his wife and child. But when Sabine found out that he had quit treatment, she took their daughter and moved in with Niedrig's sister, Conny.

Living on the streets, Niedrig found enough money from crime to pay for hotel rooms. But he soon he was broke and sleeping in an old mobile home in a junkyard, then in an unused railroad car. The situation got so bad that he realized he had to give rehab a second try or lose his young family—or his life.

In November 1990 he entered the Fredeburg clinic in Sauerland, Germany. Not only did his wife promise him a second chance if he lasted through the 14-month program, but the district attorney agreed to drop charges if he completed the treatment. More than anything else, his love for his wife and daughter motivated him to battle the addiction.

There was no way he could even think about sports at the time. He weighed 106 pounds when he entered the clinic. Just over a year later he went home weighing 200. He still hadn't kicked his cigarette habit and was a long way from any kind of form or fitness. "We lived on the fourth floor at the time, and I couldn't even carry a crate of mineral water up the stairs without stopping to rest," he recalled.

Getting up the stairs was the least of his problems. He urgently needed a job in order to feed his family. Surprisingly—especially for an addict—somewhere during his return from rehab he had acquired an iron will. He took a tough quarry job as a day laborer, dismantling a torn-down smokestack by hand. His good work wasn't lost on the foreman, and soon he was driving a forklift. Then he found a job driving a meat truck, transitioned into transporting furniture, and eventually went back to school to become an orthopedic technician.

He was 25 when he finally accepted one of his father's repeated invitations to go running in the nearby woods. It began with a 7-kilometer loop, but when his son still looked fresh after that, Hans-Werner—who could run a marathon in under 3 hours—kept running. After almost 17 kilometers he felt he'd finally made a breakthrough with his son. "I felt like a small, fat dachshund running after its owner, panting," remembered Andreas.

After many years of feeling lost, frustrated, and lonely, Niedrig took stock of his future and resolved that never again would he let someone tell him what he could or couldn't do. That run with his father proved to be life-changing. More than a decade after he left the swim team, Niedrig began training again. Three months later he ran his first marathon. He smoked a cigarette right before the start, but it would be his last.

With a fast time of 2 hours 43 minutes, he reached the finish long before his father. Soon afterward he ran into an old friend from his swimming days who had become a triathlete. He suggested that Niedrig come watch his next event. "Back then I still thought that triathlon consisted of swimming, cycling, and shooting," Niedrig confessed, confusing the new summer sport with its older, military-based winter Olympics cousin, biathlon.

When his buddy got sick a few weeks before the event, Niedrig finished his first triathlon alone and made it to the finish in 13th place. That would have pleased a lot of other athletes, but it disappointed him. *Only 13th*, he thought at the time. But the disappointment didn't last long. Soon he was sitting in his parents' living room announcing that he wanted to become a professional triathlete. When his parents pointed to potential health problems due to his years of drug use, he said he didn't care.

Barely a year later he was one of the best short-course triathletes in West Germany. Twelve months later he would start the European championships as a member of the German national team. But that event didn't end with a top finish, so he decided in 1997 to try his luck at long-course events.

He took 7th at the ITU long-course World Championship in Nice. A few months later he started his first Ironman in Roth, where he caused a sensation. The organizers gave him a start number outside the first 1,500 because he wasn't well known, but he emerged from the 2.4-mile swim in 2nd place just behind Luc Van Lierde of Belgium, the most recent Ironman Hawaii winner. Spectators and journalists alike couldn't believe their eyes when a rider with such a high start number was the first to ride onto the bike course.

Bolstered by the cheers of thousands of spectators, Niedrig gave it everything he had. He knew he was riding fast, but when the other top athletes caught him, he couldn't have known that it would prove to be the fastest Ironman of all time. Van Lierde reached the finish in 7:50:27, establishing a course record and a new world-best Ironman-distance time that has stood for 12 years. Three other athletes finished under the magical 8-hour mark: Jürgen Zäck (7:51), Lothar Leder (7:56), and Thomas Hellriegel (7:57). Behind them, Andreas Niedrig finished 5th at 8:06:59 in his first Ironman, a sensational, unbelievable accomplishment.

That same year he traveled to Hawaii. Looking back, he said he didn't feel at all ready for the race. In the end he allowed himself to be talked into starting by other athletes. As he had feared, it was a hard day in Kailua-Kona. While fellow Germans Hellriegel and Zäck finished 1st and 2nd, Niedrig hung tough and crossed the line 17th in 9 hours 1 minute. He was tired, happy, and driven by a new, clear goal: He wanted to be a top competitor in the mecca of Ironman triathlon.

He began to have one good result after another. At Roth he took 2nd place once, 3rd place three times, and a 4th place. He also placed high in other Ironman events. Most important, he became a father again in 1998, welcoming his son, Lorenz.

Perhaps his best performance came at the 2001 edition of Ironman Hawaii. Although he was a star at Roth, the second-most-prestigious Ironman event in the world, he ached to crack the top 10 on the Big Island and be counted as one of the best athletes in international triathlon. When the start cannon fired, he began swimming with the other top athletes. A school of dolphins accompanied them, but each of the athletes had to stay focused on his technique and effort—no time for sightseeing.

After the swim Niedrig was riding with the main contenders in the early part of the bike leg. But after 30 miles he realized he wouldn't be able to stay with the fastest cyclists. "I would have blown up if I had kept riding at that pace," he said. "So I eased up a bit."

Despite his measured pace, he reached the second transition area just 5 minutes behind eventual winner Tim DeBoom. "I felt completely spent," he said, describing the opening miles of the marathon. It was torture, but he made the best of it. When a competitor who had already made the turnaround at the Energy Lab came toward him, Niedrig put on a relaxed smile. He didn't want anyone to know how he was feeling.

But running in 7th place overall, he was suffering mightily. Three miles from the finish he was passed by fellow German Lothar Leder and then by Marc Herremans. It was the Belgian who gave him a pat and encouraged him, saying, "Come on, keep it up!" In fact, hanging tough would serve him well. Soon after the encouraging exchange Niedrig passed Americans Cameron Widoff and Steve Larsen, whose strength was flagging after bursting into the lead with a sizzling bike split.

When Niedrig reached Ali'i Drive, he heard the spectators cheering in the stands. Shortly before the finish he raised his arms and, looking up into the clear blue sky, celebrated as he crossed the finish line 7th. "For me, it was a dream come true," he said. It was one of the greatest moments of his triathlon career.

In the ensuing years he was dogged by bad luck. In 2003 he had an operation on his left foot due to an infected bursa behind his Achilles' tendon. What was normally a routine intervention led to an ongoing nightmare: Something went wrong during the operation, and in the following weeks the tendon detached from his heel and his foot became infected. "It almost exploded," he recounted. Pus ran from the wound, and he was in terrible pain.

He traveled to several countries trying to find a doctor who could help him, but none was willing to try to correct the original mistake. He finally found a doctor in the Bergmannsheil Hospital in Gelsenkirchen who had the courage to operate on him a second time.

In February 2005 he had recovered enough to finally restart his training. But when he stepped on a small piece of glass, his foot became infected again. The new wound remained open for more than two months while pus drained from it. Niedrig was 37. He knew a career at the highest level of international triathlon was no longer realistic. But he wanted to compete in one final event so as not to let an injury determine the end of his career.

In June 2006, after three years of frustration and uncertainty as well as pain and setbacks that seemed to outsiders to be far too much for any individual to overcome, he made a start in Roth again. He wanted to soak in the great atmosphere of that Bavarian event and say good-bye to the spectators who had supported him all those years.

With 5 kilometers to go, tears of joy and emotion ran down his cheeks. Overjoyed, he found his wife at the finish after 9 hours of racing and embraced her. When it was all over, he said in an interview with the German magazine *Stern*, he wanted to marry his wife again—this time in Hawaii, in white.

Since then Niedrig has spoken at countless management seminars, encouraging people to set goals and pursue them to the end. He has organized preventive seminars on drug addiction in an effort to help young people avoid his mistakes.

It seemed that his young son, Lorenz, already had it all figured out. In anticipation of the 2006 soccer world championships in Germany, Lorenz entered a drawing along with hundreds of thousands of other kids in the hope of being selected to run out onto the field with members of the national team. His father didn't want him to get his hopes up too high since the odds were so impossibly steep.

Three weeks before the championships started, a letter arrived at the Niedrig residence, informing the family that Lorenz had indeed been selected. Still, there was no guarantee that the German team would be playing that day.

In the end the little soccer fan got to run onto the field before the quarterfinal match between Germany and Argentina, holding on to the hand of South American player Roberto Ayala. Andreas Niedrig could hardly believe it. But Lorenz said simply, "You always say at your seminars that a person can do anything if they really want to."

ELEVEN | **ROBERT McKEAGUE**

"When something really grabs you, it keeps you alive."

ON A WINTER day in his fifty-seventh year, Robert McKeague decided to change his life. "I had been skiing with my kids the day before and was able to keep up with them," he recalled. But the next day he couldn't get out of bed because of muscle cramps. As he struggled to his feet, he realized he had to do things differently if he wanted to keep up with his children.

McKeague, a Chicago-based financial auditor, had come a long way before he took even a modest interest in sports. He was born in 1925, during the era in which Babe Ruth and Jack Dempsey headlined the sports pages, the movies were silent, and the very first triathlon was 50 years in the future. Throughout his youth and college years he stood a modest 5 feet 6 inches tall and didn't play any sports. Survival took priority. His father was hit hard by the Great Depression and found only occasional jobs. The family subsisted largely on government relief. During World War II McKeague enlisted in the U.S. Army and served in a tank battalion in Europe before turning 20.

After the war he studied accounting at Loyola University, married, and had five kids; for the next 30 years he participated on a very casual level in softball, golf, bowling, diving, sailing, and skiing. Goal-oriented, serious training was still foreign to him. But after the day he fell behind his children on the slopes, he started jogging and participating in local running events. Just 18 months later, at age 59, he ran his first marathon in Chicago and finished in 3 hours 50 minutes. A year later he won the 60-plus age group in Chicago in 3 hours 18 minutes, a 32-minute improvement.

Soon running wasn't enough. He watched the television coverage of the 1982 Hawaii triathlon and was one of thousands deeply impressed by the determination shown by Julie Moss in her crawl to the finish line. Triathlon, thought Robert McKeague, might also suit him. It wouldn't need to be iron distance, of course. He liked the idea of an Olympic-distance triathlon one-fourth as long—and the fact that such a race was held annually in the Chicago area.

Almost 10 years later—10 years in which he covered thousands of training miles on land and water and participated in countless Olympic-distance events—Robert McKeague won the ITU World Championship at Cancun, Mexico, in the 70–74 age group. "Up to that point I had ignored all the encouragement of friends who thought I could also make a good showing in Hawaii," he recalled. Now, with a shiny new age-group world title on his résumé, he decided to give Hawaii a go.

Although he didn't know what was in store for him at the race and didn't have training guidance for the still unfamiliar challenge, he won his 70–74 age group on his first try at the 1997 Ironman in Kona with a time of 15 hours 42 minutes. "It wasn't nearly as hard as everyone had told me it would be," he explained. On the contrary, it seemed surprisingly easy.

In his second race on the Big Island he paid for that casual attitude. He suffered from the heat in the lava fields and could manage only the third-best time among the competitors in his age group with a time of 15 hours 51 minutes 2 seconds. It was his first defeat in a long time.

Two years later, in 2000, he returned at age 75 to win in 15 hours 53 minutes 40 seconds. But he was the only starter in his new 75–79 age-group category. He realized that he no longer had competitors and wondered how he should move forward. "Only those who set goals stay motivated," he said. Since he knew it would be more difficult to come up with goals as he got older, he set one that would prove truly compelling.

It wasn't enough for him to share the age record with Jim Ward, who had competed in Kona in 1994 at age 77. He wanted to be the first 80-year-old to cross the finish line on Ali'i Drive. "When something really interests you, when it really grabs you, then it keeps you alive," he said. From that point forward he worked for five full years in order to reach his goal. As illustrated by 70-plus stars like Jim Ward and Madonna Buder, triathlon was proving to be a fountain of youth as training and racing lopped years off the physiological age of its best practitioners. The contrast with inactive seniors is dramatic: Couch potatoes lose about half a percent of muscle mass and fast-twitch speed from age 25 through 60. From age 60 to 70 the rate of loss doubles to 1 percent a year, then doubles again to 2 percent annually from age 70 to 80. On this scale an 80-year-old man has lost 57 percent of his muscle mass from his 25-year-old peak. Even among the most active Ironman triathletes, the inevitable loss of muscle and aerobic capacity, though smaller, accelerates with cruel intensity from age 70 on. So fine senior Ironman competitors such as Ward and Bill Bell had found that they were willing in mind but unable in body to meet the 17-hour cutoff for an official Ironman finish at age 80. In short, McKeague had set a goal that was every bit as challenging to the 80-year-old athlete as being the first to climb Everest or to run the 4-minute mile.

To illustrate the difficulty of breaking similar barriers against the unforgiving limitations of aging, note that only one man, Eamonn Coghlan, has been able to run the mile in under 4 minutes after age 40. McKeague did have a clue that he had some advantages in addition to self-discipline. His mother had turned 102 years old. Good genes seemed to play a role. He was in good health and certainly seemed to have the right physiology. He didn't take any prescription medications, his blood pressure was normal, his resting pulse was just over 40, and during competition his heart could beat steadily at a rate as high as 165 beats per minute. Furthermore, he pointed out that having over 20 years' experience as an endurance athlete helped. During those last months he trained well, including climbing an 11,000-foot peak in Bolivia. He also proved his toughness by emerging with undiminished zeal from a May bike crash that briefly knocked him out.

In October 2005 McKeague traveled to the Big Island, accompanied by 17 family members. His wife, his children and their spouses, and his six grandchildren wanted to be there when he dared to accomplish something no one had done before. "It was fantastic to have everyone supporting me," he said. At the same time, he said, behind all the enthusiasm lurked the risk of disappointing his family.

Marianne, his wife of more than 40 years, had no such thoughts. "I admire him just for his perseverance—training for so long, day in and day out, and staying so fit," she said. His daughter Arroyo certainly didn't need the validation of Hawaii. "Dad puts us all to shame," said the 37-year-old. She was half his age but couldn't keep up with him. Nevertheless, her father was feeling the pressure of breaking 17 hours. "I don't care if I reach the finish an hour, a minute, or just a second before midnight. The important thing is that I make it," he explained. The biggest obstacle, as he saw it, was finishing the bike segment within the time limit. According to the rules, he would need to be off the Queen K Highway by 5:30 p.m.—within 10.5 hours of the start. Otherwise the race officials would not allow him onto the marathon course.

"When I came out of the water I was already 10 minutes slower than I had planned," he explained after finishing the swim in 1 hour 55 minutes—25 minutes under the cutoff for the leg. He realized that 10 minutes slower in the swim meant he would need to go 10 minutes faster on the bike, which was his most vulnerable discipline. In tough years, when the winds could blow even the strongest competitors off their bikes, he calculated he might need more than the roughly 8 hours 30 minutes left before the cutoff. But this year, the infamous *mumuku* winds, whose brutal force has caused many a cyclist to despair, never materialized. The climb up to the turnaround in Hawi was the only section that caused him any problem. When he reached it he already knew his time would be good enough. "I even had the energy to encourage other athletes who were worried about the time cutoff," he said.

About 5:15 p.m. McKeague pushed his bike into the transition area to the cheers of his 17-strong family and thousands of fans. He had beaten the cutoff by 15 minutes. The significance of his arrival was lost on no one. Every spectator knew this was a special competitor—and not just because he was being followed by television crews and photographers. "The TV crews were certainly a motivating factor," he admitted. Otherwise, he explained, there were sections of the marathon course he probably would have chosen to walk rather than run. "I didn't want the cameras to film me while I was walking."

It was 11:20 p.m. when thunderous applause broke out along the final yards on Ali'i Drive as Robert McKeague, together with his six grandchildren, made his way toward the finish. He maintained an average of 13 minutes 35 seconds per mile for the marathon, finishing that segment in 5 hours 55 minutes. He hadn't broken the 80-year-old barrier at Ironman in a nail-biter; he had smashed it with plenty of time to spare, having finished the Ironman in 16 hours 21 minutes 55 seconds. Moreover, he did it with casual grace, ignoring the bloodied right elbow and knees and a road rash on his side inflicted when he tripped and fell on some rumble strips in the Natural Energy Lab at mile 17 of the run.

"To see all of those people cheering in the stands was unbelievable," he said. Although he shared the stage with two other remarkable barrier-breaking athletes—Sarah Reinertsen became the first female double amputee to finish Ironman Hawaii, crossing the line in 15 hours 5 minutes 15 seconds, and Sister Madonna Buder at age 76 became the oldest woman to finish the Ironman when she crossed the finish line in 15 hours 54 minutes 16 seconds—McKeague's accomplishment may have been the most vivid proof of the endless capacity of human determination.

Anyone who was able to take his or her eyes off the finish line and look up into the crowd would have seen a lot of shaking heads. Admiring spectators clapped their approval for a person whose perseverance had brought tears to their eyes. As McKeague crossed the finish line, chief Ironman commentator Mike Reilly announced that McKeague looked as though he could run another kilometer or two. McKeague just laughed. When Reilly asked whether he would be starting the race again next year, McKeague summoned all the strength he still possessed following the 140.6-mile race to say, *"Noooo, no way!"*

"This event was a one-time challenge for me. That's the way it will stay," he later confirmed. But he did not become inactive after his triumph. In 2006 he tackled the half-iron-distance world championships. During that time two of his sons also participated in iron-distance triathlons, although they hadn't yet qualified for Hawaii. Perhaps one of his grandkids will do so in the future; three of them have already begun taking part in children's races. But they are not the only ones to have been motivated by their grandfather's accomplishments. Robert McKeague has become a source of inspiration for thousands of people across the world. He proved that individuals in their senior years can continue to accomplish things that it sometimes seems only the young can do.

According to McKeague, what matters most is pursuing goals in an enjoyable and motivated fashion. "When something really grabs you," he said, "it keeps you alive."

TWELVE | **SARAH REINERTSEN**

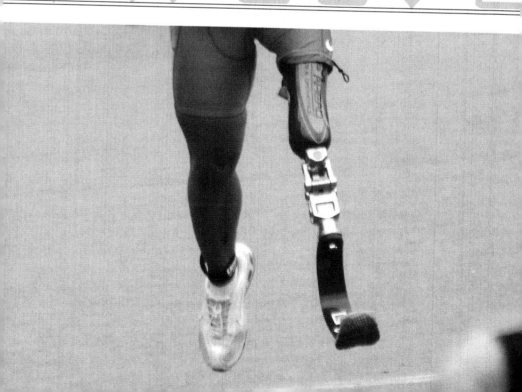

"Tougher than the rest."

NCE SARAH REINERTSEN decided she wanted to do the Ironman, her only problem was that she had never really learned to ride a bike. How was it possible that an athlete in her late 20s who had already set a sprinting world record did not know how to ride a bike? Sheer laziness? Lack of desire? Vertigo?

Sarah Reinertsen had a compelling reason, and it would not make her quest any easier. Born May 22, 1975, she came into the world with an illness called proximal femoral focal deficiency (PFFD). Her left leg was abnormally short.

As a young child, she didn't realize at first that she was different from the other kids in the neighborhood. Her parents treated her as they would any healthy little girl. It never occurred to them to pamper her. Her mother never ran over to pick her up when she fell; she always had to get back up on her own. This attitude instilled in her a powerful self-reliance that would become an invaluable lifelong habit. But certain challenges could not be solved alone by a little girl, even one with a huge heart, limitless courage, and an iron will.

She walked as an infant, but as she grew and became a toddler, she was fitted for braces that were equal to the length of her legs. Soon the braces got bigger and longer, and the differences between her legs became more pronounced. Doctors told her parents of two equally unpleasant choices of treatments. The first, an internal prosthetic, would involve inserting a new bone into the left leg to lengthen it. Her parents thought that would require a daunting series of surgeries that carried a high risk of complications. The second choice, said the doctors, was to leave the leg as it was and to fit Sarah with a stiff brace and shoes with lifts.

That was an especially unsatisfactory option, as Reinertsen could not forget the cruel taunts directed at her first prosthetic leg, which was made of wood and had a rubber foot. "It was clunky and made a huge noise when I walked," she said. "I couldn't really run. I had to do this hop, skip thing." Reinertsen remembered being taunted by classmates. "They would say, 'Yo mama got you a leg at the grocery store,'" Reinertsen recalled. "I used to get teased a lot, but kids are that way. They pick on the most obvious weakness."

By 1982 there had been some pioneering advances in prosthetic technology, and the doctors recommended amputation to take advantage of them. Reinertsen and her parents quickly agreed.

She was seven years old.

The day after the consultation she had the first surgery, in which doctors fused some bones. Shortly afterward doctors amputated the foot. Later that summer she went to rehab, got her new prosthetic leg, and learned to walk with it. Although the prosthetic technology had indeed improved remarkably, Reinertsen explained, "the prosthetic technology we were talking about in those days was a hollow wooden leg with two hinges on the side."

Back in school she became increasingly frustrated. She was always the last one to be picked for teams in gym class. Soccer was the worst: The coach assigned each of Sarah's friends to a position on the field, then handed her a ball and told her to kick it against a wall—alone. The extent to which the experience affected and humiliated her was apparent when, at age 30, she began to cry while recounting it to the television crew of the World Triathlon Corporation. Conversely, she didn't cry when she told how her left leg had been amputated.

"I hated team sports and did not feel like a true team member because I felt like I always let the team down," recalled Reinertsen. "After the amputation I just did what I could to get by in gym class. I didn't know how to run with a hollow wooden leg with hinges."

After the operation Reinertsen was still in limbo, still searching for a way to express her physical gifts. "I did not know very many amputees, and it was hard to find an inspiration," she recalled. "My parents did not know that my leg was substandard, even for that time. They just didn't know where to look—this was not something like asking what dentist to go to."

The link to a better future turned out to be sports. "My dad is a runner; he was one of those guys who did 10K and 5K races," said Sarah. "He was in a 10K race on Long Island and saw a woman run on a prosthetic leg. Afterward he found her and said, 'You have to meet my daughter.' She became a mentor."

Paddy Rossbach had lost a leg at the age of 6 when she was struck by a military truck near her home in southern England during World War II. Rossbach remembered that when she came out of the hospital on crutches, she slipped and fell. When her mother rushed to pick her up, Paddy shouted, "Don't ever try to help me again!" She went on to live a life of remarkable self-reliance. Rossbach had done nine marathons and was an expert equestrian. In her early 50s she worked as a nurse at Memorial Sloan-Kettering Cancer Center in Manhattan and was an internationally recognized advocate for and counselor to amputees, especially children. "She opened my world," said Reinertsen. "She told me about better prosthetics; she referred me to the guy who made her leg, and he referred me to a physical therapist named David Balsley."

During this period, the therapist took the 11-year-old Sarah to her first track meet to compete against people with disabilities. "I won!" said Reinertsen. "I was so used to comparing myself to all the able-bodied people in my PE class, and I would constantly come in last. But when I raced people like me, I found out I was not that bad. This therapist taught me that I could be a competitor."

From the beginning it was clear that she had to be tough to keep up when playing sports. In the moment after that first victory, Sarah realized she could be a real athlete. As her athletic accomplishments grew, she resolved to raise public awareness of the fact that amputee girls could do more than kick a ball against a wall.

With a lot of training, even more determination, and a state-of-the-art flex foot made of carbon fiber and Kevlar, Reinertsen made a big international mark in running. At age 17, she was the youngest participant on the U.S. team at the 1992 Paralympic Games in Barcelona. She was the women's amputee world record holder at 100 meters at 17.99 seconds and was the favorite to win—but she had yet another heartbreaking setback. "It was awesome and amazing to represent my country, but I didn't win the medal I wanted," she recalled. "I didn't move forward from the semis because I tripped coming out of the starting blocks. It was a bad day and a really disappointing time in Spain."

After the disappointment of the Paralympics, she decided she needed a new goal. "I wanted to test not how fast but how far," she said, and spent the next five years shifting her athletic focus to longer distances. While she earned an undergraduate degree in international relations at George Washington University, she started running 5K and 10K races with an eye on the marathon. "The biggest challenge was getting used to being on my artificial leg for long amounts of time," she recalled. "I didn't want to get bogged down in mileage or in ego. So three times a week I'd run for an hour and a half. Then on Saturdays, I'd go for a long run-walk that started at 3 hours and built to 6 hours to see how long the stump could stand it." In 1996, her senior year, she finished the New York Marathon with a time of 6 hours 30 minutes. The next year she established a new world's best time for above-knee-amputee women of 5 hours 27 minutes at the London marathon.

In the next few years she attended the University of Southern California, graduated with a master's in broadcast journalism, and a got a job as a sports reporter for NBC in New York City. During that period she did seven marathons and gradually found herself attracted to triathlon, fueled by a series of small encounters. When she first started endurance running, she met inspirational speaker Jim McLaren, who held the physically challenged record at Ironman Hawaii before a second traumatic accident left him a quadriplegic. "I thought about doing the Ironman for years," she recalled. "It has this mystique about it, and I am sure like many athletes out there, you watch it on television and you get drawn into the event even before you become a triathlete.

"I had the marathon down, but I hadn't done much swimming and hadn't ridden a bike since I was 11," she continued. "I was traveling a lot for my job interviewing athletes for the 2002 Winter Olympics, but I still carried that Ironman dream. So one day I bought an old mountain bike, fitted it with some slick tires, and set it up as a trainer in my apartment in Brooklyn so I could get fit and strong first without worrying about balance. At the same time, I swam at a New York City pool that was cheap to join, but dirty. I would go on Friday nights just after it had been cleaned and everybody was out on dates so I had it all to myself. I was bashful about hopping out to the pool and about my swimming. At first I could not do three or four laps without stopping. When I'd get discouraged flailing around, I told myself I had to do at least 15 minutes. Later I worked it up to 30 minutes. Then I started to buy the triathlon books and magazines. Still, it was hard with travel and my job and time restraints. I still hadn't gone out to ride on the roads."

Fate arrived in the form of a 2003 job offer from the Challenged Athletes Foundation in sunny San Diego. Soon she was riding outside with fellow athletes in bike lanes and taking masters swim classes with famed coach Roch Frey. "He said I swam like a bumblebee because my arms were moving 100 miles an hour in the water and I wasn't going anywhere," said Reinertsen.

Actually she was moving fast on a collision course with her dream: competing at Ironman Hawaii.

On October 16, 2004, she was standing on the pier in Kailua-Kona, looking out over the Pacific. She wanted to be the first above-knee amputee to reach the finish line at Ironman Hawaii. In the days leading up to it she wondered what it would be like to arrive for an official finish on Ali'i Drive within the allotted 17 hours. "If I can do it, I'll be laughing and crying at the same time," she told the NBC television crew.

After 1 hour 36 minutes, she emerged from the 2.4-mile swim in the Pacific, ran to her bike, pulled her hydration pack over her shoulders, and took off for 112 miles of cycling under the blazing Hawaiian sun and into the notorious *mumuku* winds.

Reinertsen had always been one to knock down barriers. In Hawaii, however, the 29-year-old faced a relentless obstacle: the time limit. She was racing to make the bike cutoff, which stipulated that only those athletes who pushed their bikes into the transition area on Kailua Pier by 5:30 p.m. would be allowed on the marathon course.

Like all physically challenged athletes, Reinertsen had to work harder to overcome some severe challenges posed by her amputation. Because the right side of her body and her natural leg carries much more muscle than the left, her body power is not equal. A CompuTrainer analysis of the watts produced on the bike showed that 80 percent of her power came from the right leg and just 20 percent from the left. Two factors made the bike portion extraordinarily rough for Reinertsen that day. One, quartering winds blew hard into the faces of riders headed toward the halfway turnaround. The wind made the large, rolling hills on the Queen K, including a final 600-foot climb to Hawi, even more strenuous than usual.

Second, instead of providing a compensating tailwind on the return trip, those winds cruelly shifted on the way back to town.

"There were headwinds both ways!" said Reinertsen. "Unbelievable. And crosswind gusts were especially rough with my size—about 100 pounds minus the weight of the prosthetic leg, really about 90 of body weight. I thought for sure I'd go down coming downhill from Hawi." By the time she got to Hawi, with roughly 52 miles left to go, it was 2 p.m. and she had to average a little over 15 miles per hour to make the cutoff. "I was pushing hard to make up time and let the brakes go. I thought, *Whooh! Let the gusts come!* Then it was *Whoa!* Roch Frey told me not to use up all my strength with a death grip on the downhill. But he also reminded me that

Sister Madonna was too far over to the right during bad crosswinds in 2000, and she went off the road."

Racing the sunset to get back to transition by 5:30, she became elated during a brief lull when she was sailing along at 16 miles per hour. But shortly after that, the wind shifted. "Then the headwinds kicked in again, and boom! I was back down to 9 mph on a hill and then could only maintain 13 mph on the flats. I knew that wasn't gonna cut it. Then I was vomiting much of the last 20 miles, trying to figure out how to puke and keep pace."

Sarah Reinertsen fought like a lion, but time ran out. She rode into the transition area at 5:45 p.m., and as she rolled up to one of the volunteers, she already knew she hadn't made it. The first tears filled her eyes. After she got off her bike and her friends put their arms around her to comfort her, she wept uncontrollably. "For me, it was totally devastating that I didn't do it, that I hadn't become an Ironman," she said.

The portion of the NBC Ironman broadcast on Sarah's battle to finish echoed the historic courage of Julie Moss. Reinertsen was already planning her return. She referred to the experience as "unfinished business" and declared that her first ill-fated attempt would not keep her from turning her dream into reality.

Together with a new coach, optimized nutrition, and a custom bike given to her by Cannondale, she began training again after a short break. Based on her experience the previous year, she knew her performance on the bike course would mean the difference between success and failure. "I focused all of my efforts on the bike, training for hours and hours," she explained.

One year later, she stood once again on Kailua Pier in the early morning. She was confident, having improved in all three disciplines. What she didn't tell anyone was that for a year she had been carrying a key-ring pendant engraved with the time of 16:05.

At 7 a.m. the cannon sounded, and 1,800 triathletes began the traditional charge. It is always a cross between a washing machine and a boxing match, with the athletes' extremities in a frenzy to move their bodies forward as quickly as possible. In the middle of all that disorderly splashing swam Reinertsen.

She reached the halfway point of the swim course in just 40 minutes and finished her swim in 1 hour 26 minutes, 10 minutes faster than the year before. Six minutes later, after she had used her running prosthesis to get to her bike and then switched to her special cycling prosthesis, she rode out on the course.

She felt good on her new bike—more comfortable, powerful, and efficient. Even the weather cooperated; there was almost no wind this time.

A new nutritional approach was also crafted to help her succeed during the ride. Her coach had advised her to eat only while climbing, which would automatically keep her from going too hard. Then she was supposed to focus on her aerodynamic position on the descents in order to sustain higher speeds.

Along with all of those improvements in efficiency and race tactics, Reinertsen enjoyed the enthusiastic encouragement of fellow competitors. "Sarah, this time you are going to finish Ironman," one friend called out as she approached the turnaround in Hawi. Many expressed admiration for what she was doing. "I had a magical day," she remembered. After 7 hours 34 minutes on the bike she reached the second transition at 4 p.m., 90 minutes before the cutoff. On those few meters of asphalt where she had experienced her Waterloo the year before, she was now being cheered by thousands of spectators.

"When I got off my bike, I knew I could do it," she said. She still had the marathon in front of her, but she had already demonstrated in countless races how well she could run.

She was in high spirits over the opening miles of the marathon. She enjoyed being able to run for a good hour in daylight, she explained, and considered it to be a kind of reward for her efforts on the bike. When dusk fell and the endless straightaway of the Queen

Ka'ahumanu Highway lay before her, a mantra looped continually in her head. It wasn't "Be tougher than the rest," which she had recited over and over during her training. No, this time it was "Soon I am going to get a mai tai!"

She faced only one moment of weakness. When she came out of the Energy Lab and back onto the highway at mile 19 of the run, she was so exhausted that she was dragging her feet and couldn't read her watch. Uncertain, she asked spectators for the time. "Just a little past 8 p.m.," someone said. In that moment she got a jolt of adrenaline. "Oh, my God, I can make the finish by 11 o'clock!"

Her dream in hand, she ran the final 7 miles on wings and beat her prediction and that Energy Lab estimate by almost an hour. High over the city and the finish, where Palani Road angles off from the highway with only a mile still to run, she heard the noise of thousands of spectators cheering for athletes nearing the finish. A few minutes later she turned right onto Ali'i Drive, the final 400 meters of the race.

She recounted that she simply lifted her arms and tried to soak in all the images, the cheers of the crowd, and her own feelings. After exactly 15 hours 5 minutes, she heard from Mike Reilly the words she had yearned for: "Sarah Reinertsen, you are an Ironman!"

The next evening she was honored along with 1,800 other triathletes and those who came to support them. She went over to a Cannondale executive who, like members of her family, was wearing a T-shirt that read, "Unfinished Business." Laughing, she crossed out "Un."

Finished business.

At Ironman Hawaii, Sarah Reinertsen once again proved that she is a remarkable athlete, not because she has one leg but because she is tougher than most. Her accomplishments required an abundance of determination and persistence, which has made it all the more difficult for her to understand people who are sedentary day in and day out. While being interviewed for the television program *Nightline*, she shook her head over able-bodied couch potatoes: "What a waste of two legs! You have them and don't even use them."

"You take the joy as you can."

FOR A TALL, muscular Canadian who looks more like a beach volleyball pro than the skinny whippets who occupy most professional triathlon podiums, Peter Reid has had moments of remarkable fragility. While the hardworking, iron-willed competitor saw himself making up for average talents with an unrelenting work ethic that made him the best bet to win Ironman Hawaii from 1998 to 2005, Reid often found his toughest opponent was his own body.

For Reid, Ironman Hawaii was a challenge he loved and first met by learning from old-school, high-mileage, hard workers such as Thomas Hellriegel of Germany. But as the work and hard-headed focus took its toll, Reid learned from other masters such as Mark Allen, who taught Reid to combine physical science with a respect for the mystical spirit of the island. It was on this inner journey that Reid won personal victories perhaps even more important than even his 3 Ironman Hawaii wins and 10 Ironman victories overall.

Born May 27, 1969, in Montreal, Reid enjoyed downhill skiing and cycling through his high school years in Ottawa and his college years at Bishop University in Montreal, where he studied political science. When Reid started to obsess about cycling, his parents forced him to rearrange his priorities. "Fortunately, my grades started to suffer, and my parents pressured me to focus on schooling," said Reid. "I am definitely a one-track person. I have to either be in school or out." In 1989 a friend talked him into trying a local triathlon. "I had a racing bike, but I didn't know how to swim," he recalled. "I suffered through it, and I loved it, and I was moved by the atmosphere, how friendly it all was. I liked that all my races were about competing with myself. The cycling team was oriented to work for other people or have others work for you. But in triathlon you showed up and did three events yourself."

When Reid graduated with his degree in political science, he announced that he wanted to pursue triathlon full time. "My parents weren't too sure about triathlon," said Reid. "When I graduated from university I wanted to see how far I could go in the sport, but my dad never really accepted that. He's proud of me now, but I never forgot those days. He told me, 'When are you going to get a real job? Why are you chasing this dream?'" Those words fueled his rise.

From the beginning Reid streamlined his quest by shutting out almost all human distractions, a habit that stayed with him throughout his career. "The whole time I raced, the only thing I had time for was triathlon," said Reid. "In a little bit of off-season, I might do some other things. I was never as talented as other athletes, so I never did anything else of significance because it was all about triathlon. I did not want anything else to interfere with training. Talk to all my friends and they will tell you: Once the season started, I would just disappear. I could not go and hang with my buddies. I could not go to school. I saved all my energy for triathlon."

In those early years Reid doubted himself. "I thought maybe I don't have it in me," he told one interviewer. But after he moved west to Victoria, British Columbia, in 1994 and started to train under the direction of Roch Frey, a fellow Canadian who was coaching his wife Heather Fuhr to great success, things really started to click. In 1996 Reid won the classic Wildflower half-Ironman, finished 3rd behind Simon Lessing and Luc Van Lierde at the Nice long-course, and took 4th at Ironman Hawaii. He thought, *Hey, I can really do something in this sport.*

But reaching this plateau was just a start. Two crucial encounters at this time helped propel him to the most rarefied air in triathlon. In the summer of 1996 Reid traveled to Germany to race the Ironman and spent weeks training with the legendary 700-miles-a-week supercyclist Thomas Hellriegel. "Thomas showed me what it took to race and win," said Reid.

The second encounter occurred at Ironman Hawaii, where Reid hit the wall hard about 80 miles into the bike and was tempted to quit. "In 1997 I had not completely figured out Hawaii," said Reid. "That year I had a really bad bike and went through this dark zone about 120 kilometers into the 180-kilometer bike. Then I got mentally and psychologically tired, like hitting the wall in a marathon—only more emotional. When I got to this point I wanted to drop out of the race. Luckily, that was exactly where my coach Roch Frey stood and said, 'No! You gotta keep going!' Getting through that moment eventually became part of my understanding of the Hawaii Ironman."

Reid finished 4th and took his experiences into 1998. That summer he visited rising American star Tim DeBoom in Boulder, Colorado, and passed on the lessons he had learned while training with Hellriegel. "Training with Peter brought it to another level," said DeBoom. "It opened my eyes to the amount of work and degree of focus necessary to win Hawaii."

That year in Kona Reid outraced the three Germans who had placed 1-2-3 the year before as well as Luc Van Lierde, the 1996 sensation who set a still-standing Ironman Hawaii course record. With winds gusting to 40 mph, Reid rode a crafty split, staying with Hellriegel and outpacing Van Lierde, who was still recovering from a stress fracture and a pulled groin suffered that spring. Then Reid uncorked the first of his Kona-winning runs, a 2:47:31 marathon that held Van Lierde at bay and put the Canadian 7:37 ahead at the line.

Winning Hawaii for the first time took away the insecurity and settled some old emotional scores with his father. "It was a dream I'd had for a long time, to win the most important race in the sport, and I proved to myself I could do it," said Reid. "It was also about proving a lot of people wrong—girlfriends, my dad—who kept telling me to quit, right in the beginning."

One person who came to have absolute faith in Reid was his new girlfriend, fellow Canadian triathlete Lori Bowden. If ever a couple proved the truism that opposites attract. . . . On the surface both were Ironman triathletes at the top of their sport. Magazines tagged them "the world's fittest couple." But at her core Bowden was an outgoing, sunny person who did triathlons for fun and loved to socialize. In many ways Bowden was as happy with her early amateur finishes a hundred or more places back in the pack as when she stood atop the podium at the greatest races on the planet. But Peter the Great was seriously ambitious, with an unwavering focus on success once he was locked into his preparations for Hawaii. The epitome of his serious race face came on the run at Kona in 1999. After Van Lierde had powered away in the early miles of the run, Reid came up on his friend DeBoom, and they ran together for a while. Running up the hill at Palani, DeBoom started making a few casual jokes, as if they were training on the Switzerland Trail back in Boulder. With a trace of exasperation, Reid told his friend to shut up.

"Tim, this is the Ironman!" said Reid.

"I never said another word after that," said DeBoom. "I took it as a lesson that my focus wasn't what it should have been."

In 1999 Reid pulled a gluteus muscle that threw out his back a few weeks after setting the third-fastest time in Ironman history while winning Austria. Just as Van Lierde had been hampered by injury from giving his best performance at Kona the year before, this time around Reid had to surrender to the Belgian and finished 2nd. Revealing a deeply felt sense of sportsmanship, Reid lamented the injuries for both men and yearned for a day in which all the best men had their best race on the same day. "One day, if I were feeling as good as I did in Austria, it would be great to find out what a rivalry this could be," said Reid. "I think I could make a move on the bike, and Luc would have to come back to me on the run, and I would be stronger there, too, so we would push each other like Mark and Dave did in '89. Whoever won that one, it would be the best race."

Sadly, that vision never came to pass, as Van Lierde ran into a string of injuries that never allowed the Belgian to unlock all his vast potential again. Reid also grew aware of his athletic mortality, the unpredictable inevitability of the day he would lose the gift he had been given and worked so hard to nurture. "Before this race I had a talk with Pauli Kiuru, who told me near the end of his career his training times just kept getting better and better, but his race times in Hawaii kept getting slower," Reid said. "When my back went out, I went down to Santa Barbara to treat it, and it just didn't get better. I decided to go home to Victoria and just trust in fate. But you never know if a training ride or a race or a season might be your last. So you take the joy as you can."

During his disappointing finish in 1999, Reid took great joy in watching Bowden (by then his wife) as she achieved her breakthrough win and record-setting 2:59:16 run. As they passed one another on the Queen K Highway, Reid shouted, "Be strong! Be strong! Be strong!" at Bowden so loudly that she could only smile in return. Reid and Bowden had a finishing-order symmetry in Kona that was almost eerie. For three years they finished 1-2, 2-1, 1-2. As they exchanged finishing places for the first time that year in Hawaii, Reid vowed to step slightly aside at public appearances so that Bowden would be introduced as "the reigning Hawaiian Ironman champion" and he as "a former winner."

By 2000 Reid was fully back on his game at Kona, but the constant effort over the previous five years presented him with a past-due bill at the finish. A few months earlier he had doubted if he could even make it to the start line. A stress fracture had sidelined him for much of the year, and he'd pulled out of Ironman California and Ironman Austria. Feeling he needed one Ironman finish to bolster his confidence for Kona, he scored a solid 8:29:49 win at Ironman Canada in late August. The result was good, but the timing set him up for a shorter-than-ideal taper for the one race that really counts.

After finishing a remarkable stretch in which he'd won two or three Ironman events a year for several years, Reid hit the burnout wall head-on at Kona after successfully holding off a furious charge by DeBoom in the final miles of the run. "That was the hardest race I ever did," said Reid. "All the years of training caught up with me. And I was matched with someone who could push me over the edge. I was fading to the end of the marathon and started to fall apart. Plus I had just done Ironman Canada six weeks before. I was racing a guy who was fresh, and he was running me down. So I was really suffering the last few miles to get to the finish line."

Reid said he had anticipated that moment. "It's been a nightmare of mine to cross this finish line and pass out, and it almost happened," said Reid. "I was hurting so bad those last 2 miles."

In 2001 Reid was once again well positioned to win Ironman Hawaii. In 2nd place at the start of the marathon, he recalled, "I was starting to hurt and I was like, *I can't do this again. I can't make myself hurt that much.* So I just stopped." As he clutched his leg with a grimace and halted near Lava Java on Ali'i Drive just three miles into the run, Reid showed the other side of the coin from the triumphant exultation of his wins in 1998 and 2000.

Five months later the slide accelerated. He dropped out of the 2002 Ironman Australia and said he was contemplating retiring. His doctor convinced him that there was something more serious than burnout at work. "My doctor kinda thought I had cancer because there was some weird stuff going on with my blood tests," Reid said. "He told me, 'Peter, triathlon doesn't exist for you now. Trying to figure out what the hell's wrong with you now is your number-one priority. You're going to stop training, and we're going to figure this out.'

"That," said Reid, "really scared me."

Forced to take some extended time off, Reid started simply hanging out and riding his motorcycle. Just a sliver away from premature retirement at 33, Reid ate his way to 188 pounds by July 1. Seven weeks after the doctor's pronouncement, he started feeling better and began working out again. Not to race, he told himself, but to start dropping the 25 pounds he had packed on.

Buoyed by his progress, Reid got a clear mind and a healthy hematocrit. Tests revealed no cancer just in time for Reid to hone his body to a greyhound-thin 163 pounds and embark on a six-week training binge for Kona.

In many ways 2002 found Reid at his most magnificent.

The 2002 edition of Ironman Hawaii was a weird-weather day that began under soggy gray clouds that drizzled on the swim, then welcomed the cyclists with a torrential downpour that left the bravest of them wary and conservative in go-fast temperatures.

DeBoom, Reid, and the 2001 Ironman Hawaii runner-up, New Zealander Cameron Brown, had coolly ceded an 8-minute deficit on the bike to the year's freshman sensation, Chris McCormack; French newcomer Francois Chabaud; and three old German über-biker pals, Jürgen Zäck, Normann Stadler, and Thomas Hellriegel. "When we saw them at the bike turnaround at Hawi, they were grimacing," said Reid. "I said to myself, 'They're going way too hard, too early.' I believed the race would come back to us."

Sure enough, once on the run, DeBoom, Reid, and Brown started erasing that deficit with implacable momentum. First Zäck halted with antibiotic-induced diarrhea. Then Stadler started the Kona Shuffle, and 1997 Olympic distance world champion McCormack, the focus of intense debut hype, was felled by cramps after 10 miles.

DeBoom, Reid, and Brown started the run together in 7th, 8th, and 9th, befitting a trio who believed, as Reid did, "that this race is always won on the marathon."

Reid made a move at mile 5, evoking a painful memory in DeBoom. "Peter put in a surge, and I was like, *Aw, I'm not ready for this,*" said DeBoom. "After the morning rain you could see the steam rising from the road on Ali'i Drive like a sauna, and the heat just hurt."

"It was so humid, it was gross, disgusting," said Reid.

"I tried to avoid what happened in 2000 [when Reid made an early push to stake out a 2-minute lead] and went with him," said

DeBoom. "Then I made a move, and I got a gap." Still, the effort came at a high price.

Reid was aware of the irony. "I led Tim and Cam out of transition, and when they came up on me, the pace seemed really fast," said Reid. "At first I thought, *I'm really hurting.* Then Tim was feeling really good and went. Basically it was Ironman 2000, only the roles were reversed."

As DeBoom escaped Reid's gravitational pull, Reid licked his chops. "It was payback time," said Reid. "I was going to make him hurt like he'd made me hurt toward the end of the run."

By 1 p.m. the two premier runners in the field had whittled away all the stubborn cyclists, and DeBoom had wrested the lead from Hellriegel, the 1997 champion, at mile 14 of the marathon, just before entering the cauldron of Natural Energy Lab Road.

As Reid pulled into the Energy Lab turnaround at mile 17, DeBoom got his first look at Reid in 13 miles. "He was smiling, and I thought, *Uh-oh!*" said DeBoom. DeBoom's hard-fought 2-minute margin had shrunk to 1:50 entering the Lab, then 1:30 at the turnaround, and 1:15 with 10 km to go.

But Reid lost his drive at the Energy Lab and crossed the line 3:10 behind his old friend. Unlike the relentlessly perfectionist Reid of a year before, whose body had broken down before his relentless will, Reid was smiling and easy on himself. "After what I went through, I'm so proud of myself for getting to the line," he said. "Once you quit, it can get to be a habit. Today I felt the joy I felt in '98, the joy I felt when I got into the sport."

The next year, 2003, Reid had forgettable results at Wildflower, Utah, and Ironman Germany. At the same time, his five-year marriage to Lori Bowden started to unravel. "We had an amazing marriage for four years and then we just kind of fell apart," Reid told *Inside Triathlon.* Things got rocky in 2002, but they reconciled. In 2003, said Reid, "It just wasn't clicking anymore. We wanted different things. I used to get tunnel vision for the Hawaii Ironman.

Lori just got fed up with it, and she had a right to be. She is a people person, and I'm a bit of a loner."

At Allen's suggestion, Reid went to Kona to make peace with the island, rented a cabin 6,000 feet up Mauna Kea, and went into Kona daily to work out. He grew mentally strong, but there was one more moment of doubt. The day before the race, things looked bleak. He was flat on his back in his room, shades drawn, wracked with the flu. "I spent the day in bed and trusted my immune system would rebound. But on Saturday I found myself throwing up on the bike."

When Reid, DeBoom, and Cameron Brown got off the bike, they stood 8th, 9th, and 10th. Then, just as they had started the run in 2002, they surged, passing Thomas Hellriegel, Cam Widoff, Jürgen Zäck, Chris McCormack, Luke Bell, and Faris Al-Sultan. When Reid came up on Rutger Beke, the Belgian looked at his watch. "I had just run a 6:04 mile, and he went by me as if I wasn't there," Beke recalled.

DeBoom and Reid eyed one another, and then the Canadian pulled away. "I was worried that I had thrown up so much on the bike," said Reid. "But it totally paid off on the run. My stomach was perfect in the marathon."

By mile 9 Reid was a minute up on DeBoom, who gathered himself for another assault on the Canadian. But by mile 12 DeBoom had dropped 2:45 behind Reid; an unfortunate attack of kidney stones felt like a knife in the gut. DeBoom pulled out. Reid said he was worried when he heard DeBoom had quit but honestly felt relieved that his nemesis was no longer stalking him.

Still, he had broken that tie with DeBoom and Van Lierde at two Hawaii wins apiece. Now Reid joined Dave Scott and Mark Allen as the only men to win Ironman Hawaii more than twice.

Ironically, this was the first time that Reid and Bowden won Hawaii on the same day. Two days after the race, they split up for good.

In 2004 Peter Reid's father, Ted, died. "My dad was proud of me at the end," said Reid. "Finally my father and I grew a little closer.

LEFT: Andreas Niedrig had his best performance in the 2001 edition of Hawaii Ironman, pushing relentlessly on the run to finish 7th.

BELOW: Once a heroin addict living on the streets, Niedrig overcame his demons to become a standout Ironman competitor.

RIGHT: In 2005 Robert McKeague became the Ironman's first 80-year-old finisher, crossing the line with his grandchildren.

BELOW: Born in 1925, McKeague took up running at the ripe old age of 57, caught the triathlon bug in 1982, and won his first age-group Ironman in 1997.

LEFT: Running in the twilight in 2005, Sarah Reinertsen kept her spirits up with the promise of a mai tai at the finish; she beat her own estimated finish time by a full hour.

BELOW: With a custom bike and hours of training under her belt, Reinertsen blasted through the bike leg in 2005 with 90 minutes to spare.

TOP: Peter Reid, known as Peter the Great, was a steady force on the bike, reliably clicking off 4:40 bike legs year after year.

LEFT: Reid's breakthrough year, with a winning time of 8:24:20, coincided with the Ironman's twentieth anniversary in 1998.

RIGHT: In 2005 Natascha Badmann took her sixth Ironman victory, once again with a winning smile all the way.

BELOW: Badmann's bike speed is legendary, although, as she points out, "my first triathlons were won on the run."

LEFT: Marc Herremans was an outstanding athlete who transformed himself into a formidable wheelchair competitor after a bike crash in a 2002 training session.

BELOW: Herremans became a beast on his handbike, building a 20-minute lead in the bike leg in his 2006 championship year.

TOP: While defending his title in 2005, Normann Stadler suffered two flats and a bee sting in rapid succession. In frustration, he threw his bike into the lava fields.

RIGHT: Stadler—the Normannator—was the most formidable cyclist in Ironman history and holds the bike-leg record at 4:18:23.

ABOVE: In 2007 the question on her competitors' lips was "Can she run?" Can she ever: Chrissie Wellington turned in a 2:59:58 marathon in her first Ironman win.

LEFT: Victory is sweet! Wellington set a new women's record of 8:54:02 in 2009.

Normann Stadler, 200●

He wrote me this letter a few years ago and did say how proud he was and how wrong he had been. Which affected my racing a little bit. I had always been trying to prove him wrong. All of a sudden, I get this note about how proud he was. I think I lost a little fire then. My dad never came to any of my Ironman races. But when he passed away, it was a lot better between us."

In the 2004 championship, Normann Stadler destroyed the old paradigm in which Ironman Hawaii was always won on the run. On a nasty, windy day, the latest in a line of German überbikers blasted out to a bike that was 23 minutes 40 seconds faster than Reid's. After Reid countered with a race-best 2:46:10 run, he was still 11 minutes behind Stadler. He finished 2nd, a bit less than 2 minutes ahead of third-place Faris Al-Sultan.

The next year would prove just as tough. In May 2005 Reid was hit with an antibiotic-resistant bacterial infection, a superbug that left him "feeling like death with migraine headaches and cold sweats," bedridden, and unable to train for seven weeks. Reid's agent wasn't worried; he'd seen it happen many times before. "Peter is a human backhoe," said Murphy Reinschreiber. "He digs himself into the deepest holes and climbs out."

"No one today knows how to arrive at the starting line in Kona more ready to win than Peter," said retired 1994 Ironman champion and IronmanLive.com commentator Greg Welch.

There seem to be two types of Ironman competitors. Some see the race as a simple scientific equation in which heat, wind, and humidity must be overcome. Others see the spiritual side of the island as a crucial component. "I definitely saw . . . the spiritual value of the island," said Reid. "It definitely became a part of my race. I am not as spiritual as Mark Allen. I have gone to two shamanism seminars with Mark. I enjoyed going to them, but I am not totally into it. I think I understand it, and I enjoy being around shamans, and through that I understood that Hawaii is more than just the distance."

Reid thought the feeling was important. "For sure, to win that race more than once, you have to understand it," he said. "I think you can win Hawaii once without reflecting on its profound nature. But if you just go through the motions there, I don't think you can win it again without really getting it."

Reid was holding second place late in the run when Cameron Brown of New Zealand came up on him just 2 miles from the finish. For Reid, this was a moment of another kind of truth. "I was in 2nd place most of the marathon," said Reid. "When it was time to attack, I just didn't do it. When I was passed by Cam with less than a mile to go, it did not bug me a whole lot. When I crossed the finish line, I thought *This is not the way I race Ironman Hawaii!*"

That way, said Reid, was "attack, attack, attack!"

"Right then, I started to realize the end was pretty close," said Reid. "For me, it was not just doing the Hawaiian Ironman. It was about having the ultimate performance. And I took that commitment very seriously."

The intoxication of athletic fame almost always leaves even the brightest stars staying too long at the fair. Leading this long, sad parade are Muhammad Ali, Willie Mays, and Michael Jordan. The list of great athletes who quit at their absolute peak is extremely brief. Football star Jim Brown retired as the greatest running back ever at age 29. Heavyweight champ Rocky Marciano retired undefeated after 49 fights. Mark Allen quit at age 37, not long after his sixth straight Ironman Hawaii victory.

And on May 20, 2006, three-time Ironman world champion Peter Reid, a week short of his thirty-seventh birthday and two years shy of his own career projections, joined the rare, happy few.

"My goal last year was to race Hawaii in 2006 and finish my career with Ironman Canada in 2007," he said. "But as I started to train that year, I definitely noticed the drive was just not there anymore. I was just going through the motions."

When he saw this missing aggression, Reid tried to adapt. "I took it very easy over the winter," he said. "I hoped to win Hawaii one more time. But I had trouble getting out the door. I had trouble doing workouts."

Reid said the decision was final. "I never thought of myself as extremely talented," he said. "I worked very, very hard and never had any issue with doing the hard work. I thought they all have more talent, but I can work harder than the others with talent. But all of a sudden I lost that work ethic and drive. Without it I felt I could not truly compete. I decided not to go to Hawaii and just go through the motions."

When he retired, Reid took on the things that he had put on hold. His first desire was to go to Kona and work as an aid-station volunteer at the Natural Energy Lab. He moved from civilized Victoria to a more rugged outpost for winter sports in Squamish, British Columbia. He took up stage-race road cycling and planned to take on the Western States 100 trail race. And, recalling the triathlon experience in 1989 that had led him away from a half-formed plan to attend flight school after graduation from college, Reid took up an offer from a friend to become a working bush pilot in the Yukon.

Even though many observers saw that Reid looked fitter than ever and hoped he would get the itch that Dave Scott scratched when he turned 40, Reid instead followed Mark Allen's example and dispelled all rumors that he would take another crack at Kona in 2009. He was retired from the sport and at peace with his decision.

FOURTEEN | **NATASCHA BADMANN**

"I trusted my legs would get me there and my heart would gain for me all it was supposed to."

WHEN NATASCHA BADMANN won her first Hawaii Ironman in 1998, she didn't leave the impression that hers was a triumph over exhaustion and a narrow escape from the torture of 140.6 miles through the lava fields. When she spoke of her experience, it seemed as if she had just written an aerobic poem or sung an endurance song. In her open-hearted victory speech, which sounded more like Walt Whitman's poetry than an endurance athlete's usual terse valediction, she laid her feelings bare.

"To start the race in the swim," she said in broken but poetic English that drew thousands of hard-core Ironman athletes into her spell, "I had the feeling of the rising sun. Whooh! Such a beautiful day that is in front of me, and I was so happy. And then when I sat on the bike, I knew there could be some wind. But it was so strong at the airport, I thought, *Oh, I am probably at the wrong place. Usually the wind starts up to Hawi, not here!* Then I realized that it wouldn't help if I was angry about the wind, because wind is for all of us the same. So I tried to imagine that I have wings, and put my wings in the wind and to fly."

Having learned important lessons in her first try at Ironman Hawaii in 1996, Badmann swam 5 minutes faster than her debut, biked 17 minutes slower than 1996 (but 5 minutes faster than her closest pursuer) on a howling windy day, and ran 2 minutes faster than her 1996 marathon. Altogether, she finished in 9 hours 24 minutes 16 seconds and held off the attacking run of runner-up Lori Bowden by 2.5 minutes. At the end a roster of great competitors such as Paula Newby-Fraser, defending champ Heather Fuhr, and Fernanda Keller all looked haunted and exhausted after an enervating day in the sun and wind chasing Badmann and her elusive Cheshire cat smile.

Badmann recalled sharing her emotions with the finish-line crowd on Ali'i Drive. "Some were waving Swiss flags, some were jumping up and down, and some were crying; all of this made me feel good," she said after she pumped her fist and waved and beamed her blissful smile at everyone on the streets of Kailua-Kona. "I didn't know whether I should laugh or cry, and I had goosebumps. I felt all this power, and I wanted to give it back to everybody who was there. I had such an open heart, I felt I could hold the whole world in my arms."

At the finish she'd thrown her hands up and stared at the sky, then covered her face with her hands. "I thought, *Is it true?*" she said. "I wondered if I would wake up and someone would say to me, 'Yes that must have been a nice dream. . . .'"

Born in Basel, Switzerland, in 1966, Natascha Badmann began her amazing athletic odyssey at something approaching ground zero. In the mid-1980s, she recalled, "Some things with my family were not how it should be," so the unhappy teenager looked for love and became pregnant days before she turned 18. When Badmann delivered her daughter, Anastasia, whose name means "she who shall rise up again," the hope she held first for her daughter might have been a prayer for herself as well. "I was too young to have a child," said Badmann, who says she was depressed and unhealthy as a single, teenaged mother. "After the birth of my daughter, I did nothing," she said. "This really means nothing."

Not long afterward she was an overweight secretary working in the Swiss equivalent of a social security office. "My background was not very happy," recalled Badmann. "When I was younger I had times where I did not want to live any more. I was so sad, I didn't even realize that weather changes."

It was at that gray, faceless job that she met an extraordinarily positive triathlete working as a computer programmer. "I was unhappy with my body, and nothing was right, nothing was good," said Badmann, who illustrated those feelings in a 1998 interview by mimicking the old, sad Natascha slumped over and frowning. In the office she complained that no diets worked because "at the end of the day, I had chocolate again."

"This will not work," responded the triathlete, Toni Hasler. "If you want to lose weight, you have to eat, and you have to move." Although she preferred the eating to the moving part of Hasler's prescription, she was willing to try when he offered to show her the way.

Badmann told San Diego *Union-Tribune* writer Don Norcross that the first time she went running with Hasler, "I went maybe 500 or 1,000 meters. It was 10 minutes at the most, and I thought, *Boy, I did this great workout.* Compared to what I do today, I don't know how I ever got to this point."

The first time Hasler took her cycling, Badmann rode a little, but when they turned around and she tried to ride up a little quarter-mile hill to home, she couldn't make it on her own. Badmann yelled, "Help me!" and Hasler rode alongside and pushed Badmann up the grade. "They still call that 'Help Me Hill,'" said a friend.

Most important, Hasler brought her out of her depression. "I would not be the person I am today without Toni," Badmann said. "Toni helped me realize that how I was was not the right way of thinking. So I started to think in the mornings: *What is going to make me happy?* I start with a smile. The first people you see in the morning when you get up, you give a smile to them. And that smile will come back to you, and your day will be completely different. That is a very big thing. So simple but so useful."

Badmann's training progressed quickly, and she entered her first race about six months after that first run and bike. The duathlon was a run-bike-run affair. Badmann led after the first run loop, but near the end of the second she was fading and told Hasler, "I'm tired. I don't want to do more today." Hasler encouraged her to press on, and she took 3rd.

Continuing a story line that would be rejected as preposterous at any Hollywood pitch meeting, Badmann developed formidable bike form to go with her strong running talent and won the 1995 short-course duathlon world championship in Cancun, Mexico. In 1996 she won the prestigious long-distance Powerman Zofingen duathlon (held near her home), defeating Ironman Hawaii champion Karen Smyers. Then she made her Ironman Hawaii debut, pressing the legendary Ironman champion Paula Newby-Fraser for most of the 1996 marathon before Newby-Fraser pulled away at the end for her eighth and final Kona win.

In that Ironman Hawaii baptism Badmann took the lead with a sizzling bike split of 4:53:47 (22.87 mph), but was passed by Newby-Fraser at mile 6 of the run. In a reversal of the normal rhythms of the race, the exuberant Swiss novice surged, made up a 45-second deficit, and repassed Newby-Fraser at mile 13, whizzing past at a 6:30 pace, some 30 seconds per mile faster than her adversary. "She blew by me," said Newby-Fraser. "I was surprised because I didn't know she was closing. But I just let her go. It was a big rookie mistake. I knew it wouldn't last."

Fifteen minutes later Badmann arrived in the Energy Lab a quarter mile ahead of Newby-Fraser, and she wore a beatific smile. "I was excited," she told *Triathlete* writer Roy Wallack. "I'd heard the Energy Lab was like Hell—hot like an oven. I wanted to see it; I wondered what happened there. And what I saw was so great, so beautiful: the lovely, shimmering blue water of the ocean. As I ran downhill, inside my body I was singing." The tune was Rod Stewart's "Smiling," which she switched in her head to "flying." But, said Badmann, when she started to climb back out of the Energy Lab, "I didn't feel so good anymore. Soon I see three helicopters, so I know Paula is coming." Newby-Fraser's prediction of a rookie mistake proved prescient, and Badmann finished 2nd, some 4.5 minutes in arrears.

In 1997 Badmann repeated her victory at the Powerman Zofingen duathlon; then came her 1998 Ironman Hawaii triumph. Following that breakthrough victory, Badmann embarked on a quest to make Switzerland's 2000 Olympic triathlon team, so she reluctantly passed up the honor of defending her Ironman Hawaii title. Women representing Switzerland ultimately won gold and bronze Olympic medals, but Badmann didn't make the team. However, her training for draft-legal, short-course racing improved her swim considerably and gave her run increased speed.

In the wild winds that plagued Ironman Hawaii in 2000, Badmann's new strengths didn't show in her swim and run splits, but her bike prowess dominated as never before, putting her 15 minutes ahead of runner-up Lori Bowden. Her technical and fitness improvements in the swim and run became obvious in the following year, when she had to overcome strong challenges from her rivals.

A stab of fear afflicted even defending champion Badmann in the second consecutive year of disheartening 40-mph winds along the Queen Ka'ahumanu Highway during the 2001 Ironman Hawaii. "When the first wind hit today, it really frightened me," admitted the Swiss star, whose biggest advantage had been a killer bike and a mystical imperviousness to wind. "Then I remembered I stood up on stage and told all the athletes when the winds hit, I spread my wings and fly. I thought, *You said that to all the others. Now you can't stop; you must fly.*"

Despite her formidable power, Badmann was temporarily rendered human on two wheels and for a few moments lost her aura of invincibility. "I came up on Fernanda [Keller], passed her, and she passed me back," said Badmann of the tenacious Brazilian. "We had a fight."

Badmann next overtook the on-form legend, Newby-Fraser, who was running second to rising sensation Nina Kraft, Ironman Germany's two-time champion. "I passed Paula, and she passed me back, so we had a fight also," said Badmann with a smile.

The resistance, though brief, was significant. Then Badmann's vulnerability vanished like a mirage.

Somehow reinvigorated after the contact, Badmann pushed on with her famous focus and positive attitude that, married to her superior technique, have made her so powerful at Kona. She knifed through the winds, and her 5:16:07 bike outdid Karen Smyers and Kraft by 13 minutes, Newby-Fraser by 12, and Lori Bowden by 9. As Bowden charged to a race-best 3:03:09 run, Badmann answered with a second-best 3:09:33 marathon that gave the Swiss star a third Ironman Hawaii win, second only to Newby-Fraser's eight.

No less a legend than Smyers, who beat Newby-Fraser in the horrible winds of 1995 and won two ITU Olympic-distance World Championships that Badmann could only dream about, pumped harder when Badmann went by on the bike—not to fight but to study. "Her form is so perfect, her pedal stroke is so even, I just watched her from behind for several miles," said Smyers, who finished 5th that year. "Her focus is so complete, she wastes so little energy, her line is so unwavering. For the rest of the race, my mantra was 'Bike like Natascha; bike like Natascha.'"

Badmann continued her Kona winning streak in 2002. But in 2003 Lori Bowden, after finishing 2nd to Badmann in 1998, 2000, and 2001 and 3rd behind Badmann and Nina Kraft in 2002, finally ran down the Swiss star, and her 7-minute advantage after the bike, for the win. Badmann, who had vomited several times on the bike, may have been off her best game but proved as gutsy as she was ebullient. After Kraft passed her early in the run, Badmann reeled her in and ran side by side for the last 2 miles, prevailing at the line by 8 seconds for 2nd place.

In 2004 Badmann had a crisis of confidence ignited by a seemingly overwhelming defeat. When she finished the bike at Kona nearly 20 minutes behind leader Nina Kraft, Badmann was so discouraged that she confessed she considered dropping out. "Before in races, I had a devil on one shoulder and an angel on the other," she explained. "This day the devil was so much bigger, I couldn't hear the angel. The devil was tempting me to quit. And that devil always says, 'Maybe you'll feel much better if you stop.' But I would have never forgiven myself if I'd stopped. Instead I completed the race and did not let myself look at how far ahead she was. Afterward, when I learned I was 17 minutes behind, I studied about it for 30 minutes. I thought, *Geez, I trained well. I raced good and hard. My nutrition was OK. It could be perfect. My mental ability was strong, too. Where can I get those 20 minutes? Maybe she had a great day? But I never improved 20 minutes from one year to the next. Why am I not 20 minutes faster, too?* I asked Toni [Hasler], 'Do you think I am too old?' He started laughing and said, 'No, you're not.' So that moment, yes, I doubted, yes."

As it turned out, the superhuman performance by Kraft that made Badmann doubt herself was in fact not truly human at all. After the race Kraft tested positive for the blood-boosting drug erythropoietin (EPO). Kraft admitted that she had started the drug regimen three weeks before the race and had taken her last dose five days prior to the start.

The news that she had won after all left Badmann deeply troubled. "When I heard that Nina had tested positive and that I had been given my fifth win, I was happy, but in a way I wasn't happy because I didn't want to win like this," Badmann told IronmanLive.com. "I felt sad that triathlon and doping would now be spoken of together. Sport should be about being happy and healthy."

Finally, Badmann added, "I was sad because of what was stolen from me. They are reporting that I now will have earned another $50,000, but that's not important. To walk across the finish line as the winner is special. I'm also sad that I didn't get to enjoy the awards ceremony. All of that would have been mine, but it was stolen from me."

Badmann has always been known for her sunny positivity and generous, inspiring, spiritual nature. But this experience showed another side of the Swiss star, one with a fierce sense of justice. Badmann added, "I hope that they use blood controls next year. I hate needles, and I can't stand the sight of blood, but I would do it for the sport."

And so it was in 2005, with confidence in her own abilities restored, that Badmann enjoyed one of her greatest victories when she met the great Michellie Jones, a two-time ITU short-course world champion, Olympic silver medalist, and winner of every major U.S. nondrafting event. Urged by her friends and coached by none other than Paula Newby-Fraser, Jones brought a formidable swim, a strong bike, and breathtaking short-course run speed to the task.

Badmann started chopping down Jones's 7:30 swim lead splinter by splinter, cutting the margin to 5:42 by the end of the 112-mile ride. Jones had ridden a brilliant 4:54:13, but Badmann had erased any question that her bike prowess might be slipping with her swifter 4:52:00.

Making her task more difficult, Badmann took too long to pass some age-group men and was cited by course marshals for drafting, costing her 4 minutes in the "sin bin" and leaving her with a 9:42 deficit to Jones to make up on the run. Most observers looked at Badmann's early Konas with run times of 3:14 and 3:19 and thought the task was too much. But Badmann knew better. "People say I'm just a cyclist, but my first triathlons were won on the run," said Badmann. "I always think if you have enough lead, why run any faster than you have to?"

This day Badmann had to. "If you had asked me before the race, could I catch her with a 10-minute lead, I would have said no way," said Badmann. "But I never doubted I could do it. I trusted my legs would get me there and my heart would gain for me all it was supposed to."

When Badmann set out, Jones's big lead began to shrink inexorably. By mile 3 it was 8:40. By mile 6 it was 7:13. By mile 8 it was 6:45, and by mile 9 it was 6 minutes flat. By then Jones was walking through the aid stations and carefully splashing her head with cooling water while Badmann seemed to be gathering strength and speed.

By mile 17 the lead was 50 seconds, and just before she came out of the boiling-hot Energy Lab Road, the shorter, slighter woman who had failed to make the Olympic team gently passed the taller, silver medal–winning star of Sydney. "You did a great job all day," said Badmann.

"You should just go," said Jones.

Badmann never looked back as she pressed ahead to her best-ever Ironman Hawaii marathon. Badmann's win put her in heady company, tied with Mark Allen and Dave Scott with six Ironman Hawaii victories and just two behind Newby-Fraser's eight.

Badmann's 3:06:25 run was 12 minutes faster than Jones's marathon, leading to a 9:09:30 finish, just 1:36 slower than her 2002 best overall time.

Measured by guts and gallantry and not by the victory wreath, Badmann's greatest effort might have been 2006. Battling a stomach virus, she emerged from the swim in a career-worst 66 minutes, 12 minutes behind Jones. She recouped 7 minutes with a 4:59:04 bike and advanced to 3rd place after 9 miles of the run—just the spot she was in the year before when she had run down Jones for her sixth win. Had a healthy Badmann mustered a 3:06 marathon, as she had in 2005, she and Jones, with her 5-minutes-faster 3:13 run, would have been on schedule to hit the line in a photo finish.

But just as Badmann headed out on the Queen K at mile 9, her stomach revolted and she stopped and threw up. "Everything got quiet," Badmann recalled to IronmanLive.com. "There was no more cheering. I started shaking. I was feeling horrible. I thought I might faint. People were staring at me, and a voice inside my head said, 'Sit down somewhere.' Everyone looked at how I was breathing, so I said, 'C'mon, keep it going. If you can't run, just start walking.'" She continued, crying, finishing 10th with her all-time worst 3:27:54 marathon. But when she crossed the line, Badmann gave the crowd the same joy and exultation she had expressed during her six wins and two 2nd places. "I was so happy at that moment when I crossed the finish line," she said in the interview. "I had that inner light in me. I was proud. It was the very best I had that day. I don't want to turn in that 10th place for a victory because what I got back from the crowd was fantastic."

Badmann turned 40 in December 2006 and approached the 2007 season on a mission. She told an interviewer that "age is only a number. Like a race number. It doesn't mean how many years you have in the sport or how much you put into your training."

From the start of the year, Badmann backed up her words with six victories in six races. She won Ironman South Africa in March by more than 25 minutes and placed 8th overall, which would have earned her a check in the men's category. In June she set a new world record of 4:08:17 in the Ironman 70.3 distance at Eagleman 70.3. Badmann left hot younger competitors at the middle distance, such as Mirinda Carfrae, Samantha McGlone, Becky Lavelle, and Julie Dibens—some of whom were a dozen years younger than she—in her record-shattering dust.

At Kona Badmann was aiming for a seventh win and meeting the challenge of the new wave represented by Jones, McGlone, and an as yet unknown phenom named Chrissie Wellington.

The day before the race Badmann looked formidable testing her extreme aerodynamic position on her Cheetah bike, riding with and into the brisk winds on the lava fields. But on race day she never got that far.

Anticipating stiff opposition from the likes of Kona rookie McGlone, Hasler was elated when Badmann broke fast on the bike after a mediocre 63-minute swim. "The first 12 km, Natascha was almost flying," wrote Hasler on his web site. "She made up already almost 90 seconds on the recent world champion Michellie Jones and remained behind the leaders about 6 minutes 30 seconds. During her last three Ironman Hawaii victories she was between 9 and 12 minutes behind the leader at this same point. At Ironman South Africa this year, she turned a similar deficit into a 25-minute lead. Everything seemed perfect."

Then Badmann entered a construction zone where competitors had to zigzag into another lane separated by traffic cones. Riding at an estimated 36 mph in full aero position, Badmann clipped an orange cone and went down hard. "Her helmet and the frame of her bike were totally broken," wrote Hasler. "She suffered skin injuries and abrasions on her whole body, and she had a lot of pain on both shoulders and her back. But Natascha didn't want to give up—that would be far more painful."

When a substitute bike was found 30 minutes later, Badmann threw a leg over it, strapped one good arm to the aero bars and tucked her most painful wing under her chest, and pedaled 30 more miles until Hasler finally, gently, convinced the great Swiss champion to call it a day.

Upon returning to Switzerland's Zurich airport on October 20, a sore and emotional Badmann was greeted by fans and media as "the fallen Iron Lady of Hawaii." A local newspaper noted that Badmann was not able to move her left arm and could move her right shoulder only with great pain.

Badmann underwent surgery at the Cross Clinic in Basel, Switzerland, for injuries that Dr. Andre Gösele, chief of the Olympic Medical Center in Basel, diagnosed as "very heavy and very complex injuries on both shoulders, especially on the left side." Gösele added that the shoulder injuries "affected the capsule, ligaments, and tendons" and also involved a broken clavicle and a broken back rib. He noted that Badmann's "heavy skin injuries [almost compared with] burned skin."

In a statement on her web site, Badmann stated that her goal was now "to come out of the deepest valley of her sporting career and come up even stronger." Her main goal, according to the statement, was participation at the thirtieth anniversary Ironman Hawaii in 2008.

"Natascha was so much looking forward to this season's highlight, as she was in amazing shape," wrote Hasler. "The results of her [2007] races and training showed she was in even better shape than when she broke the [half-Ironman] world record."

Badmann's rehabilitation was far more extensive, painful, and excruciatingly long than the U.S. public knew. Her determination undiminished, Badmann hooked herself up to a bike trainer while still in her hospital bed, just after the first extensive operation to repair tendons in her left shoulder. During that operation, the surgeon reconnected the biceps muscle and tendons with a metal anchor to the bone. This procedure allowed Badmann for the first time to hold her arm close to the body and to move the arm in physical therapy. Still, it took four weeks before her left arm was reasonably movable.

Determined to take part in Kona's thirtieth anniversary event, Badmann beat the odds simply by starting. "I am proud and happy that I could start in Hawaii," said Badmann. As recently as the preceding July, she said, "that was still a dream." Badmann said the first mile of the swim went well; "then the missing training became apparent. I felt empty, had little strength, and could not maintain the tempo anymore."

On the bike she controlled her nerves when passing the site of her 2007 accident and was moving well until she hit the 60-mile mark. "Then I did not have the strength to hold the aero position anymore, and I had to stand up," said Badmann. On the way back to town, she added, "I could [only] hold the tempo for about 10 km with good body position; then my strength faded." Badmann also had to cool the overheated musculature of her shoulders in the aid stations and gave up after 10 miles of the run.

Although her race ended in anonymity, Badmann once again proved there was no use-by date on her courage and determination.

Friends of Badmann said she might have considered retirement. After all, they pointed out, Dave Scott made an excellent curtain call at age 42, two years after his great 2nd-place finish to Greg Welch, and finished 5th at Ironman Hawaii. But even at age 42, Badmann felt she could not depart the Kona main stage on such an anticlimactic note.

In April 2009 Badmann shocked any remaining doubters by winning Ironman 70.3 New Orleans, breaking the course record with an impressive time of 4:17:50 and beating a strong field led by

2008 Ironman 70.3 world champion Joanna Zeiger and 8:47 iron-distance finisher Catriona Morrison. She also soundly thrashed old rival Nina Kraft and Kona podium finishers Kate Major and Lisa Bentley. Although her 18 months of painful rehab showed on the swim and on the run in a 2nd-place finish at Eagleman 70.3 and a 3rd-place finish at the half-Ironman-distance Rev3 Triathlon, Badmann still had the killer bike and a gleam in her eye at the prospect of finally meeting the new Ironman sensation Chrissie Wellington head to head on the Queen K.

Unfortunately, the expected battle between these two megastars was not to be. After a 63-minute swim, all Badmann could manage on the bike was a 22nd-best 5:19:48 bike—in good weather conditions. For almost anyone else that bike split would have been acceptable. But Badmann's reference point was winner Chrissie Wellington, who rode 4:52:06. Badmann's 5:19 split was evidence that something was seriously wrong, so she abandoned the race early in the run. To put this result in perspective, Badmann was joined in the ranks of those who did not finish by certified Ironman stars Yvonne Van Vlerken, Michellie Jones, Lisbeth Kristensen, Charlotte Paul, Belinda Granger, Bella Bayliss, Gina Crawford, Tamara Kozulina, and Tiina Boman.

But to Badmann, whose pride is enormous, such an anticlimactic result did not constitute a proper farewell to the race she loves more than any other. In the clamor and bustle of the finish, Badmann left Kona quietly, offering no excuses or explanations. In contrast to the numerous items about her progress after her accident, her blog has been silent since the race. Given the heroic efforts she made to rehabilitate her broken body to her accustomed level, the odds are heavily in favor of a return at age 43—and not for a ceremonial appearance. Friends who have seen her in Switzerland say she is completely focused, and committed to a return engagement on the Queen K in 2010.

"Nothing is impossible."

BELIEVE IN YOURSELF, never give up, and enjoy life!" Not everyone who says such things can thoroughly embody them, but Marc Herremans does. At age 36 the Belgian athlete continues to personify courage, competitive drive, and positive attitude—a true example for anyone who has ever doubted him- or herself.

Born in Merksem, Belgium, in 1973, Herremans was an outstanding athlete who played on the national junior soccer team. On his sixteenth birthday, however, something happened that would change his life forever: He watched Sylvester Stallone's performance in *Rocky*, the film about an underdog fighting his way to respect, honor, and fame. Although his parents forbade him to fight, the movie was a starter's pistol for Herremans's athletic life. From that day he spent hours jumping rope and running through nearby forests wearing ankle weights. Even before he knew what sport he was actually training for, the teenager knew that one day he would be a world champion.

At age 18 he left school and flew to the United States with two friends. Traveling, hiking through woods, climbing—adventure was on the menu. When he got back, Herremans took a job with the national forest service. He then signed up for military service in one of his country's elite forces, the Belgian Storm Commandos. "Sports, climbing, paratrooping: I had found an ideal situation for myself," he later said.

Then he saw television coverage of Ironman Hawaii. "All at once I knew that this was the sport I had been training for since I was 16," he recalled.

Alongside his new jobs as a fireman and a woodsman, he started training as a triathlete. Soon he realized that he would never achieve his goal of winning Ironman Hawaii unless he could focus solely on the sport. After he quit his jobs and dedicated himself to training for triathlon, success came quickly. He won races all over Europe and won the Belgian Olympic-distance triathlon elite championship in 1998 and 1999. All was going well for Herremans, and in 2001 he took a crack at the Ironman course in Kailua-Kona, Hawaii. It was the first year he trained under the direction of his new coach, Paul Vandenbosch, and good friend Dirk van Gossum, a five-time Belgian long-distance-triathlon champion who had earned wins at Lanzarote and Almere.

Herremans, then 27, had placed 4th at Ironman Australia; at Ironman Hawaii he finished just 2 minutes behind Ironman stars Normann Stadler and Lothar Leder, finishing 6th in 8 hours 51 minutes 19 seconds.

From that day forward he felt sure he would win that race one day. "The bike was my most lethal weapon," he explained, adding that due to his inexperience he had held back considerably. That he still finished just 5 minutes out of second place showed him that his dream was within reach—perhaps even the following year.

But on January 28, 2002, fate took a dark turn. During a ride with van Gossum as part of a training camp on Lanzarote, Herremans lost control of his bike on a curve during the descent from Haria. He flew over his handlebars, off the road, and down a rocky hillside, slamming his back against a rock. "I wanted to get up," he said, describing the seconds following impact, "but I couldn't."

He was brought to a hospital on the island and received a devastating diagnosis: His spinal cord was severed between the fifth and sixth thoracic vertebrae.

But he refused to accept defeat. *Maybe they're wrong,* he thought. He was flown to Las Palmas to undergo further tests. When the doctors there came to the same conclusion, he still resisted. He flew on to Belgium, to the hospital in Ghent. The medical staff there, too, was sure that he was permanently paralyzed.

"In a matter of seconds my life was ruined," he said. "All I had ever worked for was to win Ironman Hawaii. Everything else was less important. Now, at only 27 years old, it was no longer possible. My life was over."

The following days were terrible. A rising triathlon star who had always looked for adventure, who had always been active and healthy, who had wanted to write his name in the annals of Ironman history as the world's best triathlete, could now move only his head and arms. It was difficult for him to deal with the situation, and it seemed impossible to find meaning in his new life.

He experienced his first ray of hope when his sister and her children visited him in the hospital in Ghent after surgery. "It was very important for me mentally," he explained. He realized he was still alive; he could still play with the kids, could still watch them grow up. In these moments it was clear to him that he had to fight his way back into an active lifestyle. He began his new life with some easy training while still in his hospital bed.

A few weeks later, on April 11, 2002, he called Vandenbosch and asked, "Do you still want to train me?"

"Why? What for?" asked the coach, who didn't understand what his protégé was asking.

"I want to compete at Ironman," came the answer.

"As a wheelchair athlete?" responded Vandenbosch. "How are you going to do it? Something like that takes two or three years of preparation."

"I want to do it this year," Herremans said, challenging his trainer. Receiving only a dumbfounded silence in reply, Herremans said, "Okay, then I'll look for another coach."

There was nothing for Vandenbosch to do but get on board, though he had no experience with the required equipment. "We had never even seen a handbike up close before," he admitted.

His athlete was undeterred. More and more, Herremans was developing a new attitude, and his credo was "Nothing is impossible." He learned that steering a handbike wasn't all that easy when he tried it for the first time. He reached an average speed of 14 kph over 30 minutes.

"One week after the accident was the lowest," said Herremans. "I was like a little child. I couldn't wash myself. I couldn't go to the toilet. I couldn't do nothing anymore. I said, 'My life is over.' But then after two weeks, I thought, *I must do something. I want to fight back.* And I thought the Ironman was my way to fight back."

Herremans then called World Triathlon Corporation officials. "I asked if I could start" in Hawaii, he said. "They said, 'Yeah.' Immediately they say, 'Yes, yes, yes. No problem.' But like everyone else, they say, 'This year? Oh, you're crazy.'"

But in a triumph of the human spirit, Herremans appeared on the starting line in Hawaii just eight and a half months after his crash. He was tan, ripped up top, and ready. Normally the energy required for surgery and rehabilitation after such a catastrophic accident is enormous, and the process of adapting to physically challenged competition after paralysis takes many years.

Although he had no fear, Herremans was in fact asking too much of his body too soon after his accident. He had trained too much. When he was lifted out of the water following the 2.4-mile swim, he was so exhausted that he withdrew from the race. But he was satisfied and happy—happy to be alive, happy to be in Hawaii, and happy to belong once again to triathlon's family. It didn't bother him much that he couldn't get through the Ironman on his first try. He knew he would be back and would make it to the finish line.

Twelve months later he was back. This time he was in better shape, but the race was difficult for him, especially the climb to Hawi. Approaching the start of the 17-mile climb at Kawaihae on the bike course, he could hardly bear to think that the pro athletes were already whizzing by on the road back to Kona, 34 miles ahead of him. "What am I doing here?" he asked himself. "There are the guys battling for the win I always dreamed about." After those initial discouraging thoughts, however, he got his head together and thought about his goals. To win here as a pro was no longer a possibility for him. But, he thought, he could win Ironman in the handbike class and become world champion on the strength of his arms alone. This thought helped him focus on his effort again. He continued to turn the cranks of his race machine with everything he had, moving himself toward his goal as fast as 19 kph.

After the 112-mile bike segment, he was exhausted. It was now difficult for him to imagine finishing the marathon in his wheelchair. It seemed even less likely as he arduously made his way up the steep hill on Palani Road to the highway. But he did it. After 13 hours 23 minutes, he was the 3rd athlete in his category to cross the finish line. He wasn't able to celebrate, though. "I was too tired to be happy about it," he said. "I was completely out of it."

The next season, he again pushed his body mercilessly to realize his dream of victory in Hawaii. He injured his spinal cord once again, this time from a fall with his walker. He didn't care. "I can't tell anyway," he told himself at the time and simply kept on training. But the wound became infected, and what he had considered insignificant was actually dangerous, taking his body to the edge of collapse. Only then did he grant himself a little rest. But in October 2004 he traveled once again to Kailua-Kona. He finished but couldn't improve his time and placed 3rd again in 13 hours 48 minutes.

Even though the injury to his back hadn't healed, he continued training as before. At some point, he thought, he simply had to be able to win the world championship. He believed he could finish significantly faster because in the previous season he had struggled against a debilitating open wound.

But the injury persisted, and then Herremans suffered a shock. Only months before, the actor Christopher Reeve, the man who had starred in the Superman movies and been subsequently paralyzed from the neck down when he was thrown from a horse, had died from a similarly infected wound. Like Reeve, whom he had met and grown to admire, Herremans was now fighting for his life. His arrival at death's doorstep helped him finally understand that he would never achieve the goal of winning in Hawaii if he didn't take better care of his weakened body.

When he arrived in Kailua-Kona in 2005, his wound had not completely healed, but he was doing much better. This time he felt ready and capable of being a formidable competitor for the 42-year-old American Carlos Moleda, a two-time Ironman Hawaii physically challenged champion. Moleda, whose paralysis began below the lamina vertebrae and who was competing in what was supposed to be his final Ironman Hawaii, predicted that this would be a tough clash.

"Carlos is an athlete and a warrior, and I dream of a duel with him here in Hawaii," said Herremans. "When Carlos came to race in my half-Ironman in Belgium, he did not like the cold, and I beat him. But he loves the heat in Hawaii, and there will be nothing stopping him. So I dream we can push each other. Carlos is to me the greatest athlete I know. So I'll have to give the best performance of my life if I want to win this year."

As predicted, it came down to the anticipated battle between the 42-year-old American and the Belgian challenger 11 years his junior.

"Since Carlos is so strong in the wheelchair, I knew I had to get a good lead in the swim," remembered Herremans. His plan started well. He exited the water about 13 minutes before his opponent and held the lead for 93 miles of the bike before Moleda came up from behind.

"You are an animal!" shouted the American.

The Belgian responded, "Okay, but what are you, then? You're passing me!"

In those moments, explained Herremans, he realized that to have a shot at winning, he had to transition onto the marathon course before the American. Moleda was too strong once he got in a wheelchair.

Herremans shifted into the biggest gear he could, employed all his strength, and surged away from his competitor at 40 kph without a word, without so much as a glance. But the two-time winner would not give up so easily. Moleda worked his way back, and the two athletes entered the transition area together.

Once seated in a wheelchair, the American showed his class. Not only did he have much more experience than the Belgian, he also had a physical advantage. Because of his less extensive paralysis, he could support his arms with his entire upper body and stomach muscles, which helped him up steep Palani Road. Herremans had only his arms. Nevertheless, he gave it his all. His strong effort was pushing Carlos Moleda up ahead. As expected, it took Moleda's best performance to date to secure him the win: 10 hours 30 minutes, a new world record for the category.

Herremans reached the finish in an excellent time of 10:57, only 2 minutes over the old world record. Moleda waited for him at the finish. "Marc, you pushed me to the world record, I will be forever grateful to you," he said. Afterward Moleda announced his retirement as an Ironman Hawaii competitor.

For the underdog, the winner's words were an honor, but it wasn't the kind of recognition he was looking for. He believed Moleda had simply benefited from superior technique, and that was no surprise. After all, in this second life Herremans was just four years old.

Things went well for Herremans in 2006. For the first time since his accident five years earlier, he was healthy and in top form. He even had time and strength for rock climbing, his former passion. In July he traveled with friends to California to scale the 3,937-foot sheer granite face of El Capitan in Yosemite National Park. He wanted to attempt a feat that was a rare triumph for even the most talented able-bodied people. Because of damage to his climbing seat harness, he had to do an unusual amount of work with his arms and hoisted his 176-pound body 985 feet above his starting point by essentially doing 1,800 chin-ups. After 12 hours of climbing, however, he had to give up.

When he arrived on the Big Island in October 2006, he was quite confident. He was now equally strong in all three disciplines, he explained before the race. Of course it wasn't a sure thing; after all, some of his four opponents were not as physically challenged as he was. Like Moleda the year before, they could obtain some power from their stomach muscles. An athlete with an amputation below the knee could even utilize his upper leg for additional leverage in the swim. In contrast to the Special Olympics, where participants compete for gold within distinct handicap categories, at Ironman Hawaii there was only one division for athletes who would tackle the course on handbikes and in wheelchairs. For Herremans, it was all the same. "I don't worry about it; those are the rules here," he explained. He faced life's challenges as a paraplegic, and the important thing was being willing to accept those challenges. He claimed he would do anything to finally make his dream of winning Ironman a reality. What would he do if he won? "Then I'll stop," he said. "Then I will have fulfilled my dream and will begin my third life."

But on top of his ambition to finally win Hawaii, Herremans had one more thought. "I want to break the world record on this course," he said.

After all, wrote Robert Browning, if a man's reach cannot exceed his grasp, what's a heaven for?

The race began as he had feared. Even though he exited the water with a very good time of 1 hour 5 minutes, American Akian Aleong—a two-time Olympic-distance world champion—entered the bike segment on his handbike 3 minutes earlier. Herremans sensed that he would need to lay the foundation of a win on the handbike. "I knew Akian would be very strong on the run," he said. "And I knew I would have to finish the bike leg with a big lead to have a chance at the win." Because he had more use of his body, Aleong had an advantage not only when swimming but also when propelling a wheelchair.

Like a man possessed, the Belgian drove the cranks of his high-tech handbike hard. With every rotation he came closer to his competitor. After just a few kilometers, he was within sight of Aleong. Then he closed the gap, passed his rival, and rode away.

It took him 7 hours 16 minutes to cycle through the island's lava fields. When he entered the second transition area and got into the wheelchair he had a 20-minute lead. "Is it enough?" he anxiously asked himself.

After he fought his way up Palani Road to the Queen Ka'ahumanu Highway, his arm muscles were on fire. With his head bent low over his folded knees, he thrust the push rims of his wheelchair forward. No matter how hard he labored, his opponent was getting closer. Minute by minute his lead was shrinking. And on every small incline, able to use only his arms, he lost additional seconds.

At the 3-mile out-and-back portion of the run at the Natural Energy Lab, roughly 7 miles from the finish, Herremans saw his rival for only seconds, but those moments seemed like salvation itself. "I came out of the Energy Lab just as Akian was heading into it," said Herremans. "That's when I knew I would win. The gap between us [3 miles] was too big; he could no longer catch me." The final distance didn't provide any physical respite, but it certainly gave him some psychological relief. After 10 hours 53 minutes he rolled over the finish line. He had used up every bit of his strength but had fulfilled his dream. In disbelief, he put his face in his hands. He had done it. He was—as he had set out to become at the age of 16—a world champion. Ironman world champion.

Shortly afterward he announced his retirement. He wanted to start his third life and certainly didn't anticipate getting bored. He founded a charity, To Walk Again, which raises money for research in rehabilitation for paraplegic injuries as well as better opportunities for physically challenged athletes to participate in sports. He has also organized a half-Ironman-distance triathlon in Antwerp that has become one of the most popular events in Europe.

The primary goal of his new life was to start his own family. He believed that children were the best thing anyone could bring into the world; when the time came he was sure he would be able to give up adventures such as climbing El Capitan.

According to Herremans, the most important quality an athlete needs to contest an Ironman—and who has demonstrated this more convincingly?—is determination. "You have to believe in your abilities and potential," he said. Natural talent won't help if your head is not in the right place.

He advised those with motivational challenges that getting into a training groove can prove difficult, but it gets easier and becomes more enjoyable after a while. Sport and exercise, he emphasized, are good for body and spirit. "We are only on this planet once, and life is too beautiful to waste or to shorten prematurely through unhealthy living," he said emphatically.

When asked whether he believed he would ever walk again, he answered immediately and resolutely, "Yes!" Years ago, he pointed out, people never would have conceived of a heart transplant. In the past, people believed cancer was always deadly. Now half of all cancer patients survive. "Why shouldn't a paraplegic injury someday be treatable?" he demanded. And even if it were too late for him, he still wanted to do everything he could to make it possible for children who were now in a predicament like his.

Marc Herremans clearly embodies courage, competitive spirit, and a positive attitude: "Believe in yourself, never give up, and enjoy life. Nothing is impossible!"

SIXTEEN | NORMANN STADLER

"You have to love what you do."

NORMANN STADLER WAS blessed with prodigious physical gifts that led him to become the most formidable cyclist in Ironman Hawaii history. But the ultimate fuel behind his drive for success was the powerful emotions that either propelled him to ecstatic triumph or left the operatic, charismatic man called the Normannator wallowing in misunderstood dramas. No matter. In victory or defeat, Normann Stadler was the man to watch.

He was born on February 25, 1973, in Döllersberg, a town of 700 near Wertheim, Germany. The second of three sons of Gertrud and Friedrich Stadler, he broke the family mold. While his older brother Frank always sat at a desk in front of a book, it was tough to get Normann to come back into the house at the end of each day.

In 1984, when he was 11 years old, his father started a track-and-field team affiliated with the Döllersberg Football Club. Normann was one of the first youngsters to join the squad, which was coached by his father, a passionate rower who taught himself the art of endurance training.

Success came quickly. Stadler inherited his father's ambition and used his drive and talent to win a state title in cross-country running. If he wasn't training for track and field, he was zipping around on his bike. Recovery apparently wasn't necessary for him. When he was given his first racing bike at 13, he rode all over the countryside. Soon his father noticed that his son showed enormous endurance on his new ride.

Belying his later reputation as a supercyclist who could not run, Stadler finished 16th out of 100 as a young teenager in the national junior cross-country championship. During this time he posted a promising 1:58 in the 800 meters.

Two years later the Stadlers read a notice in the newspaper about a training camp for German triathletes in Würzburg. Father and son were curious, so they set off to see for themselves what this new sport and its players were all about. "The athletes wore cool clothing and their high-tech race bikes really got me excited," remembered Stadler. He began some sporadic swim training but focused primarily on the bike.

Stadler took on the 1988 German junior Olympic-distance championships in Kötzingen as his first triathlon, shaking off a broken collarbone suffered just six weeks before. The evening before the race, he and his father were chatting with some of the athletes. "Normann is going to win the race," said Friedrich. Embarrassed, the 15-year-old kicked his dad in his shin, but in vain. What was said was said. Although Stadler's bike lacked aero bars and he was teased by other athletes for his outdated equipment, he made good on his father's boast and captured the German junior championship by a wide margin. "From that day forward I knew this was my sport," Stadler recalled. Confidence rising, he won the German triathlon championship series as well as the duathlon, which replaced the swim with an additional run leg.

At age 20 Stadler was asked to join the German army's national triathlon team along with established stars such as Thomas Hellriegel and Ralf Eggert. But when he encountered national coach Stefan Grosse, a high-mileage dictator from the highly regimented East German system, Stadler revolted. "I had had a lot of success training with my father, Friedrich, a former national-class rower," said Stadler. "But when I first went to training camp at Lanzarote, Grosse had us doing 45 kilometers a week swimming, and I hurt my shoulder. Grosse had us bike over 450 kilometers a week at high altitude, and I developed an infection in my inner ear, and it destroyed my balance; I could not even walk. But Stefan told me, 'Don't be a sissy! We have to do more work to get ready for the European championships.' I quit and had to drive my car 1,000 kilometers back home in that condition. My father wanted to kill him. But I said, 'Don't bother.'"

Stadler remained in the army, obligated only to do a once-a-month boot camp, and under his father's regimen had continued success. By 1994, at 21, he made another jump, winning the ITU World Duathlon Championship in Tasmania and defeating a star-studded field that included Powerman Zofingen champion Urs Dellsperger of Switzerland.

He increased his training volume and tried to improve his swim, his least favorite discipline. But just when he thought he was making progress and began to dream about the coming Olympics, the ITU changed the rules for Olympic-distance events. It was decided that drafting on the bike would be allowed.

Stadler felt that change robbed him of his greatest weapon. How was he supposed to build a lead on the bike if other athletes could get away with doing half as much work in his slipstream? He decided to leave the national team, quit Olympic-distance races, and try his luck at iron-distance events, in which drafting was prohibited.

Though Stadler saw his future in longer events, it took time to prepare his body. In 1997 he could manage only 7th at the Powerman World Duathlon Championship at Zofingen. In his first Ironman in Switzerland, he failed to finish. In 1998 he started strong in his second try at Zurich, managing a decent swim and a great ride for the first half of the bike. But near the end of the 112-mile course, he grew weaker and weaker. He described the marathon as a "nightmare." While the contenders battled for victory, he ducked into the portable toilets several times and also vomited by the side of the road. "I just wanted to sit down and never get up," he said.

Despite his suffering, he placed 4th, one spot off the podium. But that result didn't meet his high standards. "I wanted to win," said Stadler. With that bitter Swiss experience, it was clear to him that he had to work relentlessly on his fitness in order make a living at Ironman races. Even so, he was far from optimally prepared for his first start in Hawaii 18 months later.

When he stepped out of the plane in Kona in October 1999, he felt as though he could barely breathe in the tropical humidity. "It was so hot that I couldn't imagine doing any sports there, much less competing in an Ironman," he said with a smile. The initial shock was soon forgotten. He liked the island and the Hawaiian lifestyle. He loved to sit in the Lava Java café and watch the activity along Ali'i Drive. He likened this gathering of the world's best triathletes to a family reunion. And he was a little in awe of the big names of the sport.

He was able to keep up with the early leaders at Kona in 1999, riding with a hall-of-fame lineup that included Peter Reid, Tim DeBoom, Olivier Bernhard, Thomas Hellriegel, and that year's winner, Luc van Lierde. Stadler's 4:40:59 was the fourth-fastest bike split, just 2 minutes 21 seconds off Hellriegel's best of the day mark. In the end the heat and pace took their toll, and Stadler fell back with a 3:08:20 marathon, one place behind fellow German Andreas Niedrig. Given that this was his first try at the world championship, his 15th place left him temporarily satisfied. At the same time, he recognized that he had a way to go physically and mentally before he was ready to win. "You need patience to be successful in this sport," he explained.

His trials continued, especially in races in his homeland. For three years in a row he failed to finish Ironman Europe in Roth, his nation's biggest event. Once he collided with a spectator while on his bike; another time he suffered hypothermia in the cold rain and quit. On yet another occasion he was kicked in the stomach during the swim and briefly lost consciousness. His Ironman races seemed to be cursed, and it took a lot to maintain faith in himself and in his abilities. "I knew I had been training well; it had to come together at some point," he insisted.

His perseverance began to pay off in early 2000. That year he arrived seven weeks early for Ironman Australia and stayed with his brother Frank, who had been living down under for several years.

The uninterrupted training in predictably pleasant weather, much of it in Australia's Blue Mountains, left him strong, fast, and ready for a breakthrough. On a sunny day in Forster-Tuncurry, his 49:33 swim put him in the lead from the start. His race-best bike increased his lead to 8 minutes, and he hung on with a 2:58:30 run for a breakthrough first Ironman win in 8:30:37.

That victory gave him the push he needed. "It was huge," he said. From then on he knew that he could play with the big dogs. But if he needed a small dose of humility, he could look to women's winner Lori Bowden's performance. Bowden's 4:51:40 bike, admittedly earned in the helpful vicinity of fast age-group men, was just 9:16 slower than Stadler's solo mark. And Bowden's record-setting 8:55:08 finish was just 24:31 slower than that of the German, well below the average Ironman margin of 52 minutes of men over women.

He went on to take a fine 3rd place in Hawaii that same year, which gave him far more credibility than his Australia victory. In Kona he posted a race-best 4:35:14 bike—3 minutes faster than Hellriegel, 4 minutes better than race winner Reid, and 5 minutes ahead of runner-up DeBoom. His 2:56:00 run was another breakthrough that propelled him to a personal-best 8:26:44 finish on a wickedly windy day, just 5:44 behind the winner. Best of all, he got to spend a long time in the lead of the most important Ironman on earth; Reid was not able to pass him until mile 10, and DeBoom went by at mile 11.

"It was an unbelievable feeling," said Stadler. "I was best European, the best German, ahead of Lothar Leder and Thomas Hellriegel, a place on podium. It was big!" Stadler, the 26-year-old interloper, had leapfrogged over the established hierarchy with his daring breakaway on the bike and run and nearly fulfilled a prediction of victory by his training partner, friend, and Ironman mentor, Jürgen Zäck.

"Normann will win," had predicted Zäck, who had been kept out of his favorite race by a collarbone injury suffered just two weeks before. While eventual winner Reid and runner-up DeBoom ran Stadler down midway through the run, it was not at all like Stadler's collapse in the Energy Lab in 1999, which had left him an anonymous 15th overall, and merely the 5th German. Reid greeted Stadler at the victory banquet by saying, "Every year there is someone new here. Welcome to the club." By "the club," Reid meant a short list of elite competitors who could realistically contend for the win at Kona.

The pure joy was hard for Stadler to describe, but it lasted only a short time before the German media and his Ironman-crazy countrymen bored in with questions. "Some said to me, 'What is wrong with you? Were you taking "medicine" in San Diego?'" referring to Stadler's pre-Hawaii training base. "They laughed, but the implication was that I had used drugs." No matter that he had tested clean and always had. No matter that the real answer was far more boring: Stadler had worked harder, trained smarter, was ready to jump to the next level, and was simply better on that day. Stadler had toppled the established order, and that made him a target.

In 2001 he was once again victorious in Australia and put in another good performance in Hawaii, taking 4th. But once again, despite his new nickname, the Normannator, which compared Stadler to the all-powerful cyborg played by Arnold Schwarzenegger in the *Terminator* movies, he got another dose of humility.

With talk that sensational Ironman Hawaii rookie, former professional cyclist Steve Larsen, was capable of riding 4:15, Stadler was skeptical and said at the pre-race press conference: "*If* he gets by us . . ." Zäck scoffed at predictions that Larsen could overcome a 10-minute deficit after the swim by the turnaround at Hawi. "There is a lot of talking in the media, but it's wishful thinking," said Zäck. "They want an American to be the dominator on the bike and get a 10-minute lead. It's not going to happen."

Cut to the day of truth. "I had a very bad moment," said Stadler. "I thought I had no legs. I was riding at 35 kilometers per hour into those big winds, and Larsen passed me like he was riding a motorcycle." After the race six-time champion Mark Allen said this edition had the most DNFs of top contenders ever, including Reid, Van Lierde, Spencer Smith, and Zäck. Chris McCormack, on a scouting mission for his Ironman Hawaii debut the following year, said, "Steve Larsen had a lot to do with it, the pressure he applied to everyone's pre-race game plan."

Larsen wanted to shake up the old paradigm that strong runners sat in on the bike and waited. Mission accomplished. His 4:33:32 bike split on the worst day of winds in Kona history was 11:47 faster than that of next-best Stadler.

In 2002 Stadler started the year training with T-Mobile's Tour de France cycling team, then ran hard preparing for Ironman New Zealand. His abrupt increase in early-season training mileage and intensity led to iliotibial problems. Although he recovered in time to start at Kona, he accepted the suggestion from one of his sponsors for a last-minute equipment swap that changed the fit of his bike. Suffering severe knee pain, he ended up walking half the marathon.

"It was unbelievably hot, and my skin was burning in the scorching heat," he said, recalling those bleak hours. Nonetheless, he didn't want to give up—not in Hawaii. In the end he reached the finish in 100th place in just under 10 hours. "There are so many triathletes who have to give their all just to finish this race," he said. "I didn't want to simply give up because things weren't going well."

In 2003 he posted the fastest bike again (4:33:40) but faded with a 3:02:50 marathon during which Reid, Rutger Beke, and Cameron Brown all passed him as he took another 4th place. Victory in Hawaii remained maddeningly elusive.

The 2004 campaign began with a significant setback. Two days before Ironman Germany in Frankfurt, Stadler's second-most-important race of the year, he caught a stomach flu. At first he thought he was just nervous, but on race day it became clear it was much more than that. He started losing strength during the swim in

Langener Waldsee and soon could barely move his arms. He threw up in the lake, swam feebly back to shore, and abandoned the race.

"I had no more desire to do triathlons and wanted to give it all up," he recalled. Once again he had invested six months of his life in intense training only to fail. During this difficult period his father advised him not to do anything rash. After all, he had put in a lot of good training leading up to the race and had not used up significant energy on the bike and run.

Normann followed the advice. Two weeks after the disaster in Frankfurt, he lined up at the start of Ironman Switzerland, emerged from the swim in the middle of a five-man pack with all the top contenders, rode to a 4-minute lead with the fastest bike split of 4:31:07, and held on to 2nd place with a 2:56:03 marathon. With a new personal-best Ironman time of 8:21:24, he finished second just 5 minutes behind local hero and perennial winner Olivier Bernhard. Stadler's self-confidence returned, even more so over the following eight weeks in San Diego, where he set new best times on all of his favorite training loops. "I knew that if nothing unexpected happened, I would throw down a good race in Hawaii," he said.

In the week leading up to Ironman Hawaii he was feeling more relaxed than ever. When he awoke the morning of the event after a rare good night's sleep, he told himself he would win that day.

After the swim he trailed up-and-coming German Faris Al-Sultan by 4 minutes and three-time Kona champion Reid by just a minute. When Stadler got on his bike he mashed the pedals like never before. Soon he had passed the front of the group. But instead of resting briefly and sizing up his competitors, he hammered on.

While three-time champion Reid was caught in a communal torpor on the Queen K with heavy cofavorite Tim DeBoom, both biking a scandalously slow 5:01-plus, Stadler flew to a race-best 4:37:48, 9:30 better than the second-best split of amateur Kai Hundertmarck, 10:53 better than second-best pro Torbjørn Sindballe, and a shocking 23:40 better than Reid and DeBoom.

Stadler's post-bike margin over Sindballe (10:32), Al-Sultan (14:53), DeBoom (21:51), and Reid (21:58) meant the 33-year-old could virtually coast to a win on the run. While his competitors speculated that Stadler had gone too hard on the bike and would fall apart in the marathon, Stadler rightly calculated that "in order to catch me, Peter Reid would have to run faster than anyone ever had at an Ironman." He was right. Reid did run a very fast 2 hours 46 minutes, but Stadler reached the finish with a comfortable 10-minute lead.

Over the final mile, Stadler was trying to figure out how he wanted to approach the finish line. He straightened his jersey and adjusted his visor so that his sponsors' names would be clearly visible. "But in the final meters," he said, "I couldn't compose myself any longer." He ran along Ali'i Drive celebrating and high-fiving the enthusiastic spectators, raised his arms, crossed the finish line, and started weeping for joy and relief. He had finally—finally!—done what he had worked so hard to accomplish and what he had dreamed of doing for so long.

With tears in his eyes, he called his parents from the finish. "I won," he said simply to his mother in Germany, where it was the middle of the night. The news shocked his father, who could only manage to blurt out to his son, "Make sure you get some sleep." "My father may not express his feelings very well," said Normann, "but I know that there is no one who is more proud of me than he is."

"They said a biker couldn't win Hawaii, but I did it," said Stadler, who had taken the title of überbiker with fastest bike splits in 2000 (3rd overall), 2003 (4th overall), and 2004 (1st).

While Stadler's 4:37:58 split was far from Thomas Hellriegel's 4:24:50 course record set while gaining 2nd overall in rare, perfect weather conditions in 1996, the nasty, persistent cross- and headwinds in 2004 left experts in admiration. "If Normann had biked this hard in 2003 [during rare mild conditions], he would have broken Thomas Hellriegel's course record," said none other than Paula Newby-Fraser, Ironman Hawaii eight-time champion and holder of the women's bike-course record of 4:48:30.

As wonderful as his 2004 triumph was, the period following Hawaii would be terrible. Nina Kraft from Braunschweig, Germany, who won the women's race and seemed to make the German domination of the Ironman World Championship complete, tested positive for doping. It was a tragedy for the sport and inevitably cast an unwelcome shadow on Stadler's victory.

But it was only the beginning of a rough patch for Stadler. Following the 2004 Athlete of the Year voting in Germany, one of the major newspapers, the *Frankfurter Allgemeine*, published an article asserting that Stadler had a problem being ranked 9th, behind three-time Paralympics winner and 5th-ranked Wojtek Czyz. Motivated by that article, the *Bild* newspaper piled on. It featured the Hawaii winner multiple times on the cover and ran a smear campaign against Stadler for his remarks about a beloved physically challenged athlete. Even Chancellor Gerhard Schröder spoke out against him, claiming that Stadler's statement was unworthy of a true sportsman.

Stadler felt misunderstood and hurt. He insisted that both editors had misquoted him, and they eventually apologized. Nevertheless, in a telephone conversation with Czyz, he excused himself for having expressed himself poorly. With that it was water under the bridge for the two athletes. But Stadler continued to be criticized publicly and received nasty e-mails and even death threats. His victory in Hawaii, the biggest triumph of his life, seemed to have been almost forgotten in the court of public opinion.

Stadler threw himself into his only refuge, his training. He knew that only athletic accomplishments would make positive headlines again. In July 2005 he won Ironman Germany in Frankfurt. The victory was a liberation, his first on German soil after years of problems.

Subsequently he traveled to Hawaii as one of the favorites. Being a defending champion at Ironman Hawaii is not easy. There was enormous pressure, the media continually surrounded him, and a 20-minute press conference quickly turned into an hour. "I wasted a lot of time," he said. "I was exhausted."

Things started poorly on the swim, and when he got to the bike he had a significant deficit to fellow competitors Al-Sultan, Reid, and Brown; he expended a lot of energy trying to catch up. On the climb toward the turnaround in Hawi, he had worked his way up to third when he noticed that his front tire was slowly losing air. A flat tire!

He pulled over to change the tire but couldn't get it off the rim. Normally athletes leave a 6-inch section of the tire free of glue near the valve stem so that they can apply some leverage between tire and rim and pull the tire off. But Stadler had not glued the tires himself; he had asked a bike shop do it for him. Instead of getting upset with himself for leaving such an important detail to someone else, he shook his head and exclaimed, "How much glue did they use?" He ignored the cameras and microphones, which were catching it all.

He lost several minutes waiting for a new front wheel from the neutral service car. About 20 athletes had passed by the time he got back on his bike, and he had to start the game of catch-up anew. Blood had pooled in his legs during the wait, so he found it difficult to get back into his rhythm. Nevertheless, 15 miles later he had charged back to the front.

But the ghost of flat tires was haunting him that day: the replacement was now also losing air. Adding to his mounting anxiety, Stadler was stung by a bee. At that moment he realized that his training over the entire year had been for naught. Even if he were able to ride back up to the front after another wheel change, he knew he wouldn't have strength left for a competitive marathon. He rolled to a stop and, with operatic frustration, heaved his high-tech bike into the lava fields—all recorded by the NBC cameras.

Those pictures, which made their way around the world, didn't help his image. What the 2005 media coverage didn't include was Stadler's sportsmanship afterward when, despite his frustration and disappointment, he went to the finish line to congratulate his fellow German and the new champion, Faris Al-Sultan.

After his latest disappointment, Stadler didn't hide. Dancing around the issues and making excuses was not his style. He spoke openly in interviews. "I know that I've made mistakes," he offered, "but I've learned from them, and they won't happen again."

In 2006 he was back to training 35 hours each week, and in July he lined up at the start of Ironman Germany in Frankfurt. This time the defending champion swam a new personal best of 51 minutes. It took him only a few minutes to bike to the lead. But riding too fast on some curves during heavy rain, he fell twice, bruising a few ribs. Still, he picked himself up and finished with an amazingly quick 4 hours 22 minutes, the fastest bike split.

Because of the bruised ribs and the resulting difficulty breathing, the run didn't go well. But he didn't give up. "My family and lots of friends had come to the race. That's why I wanted to get to the finish no matter what," he explained. It took him 3 hours 38 minutes to cover the 26.2 miles, and he finished 11th overall with a time of 8 hours 56 minutes.

Even though his result wasn't impressive, the race convinced Stadler that his fitness was on track. Again he traveled to San Diego six weeks before Hawaii, and every day of training seemed to go perfectly.

He arrived in Kailua-Kona with a lot of self-confidence and thought those last negative experiences were behind him. But recently retired three-time Hawaii champion Reid gave a pre-race interview in which he said Stadler would not win again on the island that year or any other. Was this lingering sour grapes after Stadler had outridden the defending champion by 23 minutes at Kona in 2004? Whatever the motive, the comment became perfect motivational fuel for Stadler.

He came out of the unusually strong Pacific swells only 20 seconds behind the other favorites, a shock for his competitors, who knew they needed to bank some time against the strong cyclist during the swim. They hadn't ridden out of town when he stormed toward the front, looking for an opening.

Before they got out of Kona, fellow supercyclist Chris Lieto turned to Stadler and asked, "Are you going to wait a little bit, or are you going to start now?" "No, I start now," said Stadler, who then proceeded to kick his Kuota rocket ship into hyperdrive and leave everyone well behind.

He knew it would be difficult to ride all 112 miles alone. But tactically he didn't have a choice. "I knew that if I was suffering, the other guys would be suffering that much more," he explained, looking back.

Unlike his competitors in 2004, the field was highly attuned to Stadler's powers of the break and lost ground grudgingly at first. "My bike computer wasn't working, so I had no idea how fast I was going," said Stadler. "I just pushed and pushed harder. Heading up from Kawaihae to Hawi, I heard 2 minutes 30 seconds. By Hawi it was 4 minutes, and 6 minutes with 45 miles to go."

At this point Chris McCormack made a key decision. "I kept saying to myself, 'You're the best runner here, mate. Do you roll the dice and go with this move? Or do you do what Mark Allen used to do and sit in with that bunch and wait for the run?'" He decided to bide his time.

Alarmed by Stadler, the pack didn't have the fire to resist but turned in some fast times on the Queen K's 112 miles, with matching 4:29s for McCormack, Al-Sultan, Marino Vanhoenacker, Brown, and Luke Bell. Lieto, who chased Stadler the hardest, was worn out after his 4:25 bike, while Belgium's Beke fought off a shocking bad patch early in the bike to finish with a 4:33:33 that would have been brilliant on a customarily tougher day but left him 10th starting the run.

Two years after he had shattered the old shibboleth that no one could win Ironman Hawaii on the bike, a year after his day had gone to hell with two flats and a bee sting, Stadler roared back with a vengeance. On a cool, windless, rainy day that turned the usually fearsome Queen Ka'ahumanu Highway into Stadler's own private autobahn, the man from Mannheim arrived in the run transition with a record-smashing 4:18:23 ride.

Stadler's margin starting the run was 10 minutes and change—10 minutes closer than his runaway margin of 2004—and almost immediately talented chasers such as Lieto, Brown, Bell, Eneko Llanos, and even defending champion Al-Sultan turned into pretenders.

While everyone else was disheartened and essentially out of it, one man was still in the game. Two men were running hard and were using the tiny corner of consciousness left in their brains to calculate the bottom line.

"My legs were hurting, but I was able to run 6:25 miles at 2:47 marathon pace, and they all can't run faster," recalled Stadler. "Especially after a fast bike."

McCormack, the excitable Aussie who had spent four years of big predictions followed by frustrating performances at Kona, clicked off the numbers as he dropped off his bike and hit the run. *Ten minutes!* thought McCormack. *That's 20 seconds a mile if Normann runs the 2:57 he's historically run at Kona.* But after 9 miles running 6-minute miles on Ali'i, McCormack had taken nothing out of Stadler's lead. "I thought, *Man, this guy's on a mission,*" said "Macca." *"I hope he blows up!"*

Slowly but surely, the pressure increased. "I hate that uphill from mile 11 through 16 heading out on the Queen K to the Energy Lab," said Stadler, whose dwindling margin was troubling. Entering the long and testing out-and-back at the Natural Energy Lab Road at mile 16 of the run, Stadler had a margin of 6 minutes 20 seconds. After the long slog uphill back from the turnaround to the 6.7-mile home stretch, Stadler's edge was just 4 minutes 10 seconds.

Stadler's lead was eroding like a sand castle at high tide. It would require cool, calculating aplomb for the German with titanic emotions to fend off the twin devils of McCormack's charge and his own nerves.

Stadler simply told himself, "'OK. Let's dig deep.' For the first time I was really fighting to finish fast. And if it came to a sprint, I'd be ready. Before triathlon I was a middle-distance track runner." It was here that Stadler recalled Reid's dismissive prediction that he would never win Kona again.

A mile down the road, Macca had chopped the lead to 3:20. By the start of the long incline at mile 24 of the run, the margin was down to 1:45. "More than anything else I was focusing on staying loose," Stadler recounted. "I also had saved something for the last miles of the race."

As he had two years earlier, Stadler experienced the final yards on Ali'i Drive and each step up the finishing ramp as if in a whirlwind. After 8 hours 11 minutes 56 seconds, all of the pressure was lifted when he raised his fist in victory and let out a yell of liberation toward the heavens. Everything was that much more beautiful than it had been when he'd won the first time, he explained. A single victory was one thing, but to follow it up with another was harder and more satisfying.

Once again, caught up in his emotional breakthrough, Stadler made a mistake. When a native Hawaiian tried to present Stadler with the traditional Hawaiian maile lei victory wreath, Stadler threw it to the ground as if to say, "Take that!" The next day Stadler had to meet with a glum roomful of native Hawaiians to apologize profusely for his inadvertent insult to their traditions. Then, at a post-awards party thrown by *Triathlete* magazine, Stadler and runner-up McCormack got into a shouting match about perceived insults.

Just before the party McCormack saw an online interview on the *Triathlete* web site in which Stadler was quoted as saying, "You know Macca drafted. He was always in the pack. We all know he was cheating."

McCormack approached Stadler and said, "Normann, can I chat to you for a minute?"

Stadler said, "What is your problem?"

McCormack said, "Mate, you're saying some things about me. What's the go? If you got something to say, say it to my face."

"I never said anything."

McCormack showed Stadler the interview on a BlackBerry.

Stadler said, "The race was yesterday."

McCormack said, "I didn't have a problem with you yesterday. You beat me, man. You were incredible. But I have a problem with you now. Look, if I'm just a useless joke, then who did you beat, mate? You just beat up on a bunch of nobodies. I've raced you my whole career. I've kicked your ass more than you've ever beaten me. Come on, man! Give me that respect."

After the dustups, Stadler made peace with everyone. Macca said, "In 25 years' time, when we are talking about the fiftieth anniversary of Ironman, they will talk about Normann Stadler as one of the greatest ever. He broke that myth that no one could win Hawaii on the bike. He was the first to do it, and he is a beautiful, beautiful bike rider. And more, I love and respect his ego. I think that's why we clash. If you don't have an ego, you don't have any business out there. And I respect that he is a competitor and a winner."

Normann Stadler was proud—proud of himself and of his accomplishments. He showed what he was made of and need never prove himself again. But he still wanted to race for a few more years and to win as many events as he could.

In addition, he hoped that his success in the sport of triathlon would help to popularize it. He wanted to put a team together, as has always been done in cycling but had never really been done in triathlon. He also planned to draw from his Ironman career experiences to improve his future life. Goal-setting, perseverance, dealing with highs and lows, positive thinking—all of those things would be helpful in daily life. And someday, when he would no longer earn his living as a triathlete, he wanted to start a family. His own words would be the perfect guiding principle: "You have to love what you do."

In 2007 part of that dream came true as Stadler signed on with Dresdner-Kleinwort investment bank to head a super triathlon team that included stars Timo Bracht, Marino Vanhoenacker, and Mathias Hecht. Food poisoning ruined his 2007 defense at Hawaii. But after Commerzbank replaced Dresdner-Kleinwort in 2008, Stadler returned and led Kona until halfway on the run before fading with illness to an honorable 12th place.

In June 2009 Stadler found his greatest joy with the birth of his first child, which took the sting out of another frustrating DNF at Kona in October and may have signaled a tempering of the fire within. "My son is much bigger in my life than sport," he said. "Now I have more responsibilities for my boy. After hard training, you come home and he smiles and all the pain goes away."

SEVENTEEN | **CHRISSIE WELLINGTON**

"I never want to look back
on my life and wonder, 'What if?'"

A T MILE 72 of the bike course in 2007, a woman unknown
to even the most carefully prepared Ironman stars rode up
behind the women's main chase pack. Number 107—outfit-
ted with a borrowed bike; an old-fashioned, non-aero helmet; an
anonymous, black Lycra ensemble with modest-sized logos; and
dark shades—joined the lineup that included the sport's young coming stars: Kate Major, Joann Lawn, Rebecca Preston, Rebekah Keat
and Belinda Granger. Also in the pack was the highly touted rookie
Samantha McGlone, a 2004 Olympian and the 2006 Ironman 70.3
world champion. The veterans were rolling toward an eminently
respectable 5:10 bike split, unaware of the killer in their midst.

After the startling news that a bike crash that had taken out
six-time Ironman champion Natascha Badmann at mile 12 and the
withdrawal of defending champion Michellie Jones at mile 50 due
to the nausea caused by a recently perforated eardrum, the pack
sensed that one of them was ready to inherit the win. After a decade
of domination by Badmann, Lori Bowden, and Jones, "It looked like
there would be a changing of the guard," said Granger.

Many in the pack still expected Badmann to swoop down on
them with that beatific smile like an avenging angel, as she had done
for 11 years. But one competitor noticed the stranger. "Who is she?"
asked McGlone. "Can she run?"

Before McGlone could get an answer, Chrissie Wellington
seized the day. Wellington had suffered a 58-minute swim that
had left her unnoticed and smack in the middle of half-a-dozen of
those same favorites. She was a slow starter who took 20 miles to
warm up; by 30 miles she was still not among the top 10 women.
But by mile 72 the newcomer had arrived and faced a choice.
"At first I thought I should stick with them for a while," said

Wellington. "But the pace started to feel uncomfortable. I had more in the tank. So I took off, and I was quite happy to see they didn't come with me."

Ironman sages say the race doesn't start until mile 80 of the bike, and this was a textbook example. "I had vowed to ride my own race, and I wanted to be a little conservative on the bike to be sure I wouldn't blow up on the run," said McGlone. "I had trained to run a 3-hour marathon"—near the course record of Lori Bowden—"and I suspected [Wellington] would come back to me."

Twenty kilometers farther south along the Queen K, Wellington caught and passed the early leaders, a two-woman breakaway of Massachusetts's Dede Griesbauer and fellow Iron rookie Leanda Cave of Great Britain. "I couldn't believe I was leading, but I wasn't going to give it up without a fight," said Wellington, who charged to a race-best 5:06:15 bike split on a typically warm and windy day on the Kohala Coast. Wellington rode nowhere near Badmann's best 4:52 and far from Paula Newby-Fraser's record 4:48 bike split, but her time was good enough to carve out a 5-minute lead over Major, McGlone, and the rest of the surviving favorites.

If Wellington were then to run even a very fine 3:07 marathon, 6 minutes faster than Michellie Jones's winning run the year before and virtually equal to Badmann's best-ever Kona run, McGlone could still cash in on her instinct.

Just three years before Wellington had been a government bureaucrat pushing paper in London with a recently earned master's degree in international economic development. A self-described "sporty kid who loved soccer, netball, and running who was more interested in the social side of sport rather than exploring my limits," she tried a few local triathlons on a "10-year-old bike," wearing a bulky wetsuit that left her struggling to a 35-minute 1,500-meter swim. Frustrated with her job, she took a sabbatical to work for 18 months in Nepal, where she helped to develop a sanitary water supply system for some of the poorest people on earth.

"When I got back to England, I started work again, but thought I'd give triathlon a go," she said casually. On top of a 40-hour work week, she trained hard for the Shropshire Triathlon, qualified for ITU Worlds in Lausanne, and begged a British coach to guide her through eight weeks of "training like a beast." Just 14 months before her 2007 Kona debut, she won the ITU age-group women's overall title in a time that was 10 minutes slower than that of the elite pros.

Then she took a chance. She asked a world-famous coach to take her on, quit her latest office job when he agreed, and dedicated herself to a demanding regimen that took her from the mountains of Switzerland to the jungles of Thailand and the Philippines.

"When I came to Kona, I had no pressure because nobody knew who I was," said Wellington. "I was hoping for a top-10 finish. But never in a million years did I think I could possibly win it."

Running as if with winged feet, Ironman Hawaii rookie Chrissie Wellington hit the finish line with crowd-pleasing, contagious joy in 9:08:45, the ninth-fastest women's winning time in Ironman Hawaii history. She was faster than all but one of Badmann's six victories. Wellington's 2:59:58 marathon was the second-fastest women's run behind Lori Bowden's 2:59:16 marathon in 1999. Significantly, her run time was faster than anything the legends had ever mustered—greats such as Paula Newby-Fraser, Erin Baker, Heather Fuhr, and certified Ironman run speedsters such as Lisa Bentley and Kate Major. Wellington hit the finish nearly a mile ahead of McGlone and with $110,000 1st-place money in hand.

Just a day after her startling win, Wellington graciously said it was "a privilege to share the hallowed turf of Kona with the sport's legends and the world's best triathletes." But, she added, "I am not a hero. My heroes are the age groupers like [physically challenged] Scott Rigsby who have overcome so much to get to the finish line."

During a heartfelt awards speech, Wellington said, "I keep feeling like this was all a dream and I'll wake up and I won't really have raced and I won't really have won the Ironman World Championship. But then I feel the pain in my legs, and I definitely know I raced yesterday."

In January 2007, just before meeting the coach with the most formidable résumé in triathlon, Chrissie Wellington was nervous, excited, and filled with trepidation. She'd been briefed by friends about the controversial legend. On the plus side of the ledger, Brett Sutton had guided five separate women to ITU Olympic-distance World Championships. Sutton-coached women had also won Commonwealth Games gold, Life Time Fitness riches, two ITU long-course World Championship titles, and multiple Ironman 1st-place finishes. The scary part: old school. Drill sergeant. His critics, who are legion, say he gives his athletes an unholy workload that brings quick success followed by injuries and burnout.

And there was a question of character and conscience. A shameful incident in his past—he admitted to having had sexual relations with a teenaged girl whom he had coached a decade earlier—had made him an outcast in the eyes of many of the sport's leaders. Wellington said she weighed the sin against the rest of the man's life and got on the plane.

Arriving in Geneva on January 6, 2007, Wellington rode quiet Swiss trains to Sutton's training camp on the snow-covered mountain slopes of Leysin, high above the Rhône valley. Wellington was an unlikely candidate to join Sutton's squad of professionals. She was a government policy adviser on international development in Great Britain and a 30-year-old, late-blooming athlete who had done a mere half-dozen triathlons in her life. But that overall win at the ITU age-group championship four months before had given her the temerity to wonder how far she might take her gift.

Sutton knew Wellington posed a challenge. "When we spoke briefly over the phone," he recalled, "she told me, 'I want you to have a look and tell me if I'm wasting my time trying to make a living as a professional triathlete. I don't want bollocks. Just tell me the truth.'"

Sutton, a former boxing trainer, punched back. Immediately he said, "I don't know if you should come or not. I don't think you have the mind-set." Sutton explained, "I started the brainwashing that first phone call. I told her if she was set on making money, she was doing it for the wrong reasons. I said, 'You're not going to make it if you don't have a passion for it.' You'll find a time in a race when you're off form and running 10th or 12th place. If you're doing it for cash and not for love, a negative thought will go through your head and it will kill you, destroy you, and you'll never get back. It's particularly crucial in the Ironman, where there are six times in every race you enter a dark place of doubt and must have that passion to overcome."

Wellington said at that point "I didn't have that deep love for triathlon. But I did have a deep desire to be the best I can be at whatever I'm doing. I can't settle for mediocrity. And I never want to look back on my life and wonder, 'What if?'"

Wellington recalled in her blog how self-conscious she was during her first encounter with Sutton. "He was, I'm sure, casting his racehorse trainer's eye at my post-Christmas frame with mince pies, Christmas puddings, and ladles of brandy butter weighing heavy on my waistline." She was "incredibly nervous—I felt like I was walking on eggshells coming in. But when we met, he made me feel at ease. He was not a domineering person—he gave off a warm feeling, and he had really kind eyes. When I'd heard about this hard-nosed, brilliant dictator, I was thinking of a tall, bull-strong man. As it turned out, I was a bit taller, and it put me at ease."

Sutton's Team TBB of professional triathletes at the time was led by Olympian Andrew Johns, eventual 11-time Ironman-distance champion Belinda Granger, four-time Ironman champion Rebecca Preston, ITU long-course world champion Lisbeth Kristensen, soon-to-be two-time Ironman winner Stephen Bayliss, eventual eleven-time Ironman champion Bella Comerford, and young Brazilian phenom Reinaldo Collucci. As a whole, the team was a nomadic squad that floated in and out of Sutton's various training grounds in Switzerland, Thailand, Australia, Brazil, and the Philippines.

Monday started with a 7 a.m. set in the pool, where Sutton immediately went to work. "When she first took off her warm-ups and was down to her swimsuit, I saw she had a very strong lower body with a very weak little girl's upper body," says Sutton. Sutton told Wellington she was relying too much on her legs in the water and should immediately start using hand paddles and pull buoys to strengthen her upper body.

On Tuesday Sutton put Wellington through an hour-long treadmill session, starting with 10 minutes at a 12 kph pace before increasing to 14, 15, and 17 kph, with intervals of recovery and heart rate recorded at various times.

Although Sutton calls himself a "dinosaur" and scoffs at the use of high-tech biofeedback, he found it useful to discover that Wellington's heart rate range was wide, from 42 to 190 beats per minute. Wellington said Sutton told her she had "a high maximum heart rate that stays high even after the intensity declines and only falls off when I stop completely. The wide range is a positive, but when I hit the wall, I will be incapable of picking myself up again." His prescription? Start slowly, move up gradually, and don't surge. Save the redlining for late in the race.

Sutton immediately told Wellington, "You're a worrier. Your mind works a million miles an hour. And for this to work, you need to learn to switch it off and follow orders and not question everything."

His suggestion was a shock. "I am an incredibly independent person, and people have to earn my respect and earn the authority I give them," said Wellington. "I find it very difficult to put my ultimate trust in someone and follow without question. I wondered, 'Can I actually live like that? Can my mouth say, 'Yes, boss,' while my head says, 'Why?'"

On Wellington's third day in Leysin, Sutton had a chat with her. "He wanted to know about my job, my financial situation, my relationship history, my living arrangements, and so forth," Wellington wrote in her diary. "They all had a bearing on my mental and physical state and, hence, my training and performance. Brett continuously stressed the importance of mental strength. Am I determined? Can I remain calm and composed when things go wrong? Can I build on mistakes rather than dwell on them? Can I deal positively with injury rather than fearing it? Can I switch off and rest my mind as well as my body? If so, there are the makings of a great triathlete. If not, success will always be elusive."

In the middle of a bike workout later that day, Sutton startled Wellington with his words: "Chrissie, you've come here for a yes-or-no answer, haven't you?" said the Australian-born coach.

"I wanted him to say, 'Yes, you have what it takes,' or 'No, don't give up your job,' and based on that I'd follow his advice," said Wellington. "But he told me, 'Yes, you have the physical capabilities, and yes, I think I can work with you. But you need a lot of work on your mind.'"

Sutton was a quick study of Wellington's psychology. "Over the first three days, it struck me how highly strung she was psychologically," said Sutton. "She was all over the place mentally. She was a highly intelligent, strong personality, and we got into our first argument when she insisted on training harder. She wanted to show me how good she was. She said, 'I've only got seven days to make up my mind.' I told her, 'Physically, you can pack your bags and go home now and try to be a pro triathlete. Physically, I have no doubts, so there is no need to go on and smash yourself here. But what you find important to you now is not important to me. I see you have the interest to be a great athlete, and you have a mentality that can make you great, but you can kill yourself with expectations. Your drive and your will are all wonderful things—if channeled in the right area. If it's not channeled, it will pull you to pieces."

Three years before she started training with Sutton, Wellington didn't know what triathlon was. A county-level high school swimmer and a onetime 3:08 marathoner, she'd spent most of her 20s trekking around the world to adventurous places. During her time in Nepal, she made a three-week, 1,300-km trek on a mountain bike with some hardy local lads from Katmandu, climbing a total of 10,000 feet to the Mount Everest base camp.

When she left Nepal, Wellington decided to take the long way home. She entered the famed New Zealand Speight's Coast to Coast Multisport Race and finished second in the solo division. Next she won a small off-road triathlon in Argentina. A few weeks after returning home to Great Britain, she qualified for the 2006 ITU amateur World Championship at the Shropshire Triathlon outside London.

At the ITU Worlds in Lausanne, although suffering from a stress fracture in her foot that had limited her training runs to a maximum of 20 minutes, Wellington emerged from a "shocking" bad swim, charged the challenging hills on her bike, and hung on in the run to win the overall amateur title by a 4-minute margin.

A man in the shadows spotted Wellington amid the chaotic anonymity of multiwave starts. "I saw how strong she was on the bike and how she did a solid job on the run," said Sutton. "I thought that either the rest of them were so bad or she was that good."

Now enrolled with Sutton in Leysin, "I found it incredibly difficult initially," said Wellington. "I had this naive image in my mind that it would be like training at university, where everyone was friendly and we all got on and laughed and joked. It was not like that. I felt very much the new girl, very much like the rest of the athletes didn't want me to be there and that they would go out of their way to make life difficult."

Wellington took much of the blame. "Part of it I brought on myself," she said. "I was very keen and eager and always gave 120 percent because I wanted to show myself, them, and Brett that I wasn't just some age grouper. I tried too hard to be liked, and I tried too hard to show I was tough."

Sutton didn't intervene. "Brett hardly spoke to me," she recalled. "He didn't give me any special attention. Almost the opposite—he let it run its course and let me cope with the hard times. The boys would make nasty comments, and he saw it all, but he didn't stop it."

Although Wellington was unaware of his motives, Sutton was simultaneously hardening and protecting her. "She was a bit opinionated and a bit soft, so I put her in with the boys," said Sutton. "I knew she was tough from day one, but the guys would knock her about a little bit and take the mickey out of her."

Sutton saw more promise in Wellington after two races. At the ITU long-course World Championship in France in July, Wellington ran a sparkling 1:12:14 20-km run (equivalent to a 1:17 half-marathon and equal to the best time of any woman triathlete) to finish 5th. At the Alpe d'Huez Triathlon in August, Wellington overcame a 13-minute deficit from a flat tire and a crash on the bike to finish the ride 19 minutes in the lead. Then she blazed through a tough, hilly run at altitude and added 11 minutes to her margin of victory. "I thought, *Oh my God, this girl is unbelievable*," said Sutton. "*She needs to qualify for Hawaii this year!*"

Sutton suggested Wellington race Ironman Korea in August. "When I told her she should go to Korea, she looked shocked," said Sutton. "But without much pause, she said, 'If you say so, I'd love to give it a go.' Then I knew she was ready."

There was one more test before she got to the starting line in Korea on August 26. "It was raining, and I was walking down some steps to the pool when I slipped and fell hard on my coccyx," she said. "It was a week before Korea, and I could not run and I could not walk, and I took two days off to rest."

She told Sutton, "I can't run, and it hurts to swim, and it hurts to bike."

He said, "There's no question—you're going."

Before the race, although she could not run a step, she decided to swim and bike and see how she felt. "The conservative goal was to make the top four and qualify for Hawaii," said Sutton. "I was pretty sure she was bruised and not injured."

On an extremely hot, windy day, although she had some pain running in the first transition, Wellington finished Ironman Korea 50 minutes ahead of the 2nd-place woman and only 40 minutes behind the proven Ironman men's star Raynard Tissink. Her 3:28 run—good under the conditions but unimpressive on paper—didn't get on anyone's radar before Kona.

After Korea Sutton knew Wellington had the potential for greatness; all he had to do was keep the pressure off. When Wellington asked him if she should aim at a 3:10 marathon, he told her, "You're aiming too high. Let's think about 3:15 and work on it." He kept what he was really thinking to himself. "If she had a good day, I was looking at 3:05," recalled Sutton. "If you tell them they should run 3 hours flat and they see splits for 3:02 during the race, it fills them with negative thoughts. A lot of coaches will lie and tell their athletes they are ready to have the race of their lives, and it kills them when they cannot meet those expectations." That, Sutton continued, "is why I never lie to my athletes. When I tell them they are ready to make a podium or have a great race, I mean it and they can believe it."

Sutton held a key workout for Wellington a week and a half before Hawaii. "It went very well," said Wellington. "He told me I was in fantastic shape, that I had done all I could and was ready." He didn't tell her anything about the numbers and what they meant, and she didn't ask.

Sutton gave Wellington a note to read once she got to Hawaii. It read, "Don't defer to anybody. Race your own race and don't be scared. These people aren't as great as they think you think they are. Everybody is beatable."

And everybody was.

In her first try at Ironman Hawaii, Chrissie Wellington had had the rookie good manners to wait until mile 80 of the bike before putting her stamp on the race. But the 2008-model Chrissie Wellington charged along the Queen Ka'ahumanu Highway without any deference whatsoever. Wellington emerged from the waters of Kailua Bay less than 5 minutes behind the women's leaders and just 2 minutes behind an aggressive pack of strong riders, including her Team TBB teammate Hilary Biscay, Gina Kehr, Dede Griesbauer, comeback pro Nina Kraft, and 2002 short-course world champion Leanda Cave. In contrast to her stealth performance of 2007, Wellington carved up the last of the contenders by mile 20.

Although she had sailed through the bike during the atypically mild weather of 2007, this time Wellington faced Kona's famously daunting winds. They only added to her advantage. She had a 9-minute lead just a few miles from Hawi, the midpoint turn-around of the 112-mile bike. The only questions that remained were akin to guessing whether Secretariat would win by 30 or 31 lengths, not whether or not there would be a duel to the line. The only anticipation centered on by how much she could crack 5 hours for the bike and whether she could top Paula Newby-Fraser's 1992 course record of 8:55:28.

Then Madame Pele tested the Wellington Express. A puncture took the air out of her tire, and the 31-year-old prohibitive favorite pulled over in front of a peaceful grass field and faced reality.

"I thought, *Oh, bugger! My parents flew in from England and I might not even finish the race!*" recalled Wellington. A flat tire during Ironman Hawaii is not the minor issue that it is in the Tour de France. In the Tour, one of several technical support vans would be waiting with a mechanic and a new wheel—just 30 seconds lost. By contrast, Ironman Hawaii has only one technical support van, and it shadows the men's leader only.

With a can-do spirit, Wellington replaced the tube in her clincher tire and inserted two air cartridges. Both failed to launch. "I obviously failed to use them properly," said Wellington. "But what can you do? Panic? Get angry and sit beside the road and cry? My coach always says, 'You get a flat, you deal with it. It's not over until it's over.'"

Once her air canister failed, Wellington took stock and decided to multitask, urinating behind a nearby bush and calmly ignoring the NBC cameras. Then she stood beside the road, waving her wheel like a hitchhiker as five very surprised rivals sped past, including Team TBB teammate Belinda Granger, who pedaled on.

"I might have been stranded there until I'd be finishing with a glow stick," said Wellington later. "But then something happened that is the epitome of Ironman. Bek [Australian Rebekah Keat] stopped and gave me her spare cartridge. If not for her, I might not have finished the race."

Aussie Keat, who had finished 6th the previous year, didn't think of herself as a Saint Bernard rescuing an avalanche victim. "I just thought she's probably going to beat me anyway," said Keat. Finding better inflation technique, Wellington got the air into the tire and took off.

Once going, Wellington virtually skipped up to the Hawi turn-around and put the hammer down on the high-speed downhill dash back to Kawaihae. Bracing herself at full speed through the white-knuckle side gusts like a rodeo bronc-buster, Wellington cruised past Granger for the lead at Kawaihae and never looked back.

In the end it was Wellington's day. Underscoring the fact that she may have come to the Ironman party late in the usual athletic life but was never a fluke, Wellington crossed the line with a personal record of 9:06:23—the sixth fastest time ever—and broke Lori Bowden's Ironman Hawaii marathon record with a blazing 2:57:44. By most estimates, Wellington was parked with her flat tire for 10 minutes. Playing the if-only game, an incident-free bike leg would have made her race a finish-line dash with Newby-Fraser's record time of 8:55:28. But Wellington's sights were set even higher. At the rain-soaked, abridged awards ceremony Sunday night, Mark Allen said he wondered if Wellington would have broken 8:50 if she had not been brought to earth by the flat.

When Wellington was asked before the race if she could run faster than her near-record 2:59:58, she said "Absolutely!"

If conditions are good, what could her pace be?

"Two fifty-one!"

In 2009 Wellington continued her incredible string of Ironman success, breaking 9 hours to win Ironman Australia and shattering the world record for the Ironman distance with an astounding 8:31:59 overall time at Quelle Challenge Roth. On that day Wellington also shattered the best women's Ironman bike split with a time of 4:40:28.

There were brief bumps in the road. She left Sutton and Team TBB to take greater advantage of sponsorship opportunities. She briefly signed on with Samantha McGlone's fiancé and coach, Cliff English, before switching to fellow Brit and five-time ITU world champion Simon Lessing. But by midsummer Wellington decided to coach herself with the input of a few trusted advisers. Outsiders fervently wished she had learned Sutton's lesson not to indulge her penchant for overwork.

While the only hint of vulnerability was her loss to Xterra world and Ironman 70.3 world champion Julie Dibens at the Boulder 5430 half-Ironman, Wellington was rested and perfectly prepared for her third Kona. With no flat tires to give the crowds a thrill, Wellington gave a historic performance. After an eighth-best 54:31 swim, Wellington started the bike just 4 minutes down on leader Lucie Zelenkova and mowed through all the contenders by the Keahole Airport, just 15 miles into the leg. Although she had to grit her teeth when the shifting mumukus threw headwinds on both the outbound and inbound legs, Wellington arrived in transition with a 4:52:06 split, the sixth best ever recorded and 9 minutes faster than next-best woman Virginia Berasategui. At that point Wellington's lead was 11 minutes on Tereza Macel, 13 minutes on Berasategui, and 26 minutes on the most formidable runners, Mirinda Carfrae and Keat.

Perhaps most telling, when she passed course observers, Wellington asked, "What's the gap to the men?"

Possibly depleted by that bike, Wellington actually gave back 5 minutes and the race run record to runner-up Carfrae. But her 3:03:05 run was good enough to finish in 8:54:02, topping Newby-Fraser's 1992 record by 1 minute 26 seconds. Wellington's overall margin of victory was a stunning 19:57—nearly a 20-minute gap on second place. She was just 33 minutes 41 seconds slower than men's winner Craig Alexander, making her historic feat the second-smallest women's-to-men's winner margin in Ironman Hawaii history. She trailed only Paula Newby-Fraser's 30 minutes 1 second margin behind 1988 men's winner Scott Molina.

Wellington was not so overcome with elation that she forgot her predecessor's greatness. While still catching her breath at the finish, Wellington told the crowd and announcer Mike Reilly, "I never thought I'd come here and break Paula's record. I feel kind of guilty doing it. I had to dig so hard to do it."

While all the record numbers she has posted have been amazing, the primary impression of Chrissie Wellington has been not so much her quantum leap in Ironman performance as her devotion to making the world a better place. She told IronmanLive.com's Kevin McKinnon about a conversation she had with Sutton when she started. "I remember saying to Brett, 'I feel so selfish. All I do is swim, bike, and run, and this is all for me. I am not helping make the world a better place.' And he replied, 'Chrissie, just you wait. Before too long you will be able to effect change in a way you never thought possible.'"

Some triathlon observers joked with more than a kernel of truth that there was a greater chance that Wellington would run for prime minister of Great Britain than stick around long enough to match Newby-Fraser's eight wins at Kona.

But for the moment, Wellington does not step on any pedestals. Instead she keeps a vow to honor the legacy of the late Jon Blais, the Ironman who battled amyotrophic lateral sclerosis (ALS) and raises money to fund research for a cure. "I was struck by Jon's determination, strength, drive, and passion despite suffering from the disease that was his life sentence. He was selfless to a fault, driven by a desire to help so that others may live. I decided then I would toll across the finish line after every race that I did, regardless of whether I won or not, as a symbol of my support for everything Jon was and for the ALS Blazeman Foundation established in his memory."

APPENDIX A: YOUR IRONMAN STORY

"You are an Ironman!" announcer Mike Reilly calls year after year to triathletes as they cross the Ironman Hawaii finish line. Every one of them, whether a pro whose race costs are covered or a recreational athlete who has paid thousands of dollars for travel expenses and entry fees, experiences some kind of joy or relief—or both—in that moment. Whether the athletes have reached their goals, fallen short of them, or exceeded them beyond their wildest dreams, they are all filled with a sense of pride, from the winner, who takes approximately 8 hours, to the last official finisher, who must cross the finish line on Ali'i Drive within 17 hours of the official start.

Prior to success, an enormous amount of effort is required. In contrast to a marathon, in which most athletes encounter a low point between miles 20 and 24 that they must overcome, triathletes often experience multiple moments of crisis over the course of the long event. On Ironman day they must give it their all; no one crosses the lava fields of Kona's coastline halfheartedly. Finishers in Hawaii must traverse and master many highs and lows before—in one sweet moment—all of their struggles and suffering are forgotten.

Ironman is a metaphor for life. As with everything else, work comes before success. It pays to set goals, be disciplined, work on one's weaknesses, overcome setbacks, and avoid being diverted from one's charted course.

Spectators can only imagine the price participants have paid to reach the finish at the foot of the Kailua-Kona pier, but no one leaves without being touched in some way. Behind every laughing face and every shout of joy is a story, and any of these stories can thrill, motivate, inspire, and give others the courage to make their own dreams come true.

For many observers, such effort puts the sanity of these triathletes in question. Ironically, many of the Ironman Hawaii finishers shared that perspective only a few years or even months before their own first participation. Conquering an Ironman may once have seemed impossible, pure fiction, nothing more than a dream. But dreams can be powerful things.

No one can stop you from wondering what it would be like to take part in such an event. And wondering often represents the first step; before you know it, you are slowly inching closer to the realization of a dream. Nothing is impossible!

When, dear reader, does your story begin?

—*Mathias Müller*

APPENDIX B: IRONMAN HAWAII HISTORY

Triathlon was not invented in Hawaii. Credit is usually given to Americans Jack Johnstone and Don Shanahan. On September 25, 1974, these members of the San Diego Track Club organized the first Mission Bay Triathlon on Fiesta Island in San Diego. The event was designed as an amusing cross-training workout for runners. The race began with a 5-mile bike, followed by multiple run-swim segments totaling 10 kilometers of running and 500 meters of swimming. Forty-six athletes lined up for the start of this first-ever triathlon, with finish times ranging from 0:55:44 to 1:34:51.

The sport of triathlon became widely known through Ironman Hawaii, which was first held on February 18, 1978, on Oahu. It arose from a discussion between athletes at the awards ceremony for the 1977 Oahu Perimeter Relay Run at Primo Gardens in Pearl City; they were debating which endurance athletes—swimmers, cyclists, or runners—were the most physically fit. John Collins, a U.S. Navy commander and one of the participants in that first Mission Bay Triathlon, took part in the discussion and suggested that three of the local single-discipline events be combined. Said and done: They agreed to combine the Waikiki Rough Water Swim course (2.4 miles), the Around Oahu Bike Race (115 miles, from which they cut 3 miles to make the transitions work; thus, 112 miles), and the Honolulu Marathon (26.2 miles). The winner of the race would be called the Iron Man.

1978: The Premier

Fifteen participants took part in the first race to cover the seemingly insane distance of 140.6 miles. Twelve of them made it to the finish. The fastest man, and therefore the world's first Ironman, was American Gordon Haller, a competitive marathoner who made a living driving a taxi. He crossed the finish line in 11:46:58, 33 minutes 29 seconds ahead of early leader John Dunbar, a former navy SEAL.

1979: The First Female Starter

Word of mouth increased registered participants to 50. But when the event was postponed one day because of rough seas, only 15 willing athletes ended up contesting the race. Thirty-five-year-old Tom Warren, a tavern owner from San Diego, California, won with a time of 11:15:56. Lyn Lemaire, a cyclist from Boston, was the first female to start an Ironman, and she finished 5th against the male competition. A 10-page article in *Sports Illustrated*, written by Barry McDermott, brought widespread attention to the race for the first time.

1980: Enter TV, the Man, and Growing Popularity

In no small part due to the May 14, 1979, *Sports Illustrated* article, 108 athletes—two of them women—signed up for the event. Dave Scott, a 26-year-old masters swim instructor from Davis, California, won that year in 9:24:33—a quantum leap in the race's athletic standards, finishing 1 hour ahead of runner-up Chuck Neumann. The fastest woman was Robin Beck, who placed 12th overall with a time of 11:21:24. Intrigued by McDermott's *Sports Illustrated* article, ABC's *Wide World of Sports* broadcast a segment on the event. As a result, more triathlons of varying distances were organized in other locations.

1981: Move to the Big Island

When U.S. Navy commander John Collins was transferred to Washington, D.C., he handed over organization of the race to Valerie Silk, the wife of the owner of a Honolulu Nautilus Fitness Center who sponsored the event. She moved the race from touristy Waikiki Beach in Honolulu and the dangerously overcrowded two-lane roads around Oahu to Kailua-Kona on the Big Island. The hot and forbidding lava fields of the archipelago's largest island transformed the race into a struggle between athletes and the elements. Thus, a stage of natural grandeur, befitting the legendary physical challenge of Ironman Hawaii, was established. Silk also instituted the rule that that year's 326 athletes would no longer be allowed to provide their own support crews and vehicles and would instead be served at designated aid stations manned by volunteers. Four-time national cycling champion and Olympian John Howard won the race in 9:38:29. In the women's field, Linda Sweeney won with a time of 12:00:32. The oldest finisher, 73-year-old Walt Stack, a member of San Francisco's Dolphin Club, finished last in 26:20:00, earning the distinction of the slowest-ever recorded Ironman finish.

1982 (February): Julie Moss's Dramatic Finish

The number of participants doubled. In the men's race, a 25-year-old lifeguard and emergency medical technician from San Diego, Scott Tinley, won, beating Dave Scott with a time of 9:19:41. But the impact of Tinley's victory was eclipsed by the women's race. Cal Poly University senior Julie Moss led the competition by 20 minutes before collapsing due to dehydration with the finish in sight. When she tried to get up, her legs gave out. With unflagging determination she began crawling, only to see Kathleen McCartney pass her with only a few yards to go. The *Wide World of Sports* television broadcast of Moss's stirring finish made Ironman Hawaii famous throughout the world. The same went for Moss, who became a source of motivation for thousands of athletes.

1982 (October): The Second of Two

In order to give athletes from colder climates a better chance to train and participate, the race was moved to October. The first cutoff was also introduced, requiring participants to finish in 18 hours 30 minutes. From that point until 2000, the race was scheduled to be held during a full moon to help light the way for those who finished in the dark. Dave Scott, who had finished 2nd in February, avenged his previous year's loss to Scott Tinley by 20 minutes with a time of 9:08:23. Julie Leach, a 25-year old Olympic kayaker, won the women's race in 10:54:08.

1983: The First Qualifier

With registration for the Kona event skyrocketing, the Ricoh U.S. Ironman Championship was held in Los Angeles in May, and top finishers there earned qualifying slots for Ironman Hawaii. Also for the first time, starting slots were awarded by lottery to give recreational athletes the opportunity to compete alongside the best triathletes in the world. The cutoff time was decreased to 17 hours—selected in part because that was how long Ironman founder John Collins, who considered himself an "everyman," took to finish the race. Dave Scott won his third title with a time of 9:05:57, finishing just 33 seconds before Scott Tinley. Canadian Sylviane Puntous won the women's title and became the first participant from outside the United States to win the event.

1984: Scott Strikes a Fourth Time

Dave Scott, by then known in triathlon circles as The Man, became the first athlete to break the 9-hour barrier with a record time of 8:54:20. In the women's field, Sylviane Puntous took a hard-fought second victory with a time of 10:25:13, just 2 minutes 15 seconds ahead of her twin sister, Patricia.

1985: Multiculturalism and Aero Bars

Triathletes from 34 different countries took the start in Kailua-Kona. Scott Tinley won and set a new course record of 8:50:54 in the absence of Dave Scott and several stars who chose to compete instead in the Nice International Triathlon with its large prize purse. Scott worked as a television commentator at the event. Tinley was the first triathlete to use aerodynamic clip-on handlebar extensions;

he also wore aerodynamic shoe covers. Californian Joanne Ernst won the women's race in 10:25:22. The first international qualifying events were held in New Zealand and Japan.

1986: Prize Money

An anonymous benefactor donated $100,000 in prize money, and Dave Scott bested the previous course record by more than 20 minutes with a time of 8:28:37, beating challenger Mark Allen by 7 minutes 37 seconds. Patricia Puntous, twin sister of two-time winner Sylviane, was the first woman to cross the finish line but was disqualified for drafting in the bike segment. Paula Newby-Fraser from Zimbabwe was awarded victory with a time of 9:49:14. Another international qualifying Ironman was organized in Canada.

1987: Scott's Sixth

With 1,381 athletes from 44 countries, Ironman was once and for all an internationally acclaimed event. Dave Scott won his sixth and last title with a time of 8:34:13, topping Mark Allen by 11 minutes. In the women's race Kiwi Erin Baker wrested the win away from defending champion Paula Newby-Fraser with a new record time of 9:35:25.

1988: Queen of Kona

Paula Newby-Fraser won the women's race in spectacular fashion with a time of 9:01:01, which broke the course record by 34 minutes. With her grand performance, Newby-Fraser earned the nickname "Queen of Kona." Dave Scott withdrew from the race due to a knee problem the day before the start. Scott Molina took advantage of the defending champion's absence and defeated fellow contender Mark Allen, who suffered mechanical troubles on the bike, with a time of 8:31:00. Ironman Europe in Roth near Nuremberg, Germany, marked the fourth official international qualifying event.

1989: The Iron War

The two best triathletes in the world battled toe-to-toe for over 8 hours in this race. Not until the final hill on the outskirts of town was Mark Allen able to get away and win his first Ironman world championship with a record-shattering time of 8:09:15, just 58 seconds ahead of Dave Scott. While breaking his six-year streak of bad luck and injury, Allen ran the marathon in 2:40:04—still the all-time best run split. Paula Newby-Fraser took her third title in 9:00:56.

1990: Course Modification

Dr. Jim Gills bought the Ironman from Valerie Silk and founded the World Triathlon Corporation (WTC). The course was modified so that the marathon course included a right turn from the bike exit at the Kona Surf Hotel to the south end of Ali'i Drive into a low area called the Pit, placing the out-and-back turnaround point inside the Natural Energy Lab of Hawaii (NELH). Mark Allen won his second title, in the absence of an injured Dave Scott, by an 11-minute margin over Scott Tinley with a time of 8:28:17. In the women's competition Erin Baker finished in 9:13:42, 7 minutes ahead of Paula Newby-Fraser, winning in Hawaii for the second time.

1991: Allen's Third

Mark Allen, known by his triathlon rivals as the Grip, won his third straight Ironman Hawaii title in 8:18:32. In the women's race Paula Newby-Fraser won her fourth title and evened her Kona record against Erin Baker at 2-2 with a time of 9:07:52. Out of 1,379 starters, 1,312 reached the finish, an all-time high finishing percentage.

1992: Newby-Fraser Breaks the Nine-Hour Barrier

The 30-year-old California resident won for the fifth time with a time of 8:55:28, beating her previous best time by almost 5 minutes with a dominating 26-minute margin over runner-up Julie-Anne

White. Mark Allen won his fourth straight title, breaking his own men's course record with a time of 8:09:08.

1993: Favorites Repeat

Paula Newby-Fraser left Erin Baker behind once again, finishing in 8:58:23. It was the Queen of Kona's sixth win, matching Dave Scott's record. In the men's race, Jürgen Zäck of Koblenz, Germany, set a new course record in the bike segment with a time of 4:27:42. His competitors, however, were not much slower; by the end of the marathon he was only fifth overall. Mark Allen passed Finland's Pauli Kiuru in the seventeenth mile of the marathon, earning his fifth straight title with a new best time of 8:07:45.

1994: Dave Scott's Comeback

At 40 years old, The Man launched a comeback. At first dismissed by his rivals, he waged a riveting racelong battle against Greg Welch and ultimately finished 2nd by 4 minutes. With Mark Allen taking a hiatus from racing Kona, Welch took his first win on his seventh try with a time of 8:20:27 and became the first Australian winner. Paula Newby-Fraser won in 9:20:14, taking her seventh title, an all-time Ironman Hawaii record.

1995: Mark Allen Equals Dave Scott

After a year off Mark Allen was looking to end his career in honorable fashion. Young German Thomas Hellriegel did all he could to undermine Allen's comeback with a masterful performance on the bike in his Ironman Hawaii debut. The German started the marathon with a 13-minute 31-second lead. Allen was forced to give it his all in a thrilling chase that produced a marathon split of 2:42:09, securing his sixth victory with a time of 8:20:34. After a long stint in the lead, Paula Newby-Fraser completely ran out of energy and was passed by Massachusetts's Karen Smyers 600 yards from the finish. Smyers, who overcame Newby-Fraser's 11-minute

47-second lead off the bike with a 3:05:20 run, won in 9:16:46. Newby-Fraser, who sat on a curb for 20 minutes to gather her strength, walked in to finish 4th.

1996: Van Lierde Sets Course Record in First Attempt
Twenty-seven-year-old Luc Van Lierde surprised the triathlon world by winning Ironman Hawaii in his first attempt. Despite serving a 3-minute penalty for drafting on the bike, he caught leader Thomas Hellriegel 3 miles from the finish and set a still-standing race record of 8:04:08. Paula Newby-Fraser took her eighth title in 9:06:49 following an exciting duel with Swiss rookie Natascha Badmann, who took 2nd, just 4 minutes 30 seconds behind. At Ironman Europe in Roth, Germany, Lothar Leder was the first to break the 8-hour barrier with a time of 7:57:02.

1997: The First German Victory
After two heroic 2nd-place finishes, Thomas Hellriegel finally scored a victory. In strong winds along the bike course, Hellriegel and Jürgen Zäck were able to ride away from everyone else. But on the run Hellriegel broke away with a winning marathon. With Zäck finishing 2nd and Lothar Leder 3rd, it was an all-German podium. When Paula Newby-Fraser dropped out at mile 17 of the run, her neighbor and training partner Heather Fuhr took over the lead and outdueled fellow Canadian Lori Bowden in a winning time of 9:31:43. At Ironman Europe in Roth, Germany, Luc Van Lierde set a still-standing all-time record for the fastest time ever achieved by an athlete at an Ironman event with a time of 7:50:27.

1998: Windy Anniversary
It was the twentieth anniversary of Ironman Hawaii, and the *mumuku* winds blew hard. Thomas Hellriegel and 29-year-old Canadian Peter Reid rode away on the bike. But in the concluding marathon, Hellriegel faded to 8th and Reid ran away from the charge of

Luc Van Lierde and won his first title in 8:24:20. Swiss Natascha Badmann took her first win with a time of 9:24:16. Several of Ironman's original 15 entrants were there to celebrate its anniversary, including race founder John Collins, who reached the finish in 16:30:02, and Gordon Haller, winner of the first Ironman Hawaii, who finished in 14:27:01.

1999: Luc Van Lierde Once Again

The Belgian won his second Ironman Hawaii in 8:17:17, three years after his first victory. In the women's race, Canadian Lori Bowden won after posting a new best run time of 2:59:16 and an overall time of 9:13:02, besting runner-up Karen Smyers by 7 minutes.

2000: Stadler Leads, Reid Wins

Another year of fierce winds. Twenty-seven-year-old German Normann Stadler attempted to take advantage of the adverse conditions on his bike. After starting the marathon with a 3-minute lead he was reeled in by Peter Reid, who won with a time of 8:21:00, and then by American Tim DeBoom. Stadler finished 3rd in 8:26:44. Natascha Badmann took her second title in the women's race with a time of 9:26:16.

2001: America Again

After a six-year drought for the U.S. men, American Tim DeBoom won with a time of 8:31:18. New Zealander Cameron Brown came in second, 15 minutes later. In the women's race Natascha Badmann took her third title in 9:28:37, crossing the line with her trademark smile.

2002: Badmann and DeBoom for a Second Straight Year

Despite a superhuman effort in the bike segment, which Thomas Hellriegel completed nearly 10 minutes faster than Tim DeBoom, the German had to content himself with 4th place. DeBoom took his second win in a row with a time of 8:29:56. After 53 minutes, German Nina Kraft came out of the water with a big lead over the field. Following the bike segment, however, Natascha Badmann once again played her trump card with a race-best 4:52:26 split, winning her fourth title in 9:07:54.

2003: Reid's Third Title

Normann Stadler rode away in the bike segment and clocked a race-best split of 4:33:40. Once again, however, Stadler faded on the run as Peter Reid stormed to his third win with a time of 8:22:55. In the women's race, Nina Kraft led for quite a while, but a penalty for drafting on the bike put her 34 seconds behind Natascha Badmann starting the run. There they were both caught by Lori Bowden's typically swift 3:02:10 marathon. The Canadian won with a time of 9:11:55. Badmann finished 2nd, outdueling Nina Kraft by 8 seconds.

2004: Stadler's Tour de Force

Normann Stadler, nicknamed the Normannator for his prowess on the bike, rode away from the entire field and began the marathon with a 20-minute lead. Despite an excellent run split of 2:46:10, three-time champion Peter Reid fell 10 minutes short and Stadler won his first iron-distance world championship title in 8:33:29. When Nina Kraft reached the finish several miles ahead of Natascha Badmann, it seemed like a German sweep. However, Kraft tested positive for the performance-enhancing drug EPO and was disqualified. Badmann was subsequently named the winner with a time of 9:50:04.

2005: A Third Men's Title for Germany

Twenty-seven-year-old Faris Al-Sultan showed his strength with impressive performances in all three disciplines. At the front virtually from start to finish, he won his first Ironman world championship with a time of 8:14:17. The seemingly unstoppable Natascha Badmann took her sixth title in the women's race in 9:09:30.

2006: Stadler Dominates Again

Normann Stadler blasted to a big lead with a record split of 4:18:23 over the 112-mile bike course and began the marathon with a lead of 10 minutes over Australian Chris McCormack. The Aussie pushed close to the German but couldn't catch him. Stadler won in 8:11:56. Stadler's winning margin of 1 minute 11 seconds represented the third-closest men's finish in the history of Ironman Hawaii. Faris Al-Sultan finished 3rd with a time of 8:19:04. Aussie Michellie Jones, runner-up the previous year, won the women's race in 9:18:31.

2007: McCormack Victorious, Wellington Upsets

After five futile attempts for the title and a 2nd-place finish in 2006, Chris McCormack finally claimed victory with a time of 8:15:34. The man called "Macca" passed American supercyclist Chris Lieto at mile 13 of the marathon and became the first Australian male to win a title in Kona since 1994. After a relatively unimpressive winning time at Ironman Korea, dark-horse rookie Chrissie Wellington became the first-ever British athlete to win the Ironman World Championship with a time of 9:08:45. She took the lead 80 miles into the bike and dominated the run with a sub-3-hour marathon. More than 1,780 competitors crossed the finish line, ranging in age from 18 to 78.

2008: Crowie Succeeds Macca

A year after finishing 2nd at his Ironman Hawaii debut, Craig "Crowie" Alexander advanced from 11th off the bike to first at the line with a 2:45:00 marathon. Alexander passed Spaniard Eneko Llanos, American Chris Lieto, and German Normann Stadler by the end of the Energy Lab and won his first Ironman World Championship in 8:17:45. Chrissie Wellington's flat tire and the momentary uncertainty whether she would get it inflated provided much of the drama in the women's race. When gracious Aussie Rebekah Keat helped Wellington get back into the race by dropping her an air cartridge,

Wellington rallied from that 10-minute stop and led the race heading into T2. The Brit then posted the fastest women's run split to that date (2:57:44), taking her second title by a margin of 14 minutes 57 seconds in 9:06:23.

2009: Chrissie Tops Paula's Record

Defending champion Craig Alexander came to win and did not disappoint, despite an all-out bid for victory by Chris Lieto that put the feared cyclist (who would post the fastest bike split) out front for much of the day. Many thought Lieto might just hold on to the lead he held going into T2, but Crowie did what he had already done twice that season and ran down Lieto at mile 21 of the marathon, becoming only the fourth male athlete to repeat at Ironman Hawaii. In the women's race Great Britain's Chrissie Wellington broke Paula Newby-Fraser's 17-year-old course record with a time of 8:54:02 to take her third straight victory at the World Championships.

APPENDIX C: IRONMAN HAWAII FACTS & FIGURES

Source: World Triathlon Corporation

Men's Winning Times (1978–2009)

Year	Name	Swim	Bike	Run	Overall Time
2009	Craig Alexander	50:57	4:37:33	2:48:05	8:20:21
2008	Craig Alexander	51:43	4:37:19	2:45:01	8:17:45
2007	Chris McCormack	51:48	4:37:32	2:42:02	8:15:34
2006	Normann Stadler	54:05	4:18:23	2:55:03	8:11:56
2005	Faris Al-Sultan	49:54	4:25:24	2:54:51	8:14:17
2004	Normann Stadler	54:27	4:37:58	2:57:53	8:33:29
2003	Peter Reid	50:36	4:40:04	2:47:38	8:22:35
2002	Timothy DeBoom	52:02	4:45:21	2:50:22	8:29:56
2001	Timothy DeBoom	52:01	4:48:17	2:45:54	8:31:18
2000	Peter Reid	51:45	4:39:32	2:48:10	8:21:00
1999	Luc Van Lierde	50:38	4:41:26	2:42:46	8:17:17
1998	Peter Reid	52:04	4:42:23	2:47:31	8:24:20
1997	Thomas Hellriegel	53:08	4:47:57	2:51:56	8:33:01
1996	Luc Van Lierde	51:36	4:30:44	2:41:48	8:04:08*
1995	Mark Allen	51:50	4:46:35	2:42:09	8:20:34
1994	Greg Welch	50:22	4:41:07	2:48:58	8:20:27
1993	Mark Allen	50:40	4:29:00	2:48:05	8:07:45
1992	Mark Allen	51:27	4:35:23	2:42:18	8:09:08
1991	Mark Allen	50:14	4:46:07	2:42:09	8:18:32
1990	Mark Allen	51:43	4:43:45	2:52:48	8:28:17
1989	Mark Allen	51:17	4:37:52	2:40:04	8:09:15
1988	Scott Molina	51:28	4:36:50	3:02:42	8:31:00
1987	Dave Scott	50:57	4:53:48	2:49:26	8:34:13
1986	Dave Scott	50:53	4:48:32	2:49:11	8:28:37
1985	Scott Tinley	55:13	4:54:07	3:01:33	8:50:54
1984	Dave Scott	50:21	5:10:49	2:53:00	8:54:20
1983	Dave Scott	50:52	5:10:48	3:04:16	9:05:57
1982	Dave Scott**	50:52	5:10:16	3:07:15	9:08:23
1982	Scott Tinley**	1:10:45	5:05:11	3:03:45	9:19:41
1981	John Howard	1:11:12	5:03:29	3:23:48	9:38:29
1980	Dave Scott	51:00	5:03:00	3:50:33	9:24:33
1979	Tom Warren	1:06:15	6:19:00	3:51:00	11:15:56
1978	Gordon Haller	1:20:40	6:56:00	3:30:00	11:46:58

Women's Winning Times (1978–2009)

Year	Name	Swim	Bike	Run	Overall Time
2009	Chrissie Wellington	54:31	4:52:07	3:03:06	8:54:02*
2008	Chrissie Wellington	56:20	5:08:16	2:57:44	9:06:23
2007	Chrissie Wellington	58:09	5:06:15	2:59:58	9:08:45
2006	Michellie Jones	54:29	5:06:09	3:13:08	9:18:31
2005	Natascha Badmann	1:02:30	4:52:00	3:06:25	9:09:30
2004	Natascha Badmann	1:01:36	5:31:37	3:11:45	9:50:04
2003	Lori Bowden	56:51	5:09:00	3:02:10	9:11:55
2002	Natascha Badmann	59:40	4:52:26	3:12:58	9:07:54
2001	Natascha Badmann	59:55	5:16:07	3:09:33	9:28:37
2000	Natascha Badmann	58:04	5:06:42	3:19:02	9:26:16
1999	Lori Bowden	1:02:23	5:08:30	2:59:16	9:13:02
1998	Natascha Badmann	56:02	5:10:00	3:14:50	9:24:16
1997	Heather Fuhr	1:01:47	5:23:11	3:06:45	9:31:43
1996	Paula Newby-Fraser	55:30	5:01:34	3:09:45	9:06:49
1995	Karen Smyers	53:37	5:17:49	3:05:20	9:16:46
1994	Paula Newby-Fraser	54:19	5:02:25	3:23:30	9:20:14
1993	Paula Newby-Fraser	53:29	4:48:30	3:16:24	8:58:23
1992	Paula Newby-Fraser	53:30	4:56:34	3:05:24	8:55:28
1991	Paula Newby-Fraser	54:59	5:05:47	3:07:05	9:07:52
1990	Erin Baker	56:37	5:12:52	3:04:13	9:13:42
1989	Paula Newby-Fraser	54:19	5:01:00	3:05:37	9:00:56
1988	Paula Newby-Fraser	56:38	4:57:13	3:07:09	9:01:01
1987	Erin Baker	57:42	5:26:34	3:11:08	9:35:25
1986	Paula Newby-Fraser	57:03	5:32:05	3:20:05	9:49:14
1985	Joanne Ernst	1:01:42	5:39:13	3:44:26	10:25:22
1984	Sylviane Puntous	1:00:45	5:50:36	3:33:51	10:25:13
1983	Sylviane Puntous	1:00:28	6:20:40	3:22:28	10:43:36
1982	Julie Leach**	1:04:57	5:50:36	3:58:35	10:54:08
1982	K. McCartney**	1:32:00	5:51:12	3:46:28	11:09:40
1981	Linda Sweeney	1:02:07	6:53:28	4:04:57	12:00:32
1980	Robin Beck	1:20:00	6:05:00	3:56:24	11:21:24
1979	Lyn Lemaire	1:16:20	6:30:00	5:10:00	12:55:38
1978	—	—	—	—	—

* Course record

** In 1982, two editions were held: February and October.

Fastest Swim Splits of Male Winners (1978–2009)

Time	Name	Country	Year
49:54	Faris Al-Sultan	GER	2005
50:14	Mark Allen	USA	1991
50:21	Dave Scott	USA	1984
50:22	Greg Welch	AUS	1994
50:36	Peter Reid	CAN	2003
50:38	Luc Van Lierde	BEL	1999
50:40	Mark Allen	USA	1993
50:52, Oct.	Dave Scott	USA	1982
50:52	Dave Scott	USA	1983
50:53	Dave Scott	USA	1986
50:57	Dave Scott	USA	1987
50:57	Craig Alexander	AUS	2009
51:00	Dave Scott	USA	1980
51:17	Mark Allen	USA	1989
51:27	Mark Allen	USA	1992
51:28	Scott Molina	USA	1988
51:36	Luc Van Lierde	BEL	1996
51:43	Mark Allen	USA	1990
51:43	Craig Alexander	USA	2008
51:45	Peter Reid	CAN	2000
51:48	Chris McCormack	AUS	2007
51:50	Mark Allen	USA	1995
52:01	Timothy DeBoom	USA	2001
52:02	Timothy DeBoom	USA	2002
52:04	Peter Reid	CAN	1998
53:08	Thomas Hellriegel	GER	1997
54:05	Normann Stadler	GER	2006
54:27	Normann Stadler	GER	2004
55:13	Scott Tinley	USA	1985
1:06:15	Tom Warren	USA	1979
1:10:45, Feb.	Scott Tinley	USA	1982
1:11:12	John Howard	USA	1981
1:20:40	Gordon Haller	USA	1978

Fastest Swim Splits of Female Winners (1978–2009)

Time	Name	Country	Year
53:29	Paula Newby-Fraser	ZIM	1993
53:30	Paula Newby-Fraser	ZIM	1992
53:37	Karen Smyers	USA	1995
54:19	Paula Newby-Fraser	ZIM	1989
54:19	Paula Newby-Fraser	ZIM	1994
54:29	Michellie Jones	AUS	2006
54:31	Chrissie Wellington	GBR	2009
54:59	Paula Newby-Fraser	ZIM	1991
55:30	Natascha Badmann	SUI	1998
56:20	Chrissie Wellington	GBR	2008
56:37	Erin Baker	NZL	1990
56:38	Paula Newby-Fraser	ZIM	1988
56:51	Lori Bowden	CAN	2003
57:03	Paula Newby-Fraser	ZIM	1986
57:42	Erin Baker	NZL	1987
58:04	Natascha Badmann	SUI	2000
58:09	Chrissie Wellington	GBR	2007
59:40	Natascha Badmann	SUI	2002
59:55	Natascha Badmann	SUI	2001
1:00:28	Sylviane Puntous	CAN	1983
1:00:45	Sylviane Puntous	CAN	1984
1:01:36	Natascha Badmann	SUI	2004
1:01:42	Joanne Ernst	USA	1985
1:01:47	Heather Fuhr	CAN	1997
1:02:07	Linda Sweeney	USA	1981
1:02:23	Lori Bowden	CAN	1999
1:02:30	Natascha Badmann	SUI	2005
1:04:57, Oct.	Julie Leach	USA	1982
1:16:20	Lyn Lemaire	USA	1979
1:20:00	Robin Beck	USA	1980
1:32:00, Feb.	Kathleen McCartney	USA	1982

Fastest Bike Splits of Male Winners (1978–2009)

Time	Name	Country	Year
4:18:23	Normann Stadler	GER	2006
4:25:24	Faris Al-Sultan	GER	2005
4:29:00	Mark Allen	USA	1993
4:30:44	Luc Van Lierde	BEL	1996
4:35:23	Mark Allen	USA	1992
4:36:50	Scott Molina	USA	1988
4:37:19	Craig Alexander	USA	2008
4:37:32	Chris McCormack	AUS	2007
4:37:33	Craig Alexander	AUS	2009
4:37:58	Normann Stadler	GER	2004
4:37:52	Mark Allen	USA	1989
4:39:32	Peter Reid	CAN	2000
4:40:04	Peter Reid	CAN	2003
4:41:07	Greg Welch	AUS	1994
4:41:26	Luc Van Lierde	BEL	1999
4:42:23	Peter Reid	CAN	1998
4:43:45	Mark Allen	USA	1990
4:45:21	Timothy DeBoom	USA	2002
4:46:07	Mark Allen	USA	1991
4:46:35	Mark Allen	USA	1995
4:47:57	Thomas Hellriegel	GER	1997
4:48:17	Timothy DeBoom	USA	2001
4:48:32	Dave Scott	USA	1986
4:53:48	Dave Scott	USA	1987
4:54:07	Scott Tinley	USA	1985
5:03:00	Dave Scott	USA	1980
5:03:29	John Howard	USA	1981
5:05:11, Feb.	Scott Tinley	USA	1982
5:10:16, Oct.	Dave Scott	USA	1982
5:10:49	Dave Scott	USA	1984
5:10:48	Dave Scott	USA	1983
6:19:00	Tom Warren	USA	1979
6:56:00	Gordon Haller	USA	1978

Fastest Bike Splits of Female Winners (1978–2009)

Time	Name	Country	Year
4:48:30	Paula Newby-Fraser	ZIM	1993
4:52:00	Natascha Badmann	SUI	2005
4:52:07	Chrissie Wellington	GBR	2009
4:52:26	Natascha Badmann	SUI	2002
4:56:34	Paula Newby-Fraser	ZIM	1992
4:57:13	Paula Newby-Fraser	ZIM	1988
5:01:00	Paula Newby-Fraser	ZIM	1989
5:01:34	Paula Newby-Fraser	ZIM	1996
5:02:25	Paula Newby-Fraser	ZIM	1994
5:05:47	Paula Newby-Fraser	ZIM	1991
5:06:09	Michellie Jones	AUS	2006
5:06:15	Chrissie Wellington	GBR	2007
5:06:42	Natascha Badmann	SUI	2000
5:08:16	Chrissie Wellington	GBR	2008
5:08:30	Lori Bowden	CAN	1999
5:09:00	Lori Bowden	CAN	2003
5:10:00	Natascha Badmann	SUI	1998
5:12:52	Erin Baker	NZL	1990
5:16:07	Natascha Badmann	SUI	2001
5:17:49	Karen Smyers	USA	1995
5:23:11	Heather Fuhr	CAN	1997
5:26:34	Erin Baker	NZL	1987
5:31:37	Natascha Badmann	SUI	2004
5:32:05	Paula Newby-Fraser	ZIM	1986
5:39:13	Joanne Ernst	USA	1985
5:50:36, Oct.	Julie Leach	USA	1982
5:50:36	Sylviane Puntous	CAN	1984
5:51:12, Feb.	Kathleen McCartney	USA	1982
6:05:00	Robin Beck	USA	1980
6:20:40	Sylviane Puntous	CAN	1983
6:30:00	Lyn Lemaire	CAN	1979
6:53:28	Linda Sweeney	CAN	1981

Fastest Run Splits of Male Winners (1978–2009)

Time	Name	Country	Year
2:40:04	Mark Allen	USA	1989
2:41:48	Luc Van Lierde	BEL	1996
2:42:02	Chris McCormack	AUS	2007
2:42:09	Mark Allen	USA	1991
2:42:09	Mark Allen	USA	1995
2:42:18	Mark Allen	USA	1992
2:42:46	Luc Van Lierde	BEL	1999
2:45:01	Craig Alexander	USA	2008
2:45:54	Timothy DeBoom	USA	2001
2:47:31	Peter Reid	CAN	1998
2:47:38	Peter Reid	CAN	2003
2:48:05	Mark Allen	USA	1993
2:48:05	Craig Alexander	AUS	2009
2:48:10	Peter Reid	CAN	2000
2:48:58	Greg Welch	AUS	1994
2:49:11	Dave Scott	USA	1986
2:49:26	Dave Scott	USA	1987
2:50:22	Timothy DeBoom	USA	2002
2:51:56	Thomas Hellriegel	GER	1997
2:52:48	Mark Allen	USA	1990
2:53:00	Dave Scott	USA	1984
2:54:51	Faris Al-Sultan	GER	2005
2:55:03	Normann Stadler	GER	2006
2:57:53	Normann Stadler	GER	2004
3:01:33	Scott Tinley	USA	1985
3:02:42	Scott Molina	USA	1988
3:03:45, Feb.	Scott Tinley	USA	1982
3:04:16	Dave Scott	USA	1983
3:07:15, Oct.	Dave Scott	USA	1982
3:23:48	John Howard	USA	1981
3:30:00	Gordon Haller	USA	1978
3:50:33	Dave Scott	USA	1980
3:51:00	Tom Warren	USA	1979

Fastest Run Splits of Female Winners (1978–2009)

Time	Name	Country	Year
2:57:44	Chrissie Wellington	GBR	2008
2:59:16	Lori Bowden	CAN	1999
2:59:58	Chrissie Wellington	GBR	2007
3:02:10	Lori Bowden	CAN	2003
3:03:06	Chrissie Wellington	GBR	2009
3:04:13	Erin Baker	NZL	1990
3:05:20	Karen Smyers	USA	1995
3:05:24	Paula Newby-Fraser	ZIM	1992
3:05:37	Paula Newby-Fraser	ZIM	1989
3:06:25	Natascha Badmann	SUI	2005
3:06:45	Heather Fuhr	CAN	1997
3:07:05	Paula Newby-Fraser	ZIM	1991
3:07:09	Paula Newby-Fraser	ZIM	1988
3:09:33	Natascha Badmann	SUI	2001
3:09:45	Paula Newby-Fraser	ZIM	1996
3:11:08	Erin Baker	NZL	1987
3:11:45	Natascha Badmann	SUI	2004
3:12:58	Natascha Badmann	SUI	2002
3:13:08	Michellie Jones	AUS	2006
3:14:50	Natascha Badmann	SUI	1998
3:16:24	Paula Newby-Fraser	ZIM	1993
3:19:02	Natascha Badmann	SUI	2000
3:20:05	Paula Newby-Fraser	ZIM	1986
3:22:28	Sylviane Puntous	CAN	1983
3:23:30	Paula Newby-Fraser	ZIM	1994
3:33:51	Sylviane Puntous	CAN	1984
3:44:26	Joanne Ernst	USA	1985
3:46:28, Feb.	Kathleen McCartney	USA	1982
3:56:24	Robin Beck	USA	1980
3:58:35, Oct.	Julie Leach	USA	1982
4:04:57	Linda Sweeney	USA	1981
5:10:00	Lyn Lemaire	USA	1979

Fastest Segment Splits at Kailua-Kona

Swim

1998	Lars Jorgensen (USA)	46:41
1999	Jodi Jackson (USA)	48:43

Bike

2006	Normann Stadler (GER)	4:18:23
1993	Paula Newby-Fraser (ZIM)	4:48:30*

Run

1989	Mark Allen (USA)	2:40:04
2009	Mirinda Carfrae (AUS)	2:56:51

Course record

1996	Luc Van Lierde (BEL)	8:04:08
2009	Chrissie Wellington (GBR)	8:54:02

*Until 1997, the bike split included both transition times. From 1998 forward, only actual ride times were considered and recorded.

The 10 Fastest Overall Times

Men

Time	Name	Country	Year
8:04:08	Luc Van Lierde	BEL	1996
8:06:07	Thomas Hellriegel	GER	1996
8:07:45	Mark Allen	USA	1993
8:09:08	Mark Allen	USA	1992
8:09:15	Mark Allen	USA	1989
8:10:13	Dave Scott	USA	1989
8:11:56	Normann Stadler	GER	2006
8:13:07	Chris McCormack	AUS	2006
8:14:17	Faris Al-Sultan	GER	2005
8:14:27	Pauli Kiuru	FIN	1993

Women

Time	Name	Country	Year
8:54:02	Chrissie Wellington	GBR	2009
8:55:28	Paula Newby-Fraser	ZIM	1992
8:58:23	Paula Newby-Fraser	ZIM	1993
9:00:56	Paula Newby-Fraser	ZIM	1989
9:01:01	Paula Newby-Fraser	ZIM	1988
9:06:23	Chrissie Wellington	GBR	2008
9:06:49	Paula Newby-Fraser	ZIM	1996
9:07:52	Paula Newby-Fraser	ZIM	1991
9:07:54	Natascha Badmann	SUI	2002
9:08:04	Erin Baker	NZL	1993
9:08:45	Chrissie Wellington	GBR	2007

The 10 Fastest Swim Splits

Men

Time	Name	Country	Year
46:41	Lars Jorgensen	USA	1998
46:44	Lars Jorgensen	USA	1995
46:50	Jan Sibbersen	GER	2003
47:01	Noa Sakamoto	USA	2008
47:02	John Flanagan	USA	2008
47:04	Jan Sibbersen	GER	2004
47:15	Hiroki Hikida	JPN	2003
47:39	Bradford Hinshaw	USA	1986
47:41	John Weston	USA	2003
47:42	John Flanagan III	USA	2009

Women

Time	Name	Country	Year
48:43	Jodi Jackson	USA	1999
49:11	Wendy Ingraham	USA	1998
49:51	Barb Lindquist	USA	2000
49:52	Wendy Ingraham	USA	1997
49:57	Ute Mueckel	GER	1997
50:28	Wendy Ingraham	USA	1999
50:28	Monica Caplan	USA	2003
50:29	Linda Gallo	USA	2003
50:30	Raleigh Tennant	AUS	1999
50:31	Jennifer Hinshaw	USA	1984

The 10 Fastest Bike Splits

Men

Time	Name	Country	Year
4:18:23	Normann Stadler	GER	2006
4:21:36	Torbjørn Sindballe	DNK	2005
4:24:50	Thomas Hellriegel	GER	1996
4:25:11	Chris Lieto	USA	2009
4:25:24	Faris Al-Sultan	GER	2005
4:25:26	Torbjørn Sindballe	DNK	2007
4:25:35	Chris Lieto	USA	2006
4:26:15	Ain Alar Juhanson	EST.	2008
4:27:23	Chris Lieto	USA	2005
4:27:25	Mitchell Anderson	AUS	2005

Women

Time	Name	Country	Year
4:48:30	Paula Newby-Fraser	ZIM	1993
4:50:16	Erin Baker	NZL	1993
4:50:16	Karin Thürig	SUI	2005
4:50:41	Karin Thürig	SUI	2003
4:52:00	Natascha Badmann	SUI	2005
4:52:07	Chrissie Wellington	GBR	2009
4:52:26	Natascha Badmann	SUI	2002
4:53:47	Natascha Badmann	SUI	1996
4:54:13	Michellie Jones	USA	2005
4:55:32	Karin Thürig	SUI	2002

Until 1997, the bike split included both transition times. From 1998 forward only actual ride times were considered and recorded.

The 10 Fastest Run Splits

Men

Time	Name	Country	Year
2:40:04	Mark Allen	USA	1989
2:41:03	Dave Scott	USA	1989
2:41:48	Luc Van Lierde	BEL	1996
2:41:57	Olivier Bernhard	SUI	1999
2:42:02	Chris McCormack	AUS	2007
2:42:09	Mark Allen	USA	1995
2:42:09	Mark Allen	USA	1991
2:42:18	Mark Allen	USA	1992
2:42:46	Luc Van Lierde	BEL	1999
2:43:55	Sergio Marques	PRT	2006

Women

Time	Name	Country	Year
2:56:51	Mirinda Carfrae	AUS	2009
2:57:44	Chrissie Wellington	GBR	2008
2:58:36	Sandra Wallenhorst	GER	2008
2:59:16	Lori Bowden	CAN	1999
2:59:58	Chrissie Wellington	GBR	2007
3:00:52	Samantha McGlone	CAN	2007
3:01:25	Erika Csomor	HUN	2007
3:02:10	Lori Bowden	CAN	2003
3:02:19	Kate Major	AUS	2005
3:03:06	Chrissie Wellington	GBR	2009

The Closest Finishes

Men

Year	1st Place	2nd Place	Time Difference
1983	Dave Scott (USA)	Scott Tinley (USA)	00:00:33
1989	Mark Allen (USA)	Dave Scott (USA)	00:00:58
2006	Normann Stadler (GER)	Chris McCormack (AUS)	00:01:11
1996	Luc Van Lierde (BEL)	Thomas Hellriegel (GER)	00:01:59
2000	Peter Reid (CAN)	Tim DeBoom (USA)	00:02:09

Women

Year	1st Place	2nd Place	Time Difference
1982	Kathleen McCartney (USA)	Julie Moss (USA)	00:00:29
1987	Erin Baker (NZL)	Sylviane Puntous (CAN)	00:01:32
1985	Joanne Ernst (USA)	Elizabeth Bulman (USA)	00:01:33
1984	Sylviane Puntous (CAN)	Patricia Puntous (CAN)	00:02:15
2005	Natascha Badmann (SUI)	Michellie Jones (USA)	00:02:21

Youngest Ironman Finisher

Robin Tain, 14 years 2 months, 13:54:53 in 1981
(minimum age was raised to 18 in mid-1980s)

Oldest Ironman Male Finisher

Robert McKeague, 80 years 6 months, 16:21:55 in 2005

Oldest Ironman Female Finisher

Sister Madonna Buder, 76 years 3 months, 16:59:03 in 2006

Slowest Ironman

Walt Stack, 73 years, 26:20 in 1981
(finishing time cutoff today is 17 hours)

Finishing Percentage

Total Ironman Hawaii starters 1978–2009: 40,942
Total Ironman Hawaii finishers 1978–2009: 38,048
Total overall finishing percentage: 92.9 percent

As of 2010, there are now 25 official Ironman races and dozens more independently sanctioned races at the Ironman distance on five continents. It is estimated that there is a pool of approximately 50,000 triathletes worldwide who will attempt to qualify for or enter the lottery to gain a starting spot at Ironman Hawaii.

ACKNOWLEDGMENTS

Anna-Sophia, for her unfailing support, for driving the car, for having energy drinks at all the right times, and for the most beautiful sunset in Mauna Kea, on Hawaii's Big Island.

My brothers, for their discretion with regard to this book, and for their brotherly affection.

My parents, for everything. This book is dedicated to them. Thank you!

My boys, for their continual encouragement, their motivational help, and above all for their true friendship.

Thomas, for the trip halfway around the world, the proud glances, and for coming to the finish line party, where the idea for this book originated as Robert McKeague finished.

All of the athletes featured in this book. They invested a lot of time and effort in this project.

The World Triathlon Corporation, especially Jessica Weidensall for her tremendous support.

My colleagues: Nils for the graphics, Ben for his counsel regarding images, Martin for the lessons in photography, Nico for the long focal distance, and Carsten for the exchange of ideas.

The sport of triathlon, which has exposed me and many athletes to wonderful experiences.

—*Mathias Müller*

PHOTOGRAPHY CREDITS

COLOR SECTIONS

Page 1: Carol Hogan*

Pages 2, 5, 6, 7, 9, 10, 13, 16 (top), 17 (bottom), 22, 23, 24, 25, 26, 29, 30, 31: Timothy Carlson

Pages 3, 4, 12, 14, 15, 17 (top), 27, 28, 32: Mathias Müller*

Page 11: Don Karle

Pages 16 (bottom), 21*: Rich Cruse

Pages 18, 19: Courtesy Robert McKeague

Page 20: World Triathlon Corporation*

CHAPTER OPENING PAGES

1: World Triathlon Corporation*

2, 4, 5, 6, 9, 10, 12, 13, 14, 15, 17: Timothy Carlson

3, 7, 8, 16: Mathias Müller*

11: Courtesy Robert McKeague

*Courtesy Moby Dick Verlag und Media-Services GmbH

ABOUT THE AUTHORS

MATHIAS MÜLLER has competed in eight Ironman races and finished the Ironman Hawaii three times. In his best Ironman performance, he finished 99th overall in 9:28 at Ironman Roth, Germany, in 1998. He has written for several German magazines and newspapers over the past 15 years. In 2008, for the *Stern-TV* television program, he trained four beginner triathletes in only eight months for successful finishes at Ironman Lanzarote.

TIMOTHY CARLSON is among triathlon's longest-serving and most respected journalists and photographers. His byline appeared for many years in *Inside Triathlon* and *Triathlete*, and he currently writes for Slowtwitch.com. He is also the coauthor, with Bill Katovsky, of *Embedded: The Media Wars in Iraq*, which won the Goldsmith Book Prize.